The Culture of Punishment

The Culture
of Punishment

Prison, Society, and Spectacle

Michelle Brown

NEW YORK UNIVERSITY PRESS
New York and London

NEW YORK UNIVERSITY PRESS
New York and London
www.nyupress.org

Library of Congress Cataloging-in-Publication Data

Brown, Michelle, 1971–
The culture of punishment : prison, society, and spectacle /
Michelle Brown.
p. cm. — (Alternative criminology series)
Includes bibliographical references and index.
ISBN-13: 978-0-8147-9999-4 (cl : alk. paper)
ISBN-10: 0-8147-9999-x (cl : alk. paper)
ISBN-13: 978-0-8147-9100-4 (pb : alk. paper)
ISBN-10: 0-8147-9100-x (pb : alk. paper)
1. Punishment—Social aspects. 2. Imprisonment—Social aspects.
3. Prisons—Social aspects. I. Title.
HV8756.B76   2009
303.3'6—dc22   2009017388

New York University Press books are printed on acid-free paper,
and their binding materials are chosen for strength and durability.
We strive to use environmentally responsible suppliers and materials
to the greatest extent possible in publishing our books.

Manufactured in the United States of America
c 10 9 8 7 6 5 4 3 2 1
p 10 9 8 7 6 5 4 3 2 1

Contents

Acknowledgments

I benefited from a critical set of comments and suggestions on this manuscript in its most distant and earliest stages, provided by a wonderful set of intellectuals: criminologist Steven Chermak, sociologist Katherine Beckett, literary scholar Eva Cherniavsky, historian Ellen Dwyer, and anthropologists Carol Greenhouse and Stephanie Kane. I hope they find traces of their own work and commitments in what this manuscript is today. Thanks to my current home, the Department of Sociology and Anthropology at Ohio University, and especially to my colleagues, Joseph De Angelis, Haley Duschinski, Nancy Tatarek, and Deborah Thorne, who played supportive, nurturing roles in the volume's progress, often providing me with readings and ideas that substantively transformed this work (many times without knowing it). Many thanks as well to esteemed colleagues across the field who took an interest and supportive role in the project at various phases and in its many incarnations, including Jeff Ferrell, David Greenberg, and Nicole Rafter.

A deep note of appreciation goes out to Sean M. Kelley, program director at Eastern State Penitentiary, who generously and enthusiastically shared photos, research, history, and, not least, his time. Also at Eastern State, Andrea (Ang) Reidell, assistant program director for Education, and Sally Elk, executive director, graciously gave of their time and expertise. Pat Kleinedler, tour secretary of the Moundsville Economic Development Council, along with other staff members at West Virginia Penitentiary and the Ohio State Reformatory, graciously and enthusiastically provided detailed historical accounts and access to the prison and its daily and special events operations. Thanks also to Dr. Ellen H. Belcher, Special Collections librarian, at the Lloyd Sealy Library of the John Jay College of Criminal Justice, who assisted me in accessing Robert Martinson's personal papers.

Of course, many undergraduate and graduate students helped in bringing this volume to bear, through classroom discussions, research assistance, tough questions, and sheer enthusiasm. Special thanks are deserved by a long but not exhaustive list of former and current students: Ashley Demyan, Danielle Fagen, Tara Livelsberger, Brandon Long, and Emily Vance played key research roles. Rebecca Carson and Kristie Garrison, who serendipitously introduced me to the overnight prison ghost hunt, initiated a key turn in my research toward prison tourism. Finally, from within and without prison, spanning classrooms, living rooms, and community centers, Melissa Benton has been a long-term motivating force in the development of this manuscript, and her success is a story of the life given over to the work of punishment—as a witness, not a spectator.

In the end, this volume's existence depends upon a gesture of faith by a select group of individuals. I am indebted to executive editor Ilene Kalish and editorial assistant Aiden Amos, who provided me, a first-time author, with a supportive and superb experience through NYU Press, as did Jeff Ferrell, series editor for Alternative Criminology, and a small group of excellent anonymous reviewers. Their comments truly made this book better and taught me much as a writer. Others have taught me more than words can tell. The writing of this volume took place as my family, near and far, existed in a whirlwind of loss. Although it is difficult for me to see, I know that experience and those lives are inseparable from this text. It is my sister, Amanda Brown-Gould, who has most often conveyed this to me, reminding me that I am always my mother's daughter. Finally, one person in particular has provided a warm dwelling of support and sustenance for this project—my partner, Bruce Hoffman. Any effort to express gratitude for such space runs up against what has for a long time now been a deep, wordless thankfulness. This volume is an effort which depended in so many ways upon his time, insights, and expertise, but more importantly, on his compassionate way of looking at and building the world. For those reasons, this book is dedicated—with much love—to him and to my mother, Morgan Brown, together—as I think they would prefer it—the two people who have patiently taught me most about the promise of things that exceed what we know, of words and worlds beyond prisons.

1

Introduction

Notes on Becoming a Penal Spectator

Tipping Points

When I began graduate school, the first course I took was a proseminar on the administration of justice. The curriculum was an unprecedented experience and challenge for me, a former humanities student, in its deep survey of organizational theory through the central institutions of the criminal justice system. The last few weeks of the course were spent on classic and contemporary works in correctional research—leading me to work by pioneers in the sociology of imprisonment. I studied the first wave of social scientists who entered prisons and observed their daily life, including the work of sociologists Donald Clemmer, Gresham Sykes, and Erving Goffman.[1] Encounters with historical documents such as *The President's Commission on Law Enforcement and the Administration of Justice*, the American Friends Service Committee's *Struggle for Justice*, as well as revisionist social control histories authored by David Rothman and Nicole Rafter, led me to reconsider the entire purpose of punishment and how visions of social control have such unforeseeable consequences and often go so badly awry.[2] Contemporary work of the period, ranging from John DiIulio's high-profile prediction of a wave of youthful super-predators, Norval Morris and Michael Tonry's argument for the necessity of an interchangeability of punishment, to Nils Christie's indictment of crime control gulags, opened up issues with little resolution against the backdrop of a deepening sense of futility.[3] My final project in the proseminar examined a key debate about the role of rehabilitation in U.S. punishment, relying heavily upon the controversial work of Robert Martinson, widely recognized as having come to the infamous conclusion that "nothing works" in the field of corrections. During that time, Marc Mauer's groundbreaking Sentencing Project report was issued, which found that one out of three black men between the ages of 20 and 29 were in prison, jail, or on probation or parole.[4]

I left the course and my first semester of graduate school feeling as if these researchers were discordant voices in a strange wilderness as the United States continued to build the most massive penal system on the planet. All of this culminated in a deepening commitment to the study of punishment. It seemed clear that the U.S. penal system remained the most invisible and overlooked of justice institutions and that the reasons for this strange inattention were remarkably thin and undertheorized. It also seemed clear that a generation of criminologists and sociologists were taking on a deep sense of urgency in mapping these penal transformations and arguing their meanings. I remember thinking that, as a citizen and potential criminologist, I bore some responsibility and accountability in this new understanding, as it was developing against the relatively quiet backdrop of unprecedented prison expansion and mass, racialized incarceration in the United States.

I launched energetically into the project of visiting prisons at every security level and across the United States as part of my plan to study them. I eventually obtained a teaching position at the largest women's correctional facility in my home state of Indiana, all in order to lay the groundwork for gaining access and conducting doctoral research in the statewide correctional system. In these pursuits, I found myself immersed for the first time in the physical world I proposed to study and hoped to change. It was a claustrophobic space whose structural tensions, ironies, inertia, and contradictions were immediately apparent. All of my visions of reform and transformation quickly dissipated into a chronic kind of worry and exhaustion, alongside of an overwhelming sense of being up against something impossible to transform. The anxious awareness of the impossibility of change, after all, is in many ways the story of the prison and reform—and certainly marks its history and its sociology. The physical world of incarceration was also, in a mundane, horrific way, a space, in the late 1990s, overflowing with people—prisoners, correctional officers, case workers, mental health staff, attorneys, administrators, and brief but routine appearances by families and community members. During those long drives home from class and facility tours, through beautiful, desolate rural counties, where the roads were largely empty and the economy long gone, I continuously pondered what it meant to be a prison culture—a society committed to the construction of prisons and the warehousing of mass numbers of people with little regard for the complexities of their lives, the lives of those hired to confine them, and the communities that surrounded them. I returned home to conversations with friends, family, colleagues, and students that seemed deeply disconnected from these stark environments and their consideration, with debates and dialogues developing in which authority could be tried on freely and assertively, where declarations about punishment and the appropriateness of pain were playfully tossed about. Those same playful discourses became apparent in the programs I watched on television, the films that I screened, the video games that I played, and the commentary that pervaded the news. Everywhere I looked, the architecture and vocabulary of punishment suddenly appeared.

In the days since, I have conducted multiple research and teaching projects in prisons with the people who work and live there. Many have been gracious enough to lead me through these complex worlds. Former prisoners have permitted me to follow them through reentry, back to cities, into their homes and the lives of their parents, children, brothers and sisters, partners, employers, and spiritual communities. Others remain in the same halls, cells, and dormitories where I met them ten years ago, fighting against the effects of prolonged institutionalization and worrying about the day they have to enter a world now virtually unrecognizable, with few resources and family to support them. Some will never leave. Some have died. In that process, I have witnessed the devastating, fruitless impact of stigma, isolation, and confinement—of dead time and holding patterns that are chronically dysfunctional for people who will one day return to society, to us—the long-standing and most basic findings of prison sociology. Along the way, people who spend their lives working in this environment have discussed the stress they encounter in performing the work of incarceration on the job and off. They have spoken candidly and passionately about how they and those around them change in doing a work whose positive effects are hard to find, on how they withdraw into communities of workers who understand the day-to-day life of prisons . . . because broader society does not.[5] It is out of this experience that I decided to write this book.

Historically, prisoners and prison workers are necessarily divided by power and by function. The prison then epitomizes what it is to position people in fundamentally unequal structures. However, what prisoners, prison workers, and those who care about them share is an extreme sense of difference and isolation from society—a sense that they are ultimately disposable and most socially valuable when invisibly fulfilling the warehousing mandate of a society that has come to view incapacitation as the first and most logical political and social choice in dealing with a vast array of issues, some crime-related and many not. They are aware of broader societal attitudes, assumptions, and understandings of punishment and have, with all of us, experienced the rise of a popular punitiveness over the last four decades. Sometimes they support and internalize this turn. But even in that context, they know the work that they do and the experience of being in prison are social realities that few outside of their worlds care or wish to know about—except in connection with a certain voyeuristic sensationalism.

In this book, I argue that many American citizens access punishment through cultural practices removed from formal institutions like prisons in a manner which, although largely unacknowledged, massively extends throughout our social foundations. Across families, communities, schools, religion, the military, politics, the economy, and beyond, punishment is practiced and played with in daily life. In part, this manner of cultural engagement perhaps occurs because it is simply easier, convenient, and more accessible, but it also marks a choice. Americans choose when and under what conditions they would prefer to see prisons and, in the particularity of that engagement, invoke and reproduce specific kinds of logics and explanatory frameworks. I look to the places where this engagement is occurring, places that lie outside of the prison-industrial complex, where punishment arises popularly and culturally. Like a detective, I glimpse a lead—a film about prison that attracts a cult following or a hit television show that playfully engages penal judgment; an advertisement for a prison ghost hunt whose popularity is growing locally, regionally, and nationally; a news story whose penal images are so graphic and so immediately global as to defy previous representations of prisons, evoking international outrage; and finally, a popularized scientific publication on rehabilitation that maintains its hold across time in textbooks, popular discourse, and the common history of a discipline—and I follow it where it goes. Why? Because other people are doing this also, citizens with—and, more significantly, without—direct connections to prisons. In all of these cases, cultural fragments emerge whose hold on people is deeply bound up with the nature of their connections to punishment—but from a distance.

It is in these spaces that much of the popular knowledge about punishment is constructed—in spaces far from the social realities and the social facts that define mass incarceration. Consequently, the turn away from imprisonment, if and when it occurs, will only be meaningful if we know something beyond the political, economic, and structural forces which led to its downfall. We will need to know something about the ways in which people who are removed from punishment imagine it— and why certain kinds of political rhetorics and cultural meanings are given so much privilege. We will need to know how ordinary citizens use imprisonment, what they find fascinating about it, why it emerges at key moments in particular kinds of representational frameworks and public discourse, and finally, and perhaps most significant, what kinds of penal subjectivities develop out of these interactions. By penal subjectivity, I mean that these performances of punishment, when distant from actual punishment, nonetheless provide frameworks for ordinary citizens to step into or out of self-conscious modes of awareness as moral spectators and deliberative citizens. In those positions, Americans make decisions about the proper place and meanings of punishment and the role of pain and exclusion in society. Such a framework insists that there are specific conditions in which Americans engage the complex work of punishment. When do they recognize and act upon their own complicity in the practice of punishment? Of equal importance, when do they fail to recognize this role—or intentionally evade it—and under what conditions? In contexts where individuals only know incarceration at a distance, the dynamics of penal participation are slippery and can quickly devolve into complex, often voyeuristic frameworks which privilege various kinds of punitive, individualistic judgment. Citizens may participate vicariously in mediated worlds where pain is inflicted across television, films, recreation, and news. They may be disturbed by these images. They may find such engagement titillating. In any case, they are enthralled in a manner that is not easily conducive to analysis or self-reflection. Thus, a shadow world of moral judgment and penal logics exists beyond prison walls as a constant and perpetually growing cultural resource for people to make sense of punishment. Few other institutions encounter such a radical and momentous divide between their physical realities and cultural imagining. And without some awareness of how this separation occurs, we not only risk reproducing the worst aspects of penal history, but developing new and more awful trajectories as well.

Of course, it is also true that the scale of incarceration in the United States has brought unprecedented numbers of people into the penal system and created social networks of incarceration that exceed any in previous history. The world leader in incarceration, the United States now imprisons just under two and a quarter million people, with over 7 million under some form of criminal justice supervision. Ninety-five percent or more of those incarcerated will be released from prison at some point in the future. The nature of this pattern of imprisonment occurs in a manner fueled by the war on drugs and the disproportionate imprisonment of African American men, who are seven times as likely to be incarcerated as white men. Beyond the bare demographics of the U.S. penal system are the extensive, largely hidden collateral consequences of mass incarceration. Although these costs vary across jurisdictions and states, they include lifetime bans for those with felonies of the receipt of welfare and food stamp benefits, restricted rights to housing and higher education, limits in emergency public aid and social service access, occupational licensure restrictions, and voter disenfranchisement, all of which can add up to insurmountable barriers for individuals returning to poor, working-class communities. The costs of incarceration extend far beyond the individuals who are housed in the U.S. penal system. The future for the estimated 2 million children who have a parent in prison is stark. Among the most vulnerable of demographic groups, these children are more likely to grow up in poverty and encounter the criminal justice system far earlier and more consistently than their middle-class peers. Families of prisoners, consequently, are informed by a unique set of economic, social, emotional, and existential stressors. As well, the people and corporations who serve as the rising labor force for the prison-industrial complex point to new ways in which American towns and cities can be organized around the project of punishment with no economic motive or social investment plan beyond mass incarceration. These kinds of cumulative effects add up to structural shifts for entire communities and ultimately all of American society, exacerbating fundamental race, class, and gender divisions and inequalities and providing scarce resources or impetus to think through alternative approaches to crime and its contingent social problems. Significantly, these discussions are largely absent from political discourse. Senator James Webb, who coordinated hearings on mass incarceration in 2007, addressed this omission, arguing that "the United States has embarked on one of the largest public policy experiments in our history, yet this experiment remains shockingly absent from public debate."[6] Although mass imprisonment figures largely as the country's most critical civil rights concern, not one recent presidential candidate has identified it as a key issue.

Such developments frustrate the project of democracy in a number of ways. Social dynamics and interrelations in penal contexts are built fundamentally upon exclusionary practices and ideas of difference which divide rather than unite, turning citizens against citizens. Contemporary federal, state, and local initiatives build up last-resort institutions like prisons in a manner that renders communities economically and politically dependent upon them, while pulling resources from education, health care, the economy, and other social institutions and services. Communities then take as their most basic good a potentially limitless drive toward an impossible sense of security, founded upon governance through crime and fear. Such contexts are most disturbing in their normalization of crime and punishment, where both risk becoming pretexts or simply accepted, well-intentioned ways of accomplishing other kinds of social and political goals. How we think about privacy, personal responsibility, and the needs of others, deserving or not, may be radically reshaped. This book takes seriously the possibility of a convergence of concerns like these in a manner that changes who we are as individuals and a society. Thinking about punishment as something beyond sheer normalcy or the safety of the self-evident is a necessity given the institution's uniqueness, a social practice that has been theorized since the birth of democracy as a force to be carefully deliberated upon and limited in its application in any society that values freedom, equality, and self-governance.

We "mass" imprison in this country in a manner that is defined by sheer scale (massive, incomparable numbers of bodies and beings) and by a concentration of the social effects of incarceration upon particular groups. Because the axis of incarceration extends along distinct race and class lines, it is only a privileged group of citizens who do not know this experience. As a result, the U.S. penal system is defined specifically by a classed, racialized minority presence from which white middle-class citizens are comfortably distanced—distanced enough to support and sustain the largest punitive political turn in U.S. history, a phenomenon that most prisoners and prison workers do not view as beneficial to larger society or the operations of prisons. Although public works, prisons are not frequented like libraries, highways, memorials, parks, or state houses. Their access is carefully regulated, and consequently many citizens never encounter the overpowering tangibility of imprisonment. Ironically, perhaps, these are the very individuals who are politically positioned to facilitate the existing system through democratic processes that result in policies which exacerbate social divisions and inequalities.

This volume then is predicated upon the fact that we must examine the ways in which those who have no need to address the problem of punishment develop cultural meanings about it if we are to understand—and change—the penal route we have taken. Even those who directly experience incarceration and its impacts—prisoners, prison workers, and their families and communities—do not do so in a social vacuum without being shaped by culture more broadly. Consequently, the material reality of incarceration requires careful examination. It is, however, also an argument of this volume that culture is shaped by punishment in ways that we are only beginning to map. Performances, engagements, and representations of punishment proliferate and diversify daily, accumulating into complex logics and mentalities that will be very difficult to leave behind—as difficult as it will be to move beyond prison walls. And these logics already extend well beyond our borders. In late modernity, as citizens across the planet struggle through the contradictions of globalization and deeply riven economic and social inequalities, decisions are being made about how to deal with the potential threat of mass, unending violence and insecurity, of how and whether to engage in processes of democratization, of how to govern ourselves and others. These decisions are informed directly by imprisonment and the technologies and strategies that the United States, as both a global security force and a prison culture, has invoked and propagated. U.S. military prisons can be found the world over, with a detention facility located at nearly a thousand military bases—and this does not include secret prisons and black sites. These prisons rely heavily upon U.S. civilian prisons in design, staffing, and implementation. Moreover, they are advertised as "state of the art" facilities, planned and publicized as models for the rest of the world. These emergent ways of being risk an unprecedented diversification, extension, and permanence of penal systems across social life, in ways entirely capable of reshaping what it means to live meaningfully and to count as a social and political subject, not just at home but abroad. In the era of mass incarceration, this global subject is increasingly defined in penal terms—refugees, detainees, deportees, enemy combatants, persons under custody, illegal aliens—whose status depends upon values and frameworks for judgment which tend toward exclusion over inclusion and isolation over social commitment. This penal subject, of course, runs up against another—the distanced citizen, a penal spectator, secure in his or her place within sovereignty and the opportunity to exercise exclusionary judgment from afar.

Penal Spectatorship and the Cultural Work of Punishment

To conceive of ourselves as penal spectators asks us to consider a different set of aspects about the practice of punishment. First, it foregrounds the fact that for those of us without direct connections to formal institutions of punishment, a kind of experiential distance defines our relationship to its practice. Such distance shields us first from the most fundamental feature of punishment—its infliction of pain. This is a strangely difficult concept. Because punishment is assumed to follow a crime, an act of violence or harm against another, the infliction of pain is perceived as deserved or necessary. Consequently, the question of pain's authority and its effects rarely materializes and instead these are seen as natural and indisputable consequences of individual actions. To understand the spectacle upon which punishment depends, we must temporarily consider the act of punishment alone. Legal theorist Robert Cover famously explores why it is that any man walks into prison of his own volition.[7] How is it that thousands, now millions, of people in the United States are funneled uniformly, bureaucratically, into institutions designed to deprive them of liberty, autonomy, material possessions, family, friends, sex, and security? The answer of course is found in the sheer force and potential violence of the state, embodied in law, the kind of power that can carry the individual to the prison cell, the interrogation room, and the execution chamber. The legitimacy of this claim depends upon the idea of punishment as the only just and effective way to organize human accountability. And yet, to someone with no knowledge of such claims and justifications, punishment would always appear as violence coordinated by one human or group upon another. To talk of pain inflicted in such a context is seen as denying a preexisting pain—the pain of victims and past criminal acts. However, punishment is always a narrative about a chain of pain, one whose origin is not easily traced. The fact that contemporary imprisonment occurs against the backdrop of structural conditions of poverty and vast race and class inequalities, containing within it an immense number of narratives of pain and abuse, where perpetrators and victims bleed together, does little to challenge this fundamental logic of retribution. The remoteness of the penal spectator instead guarantees that his imagining of punishment is haunted by abstract potentialities of danger and insecurity. And this spectator as cultural agent is a formidable force in the construction of pain. In gossip and conversational chat, as well as media and political commentary, the exploration of inflicted pain as nothing other than an appropriate and desirable response to other people's pain and violence is a contemporary cultural requisite.

Legal scholars have argued for some time that the interpretation of the law, in the declarative decisions of judges and political leaders, the legal strategy and interpretation of attorneys, and the daily work of people who manage prisons, always carries a mundane and ordinary pain and violence with it. Few, however, have mapped how the routine popular interpretations and applications of punishment among citizens far removed from the justice system carry with them a similar structure and threatening potentiality. In this way declarations of punishment, those moments when we interpret the law and enact penal judgments both formally and casually, are divorced from the pain that is daily inscribed on the bodies of the punished. In fact, everything about the proper administration of punishment works to conceal this violence of the law through the façade of rational bureaucratic structures that are removed from everyday encounters with punishment's pain. And even those with closest proximity, such as judges, prosecutors, and prison guards, experience a defining distance from any sense of personal responsibility or accountability in the implementation of punishment, rather rationalizing and locating that burden with the individual who committed the crime (where certainly, but not totally, it is due). The citizen experiences an even more remote framework from which to deny this complicity. In this respect, violence is rarely rendered accountable in the deployment of punishment and consequently, a context defined by pain is one in which pain is primarily ignored or invoked figuratively and from a distance. And, as sociolegal scholars Austin Sarat and Thomas Kearns argue, at that distance, the invocation of the law and its violence depends upon "our worst fears and nightmarish beliefs about ourselves and one another—they hold us before the law and induce compliance by making us captive to our own most cynical and despairing images of human nature."[8] Sarat and Kearns continue that in order to live within the framework of law, in order to deed to a sovereign power a monopoly on force and violence, human capacity must be imagined in a peculiar way. In such a world, the possibility of living without law appears as "the specter of human nature turned cruelly against itself, ceaselessly employed in a struggle for more and more power and poised at every turn to do deadly battle,"[9] "a world of scarcity and insecurity,"[10] only domesticated through law's violence. It is this fantasy of justification that undergirds how we punish, and it is in such an imagined space that penal judgment is born.

Part of my argument in this respect is that this imagining has taken on dangerous propensities in recent times. The scale of punishment in the United States has been marked of late by a parallel rise of executive power, one in which an official and powerful form of spectatorial judgment emerges in the offices of the president, attorney general, governor, and prosecutor and seeps broadly into a spectrum of agencies that have built-in susceptibilities to the seduction of punishment, including law enforcement and a wide range of military, intelligence, immigration, and justice institutions. In such moments, the terms of debate about the meanings of punishment are increasingly difficult to alter. Rather, we see a case in which the very need to conceal law's violence and the pain of punishment erodes, where accountability in authority and legitimacy is presented as without need of democratic check, and where the pain of punishment is foregrounded as a new and acceptable currency for public exchange. In this transaction, it is the pain of punishment that speaks most powerfully and effectively for citizens, spanning in its authority as the voice for victims of crime and a new global platform from which to define human worth through torture and exclusion. The hope is that such practices will one day soon appear as anomalous, but even as the notorious post-9/11 U.S. war prisons recede from public practice, their disappearance will always only be an illusion. Rather, such processes and propensities point fundamentally to what occurs in societies where frameworks of punishment are foundationally privileged—at a distance.

Such distance then also shields us from the democratic burden of punishment as a kind of cultural work: something we do, which requires intention, deliberation, and human check, which has effects both intended and unintended—and can and should be interrogated relentlessly. In their call for a jurisprudence of violence, Sarat and Kearns insist that we develop a framework from which to better talk about, represent, and understand the ordinary worlds and experiences of law's violence and the conditions under which ordinary actors step past basic inhibitions that most of us ought to have against the infliction of pain. Such boundaries are crossed routinely in settings that span everyday conversations about punishment in the workplace, schools, political and media commentary, television and film, to the experimental settings of the Stanford prison project, the execution chambers across the United States, and the interrogation wings of Abu Ghraib and other new war prisons. Punishment constitutes one of the most precarious spaces of the human condition in its seductive invitation to rely upon the acts of others, both real and imagined, to justify our own infliction of pain rather than see our place in its problematic pursuit. Classical theorists have long argued that one of the ways in which we become human—and humane—is through intervention, through the ability to engage in social action and assume a collective responsibility. In such spaces, a cultural work is required—one that does not simply set obligatory safeguards and precautionary reminders of the problem of pain in punishment but one that challenges us more fundamentally and insists that we rethink our relationship to punishment altogether.

The Cases

Each of the chapters that follow represents a case in which we see punishment at work from the vantage point of penal spectators. In that discussion, I argue, like most contemporary penal scholars, that punishment is increasingly prolific in everyday practice, well beyond formal institutions, but in a manner that is naturalized and largely invisible. Patterns of exclusion and technologies of confinement are extensive in late modern social life but appear as common features of everyday experience, conveniently and quickly naturalized and only rarely opposed, challenged, or interrogated. Each case in this volume points to sites and instances in which this extensionality and normalcy of social control is mapped into a shift in subjectivities surrounding punishment. This shift is embodied in the worldview that the penal spectator implies, a citizen who sanctions, in her approval and witnessing, the infliction of pain. At each site I address in this volume, I explore a tension between the potentiality of a fully engaged democratic citizen against the privileging of a distanced mode of penal spectatorship. The penal spectator thus makes decisions about punishment based on a framework that depends, in many ways, on a denial of any real democratic engagement in interrogating the project of punishment. Rather, in her positioning, she is so disconnected from the practice of punishment as to be simply a voyeur, yet in a context where her experience carries profound privilege, authority, and moral justification. In each case, I explore what it might mean to move away from this position and to rethink punishment as a practice that is intentional, deliberative, and a special aspect of human agency, always fundamentally chained in its assertion to the production of human pain and its restraint.

For instance, one practice I examine, prison tourism, does bring citizens into a direct physical engagement with prisons, but these encounters occur most popularly in empty, defunct prisons. Even in functioning prisons where the incarcerated are present, these tours are carefully constructed in ways that prohibit active engagement with and interrogation of punishment. These encounters are also characterized by a casual passiveness. Removed from formal institutions of punishment and the individuals they house, the subject is afforded the convenience of the highly mediated, fleeting gaze, looking in on the world of punishment in a manner that does not force or ask observers to speak back or engage in a dialogue. This kind of looking is fundamentally voyeuristic, distracting, and yet authoritative, inhibiting a deeper interrogation of punishment. This structure of address creates a troubling framework for penal engagement which crosses popular and public spaces, developing into convention and recognizable iconography in a variety of cultural settings.

Much of this volume marks an effort to explore the spaces that are dominated by penal inflection, where non-incarcerated citizens "go" to prison, but are often perceived as not, the precise sites at which punishment is missed, overlooked, or misunderstood. In that analysis, the question that persists is, what would it take to make our relationship to punishment more explicit, more reflective, and more critically engaged? At each site, we witness how the acknowledgment of punishment as cultural work is impeded and what the effects of that prohibition are. If punishment is to be understood and conceived of, as most sociologists and criminologists argue, as the infliction of pain and a last resort among social institutions, then how must our interpretations and imaginings of its use and function change and be challenged? In the event that this engagement fails, political protections, civil liberties, and democracy itself are at stake. But, as laid out at the beginning of this chapter, other changes that are more natural and insidious in the structures of everyday life will foreshadow and run parallel beside this larger transformation, in the mundane ways in which we gradually alter our interactions, judgment, and regard of one another, ways that profoundly reshape the nature of social life—and our most common, basic responses to distant and not-so-distant others.

I believe avoiding this kind of dangerous configuration explicitly involves a move to bring discussions about the relationships between punishment lived and punishment imagined to the fore. Consequently, in this study, I look to sites that have high levels of cultural salience either through popularity (media, for instance) or authority (science, for instance) and have historically evaded analysis. The sites I have chosen are all exemplary of how meaning is made culturally, mediating knowledge about prisons often through a powerful, global visual culture. They are by no means totalizing—many other cultural sites could be included with appropriate qualification—but they do reflect a certain contemporary quality as sites that are central to popular meaning making and thus are strategic in understanding punishment at work. Each engages the cultural labor directed at working through the meanings and scripts of punishment, empirical accounts of exemplary cases which might be otherwise overlooked due to their position within the mundane routines, taken-for-granted contexts of cultural life. Here, penal subjects and regimes of truth are produced, commonly, casually. Each case reflects a site from which punishment, in its imagining, assumes a certain amount of authority and legitimacy through the judgment and interpretations of a penal spectator. Each seeks to persuade its subjects of particular truths, working to reconcile contradictions, uncertainties, and contested meanings into unified frameworks, dominant discourses, and, ultimately, narratives of truth. Such efforts may illuminate the ways in which persuasion, including proclivities toward punitiveness and retribution or compassion and forgiveness, is constructed at a distance.

In the next chapter, I explore more fully the complex relationship between penal spectatorship and the idea of punishment as a distinct form of cultural work or labor. I do this specifically through an engagement with contemporary penal and cultural theory. In juxtaposing the meanings of work in relationship to culture and punishment, I argue that a central intersection emerges from which not only to examine the fundamental properties of punishment as an institution but to push us beyond its confines. Such a theoretical pursuit opens up alternative ways in which to think through our most distant relationships to punishment, exploring its double-edged quality in the production and destruction of social life. I begin with a deep look at the way in which contemporary social life is fundamentally melded to penal concerns, thereby creating a framework for analyzing punishment at work in culture. Then, relying heavily upon a broad and interdisciplinary set of perspectives, I attempt to establish a dialogue between otherwise disconnected scholars who are speaking in a contemporary framework across disciplines to the urgency of social commitment in times of exclusion. Out of this dialogue, I point to the ways in which the practice of penal spectatorship—and the sheer extensionality of the penal gaze—implies a present moment in which dangerous social forces collide with distinctly penal and exclusionary underpinnings. I also point to how this dystopian vision opens up the potential for alternative practices and a more optimistic future through the cultural work of a critically engaged democratic citizen, an argument revisited and strengthened in the volume's conclusion.

Chapter 3 begins a survey of cultural sites where we see punishment at work. I begin with the site where punishment is most likely to be accessed popularly, the media. In American culture, the majority of citizens are much more likely to screen the prison rather than visit it. This chapter explores the meanings that circulate in this densely visual arena while simultaneously interrogating the place of the penal image in late modernity—a site where the separation of the image from reality is no longer possible. In this analysis, I surveyed over 400 prison films, defined as narratives which examine or rely upon institutional environments centered upon confinement, from 1970 to the present, while selectively reviewing exemplary classical films from the past. I also sampled a range of contemporary television programs based on their invocation and reliance upon key penal correlates: exclusion, isolation, blame, and the infliction of pain. I also attempted to move beyond classical prison texts whose settings are primarily built around prisons and instead question how penality and its meanings circulate more broadly in performances and representations generally perceived as removed from punishment. Based on this careful review, I argue that the contemporary experience of punishment is far more dominating (but not without ambivalence), wide-ranging, and deeply embedded in social life than previous studies of penal imagery or practice have permitted. Such a pursuit insists upon a much larger theoretical framework for understanding the interaction between the image and the vast variety of everyday discourses and practices that penal representations are caught within. This inquiry also forces a set of questions directed at how one interrogates the nature of this relationship and, by extension, how one approaches the image, particularly the penal image, with analytical integrity. In this regard, the penal image functions theoretically to reveal important things about the study of punishment but perhaps even more significantly the study of representation broadly. My contribution to this developing legacy, however, seeks to demonstrate not simply how crime and punishment are irrevocably and intrinsically bound up with the image but also insists that certain kinds of images, specific penal icons (images of Abu Ghraib for instance), carry with them their own unique sets of representational concerns, problems, and questions, implying a distinct ethical positionality and work in penal spectatorship.

In chapter 4, the volume moves literally into the space of the prison by way of the prison tour. Tours of the penitentiary are historically significant and present at its birth, emphasizing the manner in which both technologies of confinement and processes of looking are central to the blueprint and organization of modern social life. This chapter addresses the manner in which these early functions of spectacle are currently being revisited and revised with the increased popularity of prison tourism. Prisons may now be visited virtually through cyberspace, visually through television and filmic tours, and in person on trendy day and overnight tours of now defunct prisons with both popular and historical appeal. In these commercial tours, the politics of the gaze is primarily grounded in a key tension defined by sheer spectacle and thrill-seeking against efforts of historical education and preservation. Within this context, contradictions in penal discourse emerge which are difficult to sustain or suture. Rather, the penal spectator participates in a series of scripts and roles in which both voyeurism and civic-mindedness construct the proper place of the prison in American history and contemporary public life. I follow this pattern of contradiction into the classroom educational tour, whose politics are grounded in a similar kind of live viewing exhibition yet one which carries an even greater and more precarious source of authenticity and legitimacy in the claims of penal spectators. Here the politics of the gaze intersect with the production of punishment in ways that proliferate with little acknowledgment or consideration of what punishment may mean, but with an additional sense of veracity and moral authority, of "having been there." This chapter, based on interviews with prison preservationists and administrative staff, observations, and extensive participation in prison tours across the United States, contextualized by the analysis of public relations and tour marketing materials, interrogates the tensions embedded in the production of commercial tours of prisons and speculates as to how inherent problems in this kind of engagement might be framed more critically.

In chapter 5, issues of penal spectatorship are revisited in an international prison context defined by its secrecy and invisibility—yet one in which the visual rips into daily life. In the aftermath of the Abu Ghraib scandal, issues of penal representation reappear but in an intensely volatile and complex transnational environment defined as both a prison and a war zone. This analysis extends to an examination of punishment in post–9/11 offshore, off-limits institutional contexts, with a specific emphasis on cultural images of these new war prisons. In this analysis, I relied heavily upon news media coverage, social documentary, photography, and an extensive body of legal cases and commentary, debating the role of torture and detention. This case is particularly critical as it marks the extreme ends of distance and penal spectatorship. In a related theme, what happens in these kinds of prison spaces and the manner in which such spaces are visualized are important harbingers of the shifting meanings and possibilities of punishment in increasingly global, commercial, and postnational contexts—spaces in which what it means to punish are radically bound up with and yet outside of the force of law and sovereignty. In these border zones, troubled penal performances again reveal how the problems of penal spectatorship at a distance force us to revisit the question of what punishment means and may come to mean in postnational contexts. Here too, we are reminded of why an understanding of punishment as cultural work always depends, in its starting point, upon an awareness of its practice as a social limit and never as a source for the regeneration of commitments to social life. Consequently, this chapter, with its emphasis upon the globalization of American punishment and the problem of penal possibility—in the form of new and unregulated modes of punishment worldwide—raises questions about the necessity of a penal politics and the work of punishment in that near future.

In the final case study, I examine the role of science and the scientist in this formation. I look at criminology at a specific historical juncture, one that is routinely identified as the departure point for the failure of rehabilitation in the latter part of the twentieth century. I find that the conjugation of science across this period is fundamentally melded to a social vision of science, which when traced over the three previous decades reveals how the very distinct discourse of penal thought of this time converges with a language of futility and a politics of necessity. I trace these concerns through what I consider to be an emblematic case study of the role of scientist as both a privileged and critical penal spectator. Here, I map how the death of rehabilitation is conjoined to the life and death of Robert Martinson, the sociologist largely credited with the idea that "nothing works" in rehabilitative thinking. In analyzing the place of science culturally, I trace the genealogy of Martinson's publication and key responses to his work, and contextualize the place of this research against broader biographical information gleaned from popular media and personal archives. Such research enabled me to map the manner in which Martinson's research and biography are presented and engaged scientifically and popularly, and how this retrospective continues to construct the work of punishment, redirecting scholarly attention toward punishment through a stark realism. I argue that this shift in intellectual inquiry toward a deeply empirical, evidence-based mode of study indicates something profound about the ways in which we study punishment, the reasons why, and why science itself constitutes a key site in which we see the cultural work of punishment being performed. In this pursuit, science relies upon distinct tropes and metaphors through which to construct the cultural meanings of science rhetorically. In this process, the science of punishment is specifically invoked, analyzed, and engaged as a site for the enactment of a new politics of penality—and a new language that more directly argues for the necessity of deep theory, new questions, and a call by experts for an engaged and circumspect citizenry when it comes to punishment.

The conclusion of the volume attempts to do three things. First, I revisit the key concerns and emergent relations in the cases of the volume. Second, in our pursuit of alternative discourse and practices, I discuss some key exemplars of change, and why such exemplars may be difficult to find. Third, I specifically take on some of the implications of penal spectatorship in relation to the development of a more informed and critical engagement with the work of punishment. The chapter, in this respect, is very much directed at encouraging the pursuit of a new and more radical set of questions, methods, and imaginaries in future research on punishment.

A Final Word

This volume focuses specifically on those sites where individuals who have no direct connection to the harsh realities of punishment are more likely to access imprisonment. These individuals are by definition observers, spectators, and, often, voyeurs who are fundamentally detached from penal experience as both targets and orchestrators of punishment. They are, however, also those citizens whose imagining and intentionality feeds recursively into public policy, the politicization of crime, and the nature and quality of democratic checks upon public institutions of punishment. I very much wanted each chapter to stand on its own as a case—and an application—so that readers might try out different ways of exploring these limits, and that would encourage them to think through other sites in which to apply this framework, something like the beginning of a more critical dialogue where punishment is moved more transparently to the fore in cultural practices we often ignore. I also wanted the processes of penal spectatorship that we all engage in and their implications to be the threads that hold this volume together. In that process, this project and its many settings have reshaped my notion not only of what it means to do criminology and cultural study, but of what it means to be an intellectual and a citizen. The contours of this project—its questions, methods, and findings—are shaped according to this experience, configured through fundamental structures of modern and human thought, which in their instrumental undergirdings perpetually plunge criminologists, prisoners, prison workers, and citizens back toward the "social purposes" of punishment and position the prison as a primary metaphor for the human condition and our search for meaning. In pursuing my research, I have found no one place where my object of study exists. For better or worse, I have found it, like power and freedom, like human agency and social constraint, everywhere. At best, this is a working limit of this study—an attempt to push punishment as far as it will go, to the point where its very frames become unstable. This is importantly an analytical process and not indicative of some fundamental restructuring of the social world around punishment (which may or may not be occurring). And I am aware and cautious of, as British criminologist Lucia Zedner writes, the "danger that writing so apocalyptic . . . will further entrench a culture which penal theorists might properly think they have a duty to resist."[11] To respond to this imperative, I nonetheless push perhaps sometimes further than I should. But it is a push that I feel is necessary to better understand punishment—and its limits—and to understand what that "duty to resist" might look like.

It also explains how I came to prison in those early days thinking I would tell one story and instead found myself caught in a set of vocabularies and logics largely missing words—at the limits of representation. Punishment, in this sense, always operates at the ends of the social where bonds and commitments are severed—and so too does this volume—ruthlessly examining the moments in practice and discourse which are defined by the presence and perceptions of "human and moral problems of a profound and intractable kind—with the fragility of social relations, the limits of socialization, the persistence of human evil, and the insecurity of social life."[12] To borrow Austin Sarat's words concerning capital punishment, imprisonment, like all cultural forms caught along the continuum of punishment, engages "the limits of representation" and the recurring penal problem of not "being able to capture . . . meaning or significance."[13] For Judith Butler, it is this site to which we must return—in search of the human "where we do not expect to find it, in its frailty and at the limits of its capacity to make sense."[14] In this way, I have only come to know the darker propensities of penal spectatorship through my own inevitably voyeuristic and problematic undertakings in the study of punishment. Along the way, these places became sites where I had to persistently remind myself of the importance of an intellectual, a civic, and, most importantly, a human voice.

For these reasons (and all the reasons I lay out in this volume), I believe ultimately the practice of punishment and its study demands equally a choice to view and a process to build the world otherwise. In the midst of such penal predicaments, certain voices, essential theorists of pain and oppression, have been my guides: bell hooks reminding me that she "came to theory because [she] was hurting . . . desperate, wanting to comprehend—to grasp what was happening around and within [her]," because she could see in theory "a location for healing";[15] Patricia Williams struggling to make sense out of a life lived in the painful shadow of ambiguity, "somewhere between the Law and what one feels/intuits as truth";[16] Stanley Cohen, who also "wrote worried and confused papers about why radical theories of crime and deviance seemed 'right,' yet had undesirable, ambiguous or no implications at all for the individual business of helping (social work) or punishing (criminal justice)";[17] C. Wright Mills insisting that the capacity to imagine beyond the self-evident is never only the "task" of sociology, but more importantly "its promise";[18] the American Friends Service Committee insisting that "the quest for justice is endless—a struggle not a goal."[19] Most days, I simply repeated the anonymous words of a female prisoner to myself: "Get up, brush yourself off, and just go on. You gotta walk for the rest of your life."[20] What follows is the outcome. The writing of this work has not been an easy project, much less so than I might have ever imagined. Powerful images have haunted me and strange voices continue to echo around me as the discourse of punishment is filled with troubled texts, negative theories, blind expertise, good intentions gone bad, and lives, languages, and images embedded in painful contradictions that are sadly routinized habits. Yet, in all of this, there is the vision and hope of an otherwise, an elsewhere that could someday be here. This place and its work would be defined not by penality—that complex world of punitive signs, symbols, and practices—but by an informed agency and attention to a deliberate and informed structure of empowerment and freedom. Within this framework, an abhorrence at the infliction of pain and an understanding of its tragic qualities in every instance would no longer be ideas toward which we must work and struggle. They would simply be how we live with ourselves and others. This is the gesture to which I wish to remain faithful.

2

Prison Theory
Engaging the Work of Punishment

To punish is the most difficult thing there is. A society such as
ours needs to question every aspect of punishment as it is practiced everywhere.

> —Michel Foucault, "To Punish Is the
> Most Difficult Thing There Is," 2000

Because of the uniqueness of punishment as a social institution, theory plays a special and critical role in our understanding of
it. This chapter assesses the place of the key concepts of this volume—
penal spectatorship, culture, and work—by way of an interdisciplinary
and theoretical dialogue on punishment, pain, and exclusion. Here I
use theory as a means through which to disrupt and expand our conceptualizations of punishment and also as a model to rethink not only
the project of punishment and its alternatives but the very approaches
and assumptions as social scientists we employ in that pursuit. Perhaps
most importantly, I wish to demonstrate our own complicity in punishment's practice with a new level of depth and extensiveness. Such
an effort begins with the penal spectator who by definition looks in
on punishment and yet is also its author. In this looking, this subject
acts as bystander and outsider as opposed to an engaged participant or
witness. She may stare curiously or reflectively, peer sideways from her
peripheral vision, or gape and gawk directly, but the object of her gaze
is inevitably other people's pain. And it is this quality which complicates any kind of penal spectatorship. There are radically different ways
of looking and participating in other people's pain, ways in which we
all participate.

At their most extreme ends, these ways of looking span a continuum marked by the most profound act of observing—witnessing—to its most profane: torture and, ultimately, killing. In this way, looking is always a mode of action and human will. The witness, as the ultimate observer, is someone whose privileged status depends upon a direct proximity to experience. Bearing witness not only demands an experience of the event but carries with it an endless burden of representation and articulation. In the most extreme of human instances, the witness can say what only the dead know—I experienced the event. And yet, even at the gates of Auschwitz, the witness with an unprecedented moral authority denies himself the role of judge. As political philosopher Giorgio Agamben writes, for the witness, "it is not judgment that matters to him, let alone pardon. . . . It seems, in fact, that the only thing that interests him is what makes judgment impossible: the gray zone in which victims become ex-ecutioners and executioners become victims."[1] As Agamben goes on to elaborate, judgment, while perhaps necessary, implies a resolution or clo-sure to problems that are impossible. In professing such judgment, at the gates of Auschwitz, Agamben writes: "Behind the powerlessness of God peeps the powerlessness of men, who continue to cry 'May that never happen again!' when it is clear that 'that' is, by now, everywhere."[2]

Opposite to the witness is the torturer. Here, the vantage point extends from the orchestrator of pain, a position which requires that the punished be seen as a locus of danger and repugnance, justifiably deserving of im-mense and imminent violence. From the U.S. air base at Bagram to the military prison at Abu Ghraib, ordinary actors who engaged in the pro-duction of such pain describe a deepening ambiguity in law and author-ity which led to a confusion of proper roles and rules. In such settings, soldiers were persistently reminded that they held in their custody "the worst of the worst," that fellow soldiers were dying in the war effort, that nations depended upon an end to terror which in turn depended upon information and "intelligence" contained in the bodies before them which must then be broken. In such times, they and the American people were told, the gloves must come off and all must spend time in the shadows. This rhetoric converged dangerously with military orders, boredom, and creative horseplay. Here, distanced penal spectators actively took on the role of punisher and torturer. Soldiers later described and justified their actions through a variety of logics, including those above. They were just following orders. They did not know that it was wrong to torture. They were just messing around. They were lost. The vast majority of the over

80,000 detainees who were confined in these new war prisons have never gone to trial, had no relevant information, and were eventually released.

In each of the above cases, we approach the extreme ends of spectatorship—sites where individuals have both experience and direct proximity to human experiments in the production of pain. This volume, however, is largely about another kind of space, one safely distanced from such directness but nevertheless marked by the ambiguities, the gray zones, in judgment and action which materialize in the observation of pain as well as the sense of being "lost" in spaces whose sociality is fundamentally distorted. As Susan Sontag writes, "No 'we' should be taken for granted when the subject is looking at other people's pain."[3] Yet, and this is one of the features that defines penal spectatorship, there is often a striking amount of collective enthusiasm and energy in this looking, an inability in fact to turn away, much like passing the scene of an accident. This fervor often translates into a peculiar energy in the call for punitive modes of social response over those directed at building social capital and sustainable, humane relationships. In *The Race to Incarcerate*, Sentencing Project director Marc Mauer writes of the peculiarity of this orientation.

> When one of our loved ones is ill or in trouble, most of us rarely hesitate to employ whatever financial and human resources we can muster to deal with the problem. This might involve specialized medical care, tutors for learning-disabled children, or a nursing home for an aging relative. Deciding how to use taxpayer funds wisely is a contentious issue, of course. One is led to wonder, however, to what extent the zeal with which efforts are made to demonstrate the value of imprisonment is a reflection of the "otherness" of those being imprisoned.[4]

Mauer not only directs us to the strange passion which animates efforts to preserve and extend punishment, but also points to the ways in which such energy is absorbed inevitably from other kinds of social efforts: health care, education, resources for the most vulnerable, including the young and aging.

In this chapter, I wish to explore ways in which to theorize more broadly the energy and fervor that animates penal spectatorship and its foundations in our social order. I pull from multiple intellectual arenas, including empirical sociology, which has carefully measured and historicized the punitive turn, as well as moral and political philosophy, which, through the very power of abstraction, challenges social scientists to ask larger, starker, and more central questions about the role of punishment in everyday life. Many of the foundational thinkers in the sociology of punishment—Emile Durkheim and Michel Foucault, to name only two—powerfully crafted theoretical vistas through the merging of philosophical concerns with the empirical efforts of social science. In a field predominated by technical or narrowly specialized approaches to theory and an often uncritical empiricism, criminologists, in their attempts to get at punishment, can benefit profoundly from a call to move beyond their discipline. This chapter, although somewhat lengthy, is necessarily so in that it lays the foundation for an exploration of the cases ahead in this volume in its attempt to generate an innovative and interdisciplinary theoretical dialogue from which to configure future research.

Dimensions of Penal Spectatorship

In *Governing Through Crime*, sociolegal scholar Jonathan Simon provides us with a model of spectatorship in his analysis of the ways in which state- and subjectivity-building capacities, which privilege crime, construct dangerous solidarities and damage democracy. As crime becomes the primary way in which a broad variety of social problems and social action come to be configured, Simon finds that the penal state itself becomes a framing logic not simply for the urban centers hard hit by crime and violence through spiraling inequalities of race, class, gender, and ethnicity, but for the sites and centers for the performance of middle-class life—offices, workplaces, universities, medical centers, housing, and airports. In such a convergence, he argues, the subject position of the citizen is radically reshaped around a new identity, one that depends upon a common and active imaging of ourselves as victims, in particular, of crime. Here, Simon points to the correlates of this identity—in particular its troubled relationship to race and class.

> Crime victims are in a real sense the representative subject of our time . . .
> It is as crime victims that Americans are most readily imagined as united;
> the threat of crime simultaneously de-emphasizes their differences and
> authorizes them to take dramatic political steps . . . The nature of this
> victim identity is deeply racialized. It is not all victims, but primarily
> white, suburban, middle-class victims, whose exposure has driven waves
> of crime legislation.[5]

Simon's crime victim identity in a contemporary framework supersedes a host of other possible subject positions as citizens, including the consumer and the civil rights subject, and is reproduced and managed popularly and politically as a voice framed by "extremity, anger, and vengeance."[6] In the discourse surrounding emergent executive, legislative, and judicial frameworks, the invocation of the victim is among the most salient and powerful of discourses. As Simon continues, the logic of such an idealized political subject has "important representational consequences" in that "to the extent that activist victims define the victim subject position more generally, lawmaking will systematically favor vengeance and ritualized rage over crime prevention and fear reduction," with prisons and police supplanting other modes of social investment.[7] This opposition further removes prisoners from any secure place in the social order, as

> to be for the people, legislators much be for victims and law enforcement, and thus they must never be (or capable of being portrayed as being for) criminals or prisoners as individuals or as a class. To do so is damning in two distinct ways. First, it portrays a disqualifying personal softness or tolerance toward crime. Second, it means siding against victims and law enforcement in a zero-sum game in which any gain for prisoners or criminals is experienced as a loss for law enforcement and victims.[8]

In these essentializing contexts, it is the idea of a zero-sum framework which positions spectators in a manner where cultural scripts, meanings, and discourses that might complicate and humanize punishment and the punished are singularly closed off. In such spaces, exclusionary divisions become the foundation for social relationships and identities, and these powerful partitions extend into strategies of governance through a reductive invocation of the victim. Simon goes on to describe the insidious ways in which this imagining of the political self has inhibited the ability of the judiciary to serve as an effective check on executive power or to moderate deepening social inequalities. Here he theorizes a profound link between such logic and the reshaping of judgment generally.

> Whether yoked to a panoply of calculative rules such as the sentencing guidelines, or to their own imagined jury of vengeful victims, many contemporary judges now experience themselves as what we might call "judgment machines": people who are no more responsible for the consequences of their judgment than a pregnancy test is for the condition it

declares. It is not simply judges, both federal and state, who have suffered a decline in autonomy, power, and prestige. In a real way, all roles calling for any independent judgment—including, but not limited to, parents, school administrators, and business executives, among others—have become vulnerable to a seemingly limitless panoply of ill-defined yet emotionally powerful suspicions.[9]

Such shifts in judgment imply powerful transformations in the way we view the world and each other. Simon's reframing of the citizen's subjectivity in the United States is marked then by a cultural tendency toward a dystopian imaginary, one in which we return to Sarat and Kearns's fears of a world without law in which the only possible orientation toward one another is through violence and destruction amidst scarcity and insecurity. For Simon, these imaginings seep broadly into frameworks of social interaction and render a particular kind of judgment, one that is distanced and evasive, yet nonetheless authoritative, as an increasingly privileged logic in the organization of daily life. The penal spectator fits squarely within this logic, relying in his or her vicarious and indirect production of pain often upon a newfound authority and claim to legitimacy.

Significantly, the ways in which we see others when regarding punishment are complex and should not be treated in a static or monolithic manner. Transformations in social organization culminate in changing modes of subjectivity where inner lives reflect complex positions in response to everyday experience. In this way, subjectivity might be understood "as both an empirical reality and an analytic category: the agonistic and practical activity of engaging identity and fate, patterned and felt in historically contingent settings and mediated by institutional processes and cultural forms. . . . a strategy of existence and a material and means of governance."[10] In relation to spectatorship, the penal subject is not to be misconstrued as an individualized identity, monolithic and static in its appearance, or as a pathology but rather as a temporal possibility and proclivity, a logic that expresses durability and prevalence in a contemporary framework—one in which we all engage. In this respect, its very breadth and contradictory qualities open up key points of contest, resistance, and the possibility of transformation.

> Subjectivity is not just the outcome of social control or the unconscious; it also provides the ground for subjects to think through their circumstances and to feel through their contradictions, and in doing so, to

inwardly endure experiences that would otherwise be outwardly unbearable. Subjectivity is the means of shaping sensibility. It is fear and optimism, anger and forgiveness, lamentation and pragmatism, chaos and order. It is the anticipation and articulation of self-criticism and renewal.[11]

Because subjectivity is the ground from which we think through our lives and relations to others, it is a critical source for alternative ways of being. More often, it is a process through which to engage the ambiguities of our subject positions. For instance, it is quite possible that citizens see themselves as the targets of surveillance in a culture of control (at school, work, home, etc.) even as they see themselves in other contexts as potential crime victims. Such complex orientations make way for contesting hegemonic discourses and building empathy with groups, like the incarcerated, who are state targets in a far more dramatic physical and material way. In fact, one of the key questions of this volume concerns how to locate and display this compassion and understanding. The penal spectator as a subjectivity practice which more often denies or prohibits this kind of reflection is particularly insidious in its normalization so deeply and extensively across social foundations. For instance, penal spectatorship includes as well practices and engagements that we ordinarily do not conceive of as caught up within the spectrum of punishment at all—moments where cultural scripts and meanings about punishment are invoked in everyday conversation, ordinary events, and popular performances distanced from the formal institutions of punishment. Daily we engage in institutions that map our experiences and decision making through penal frameworks. We watch from within and across a massive mediascape in which films, television dramas, the Internet, video games, and news commentary all lay out scenarios and events from which we try out punishment—and theorize its correlates of judgment, blame, pain, and accountability. We navigate institutions designed increasingly and commonly through penal architecture, now mundane security features of everyday life—gated buildings and communities and a wide array of new surveillance techniques at schools and work, as well as in our leisure and travel. Daily the correlates of punishment and social control materialize around us—but often in a manner which obscures the nature of this practice as anything more than a distant look or fleeting glance.

The nature of this mode of spectatorship in relationship to action, I will argue, is critical to understanding the role and possibility of the social in human relations, well beyond penal frameworks. Punishment serves as an important site from which to comprehend the closing off and opening up of alternative ways of understanding one another, including accountability fostered through frameworks of compassion and forgiveness. With its structuring relationship to pain, judgment, and violence, it serves as a unique site in which collective action, the social, is fundamentally and intentionally directed at creating exclusion and suffering. And it performs this work in ways that are largely invisible. Consequently, it is a site where the cultural work that we do is vastly under-articulated, misunderstood, and evaded, and yet the stakes are profoundly high. Our encounters with punishment across this spectrum of practices are driven by fundamentally collective and thus *social* decisions to inflict pain upon one another. Importantly, this does not mean that punishment is always experienced as pain. I focus less on the experience of punishment and more on the social decision-making processes and cultural imaginings of punishment which color its implementation—and the actors who engage in this construction. When individuals explore meanings of punishment in popular culture, television news, recreational tours, military service at faraway prisons, and scientific research, they ultimately are exploring and trying out justifications for the infliction of pain or its prohibition. The motives, meanings, and attractions of the pain of punishment ultimately underlie any effort to get at how it is structured culturally and what this work of envisioning constitutes in practice.

Because punishment marks a social institution of unique and separate significance due to its proximity to pain, the treatment of punishment as a cultural labor implies much about collective understandings of pain, its limits, and its possibilities in the transformation of human behavior, social life, and notions of the self—but the work of punishment in penal spectatorship is rarely recognized as labor of this sort. Rather, its work is largely assumed and playfully, often simplistically, bound up with philosophical intention, naturalized justifications, and general assumptions about how punishment works—all within an emergent framework that privileges the politicization of punishment, thus lending this position more authority and shaping power in the nature of social exclusion. In order to understand what this work might be and why it is the kind of work so resolutely simplified or overlooked, I believe we start outside of the organizing frames for the study of punishment and instead look at contemporary sites where pain, suffering, and exclusion are argued to be central to vast reconfigurations of social life. In order to get at the place of punishment in social life, we must look first to the various ways in which its correlates, particularly pain, exclusion, and suffering, define contemporary attempts to understand ways of being in the world. In this effort, we must build upon the empirical foundations of the sociology of punishment, but to develop our inquiries and questions more rigorously and with greater depth, we must borrow from moral and political philosophy as well as literary and cultural theory. This chapter then seeks to bring together a variety of voices and theoretical frameworks in a discussion about punishment and its stakes at the ends of social life. In this regard, we are encouraged to consider just how far our penal gaze may carry.

Social Life Reshaped by Punishment: Culture, Theory, and Penal Dystopia

> There are many ways of being human, and each society makes its choices. (Zygmunt Bauman, "Social Issues of Law and Order," 2000)

Late modernity is argued by many of the theorists in this chapter to be defined by the problem of pain and suffering across complex grids of inequality and exclusion. Routinely, contemporary thinkers argue that the history of the present marks a turning point in our understanding and configuration of power. The great inequalities and tragedies of the modern world, those which can never quite achieve explanation or representation, including the concentration camps of the Holocaust to contemporary formations of genocide, are both cause and consequence of emergent propensities in the organization of exclusion and power through new modes of governance. Penal terms are not large enough to frame a full explanation of these events, but these changes have not occurred without a radical reliance upon punitive conditions. These shifts are marked by the ironies of punishment: as failures of the social and moments premised in the absence of accountability, they open up the central terms, questions, and motives of punishment. In this process, a wider account of the meaning of punishment is necessary.

Much of the contemporary and empirical literature on the sociology of punishment has begun the pursuit of this broader elaboration, one which can permit a stronger assessment of punishment's centrality to social life and institutions far removed from its formal practice. One tendency in this line of thought encourages us to consider punishment as an extensive structural force which organizes, regulates, and lends a particular set of possibilities to the dimensions of social life and human existence, again built upon exclusion.

Prison thus constitutes a uniquely important form of penal architecture, creating the historically unprecedented ability to contain thousands— even millions—of human beings, and to target and define unwanted groups. Generalizing penal space from the prison into a concept of architecture, however, allows us to think about, first, other sorts of spaces where penality works, and secondly, spaces of the prison that have either been neglected in earlier periods of study or which have only become visible under current conditions.[12]

Such an elaboration importantly points to the massive quality of penal impact, its ability to shape the lives of millions of people. Second, it strategically relocates punishment in a manner which allows us to theorize its place across social life broadly in "other sorts of spaces where penality works" and the conditions and contexts within which punishment is rendered visible. In doing so, it encourages us to think through new and emergent spaces which share the architecture and conditions of the prison. Third, in a consideration of these spaces, the primacy of punishment in relation to culture is foregrounded, replete with complex and contradictory meanings, opening up new and larger questions about the role of punishment in our understanding of the world. Philip Smith writes, "The meanings of punishment on the nonbureaucratic, nonstate periphery are not restricted to dry and dusty institutional readings but involve complex intersections with the myths of popular culture, with literature and symbolism, and involve the mobilization of emotions. We need cultural theory to understand this, not just criminological or institutional theory."[13] In such a context, punishment is much more richly and usefully explained as a complex, interactive process, where cultural values and meanings are multiple, always circulating and converging in a nexus of experiences and places, in a manner which profoundly troubles and disrupts analytical pursuits.[14] This quality is best exemplified in the concept of penality which assumes an expansive notion of punishment as present and at work in the lived spaces and practices of everyday life, well beyond the institutional forms punishment may take.

As French philosopher Michel Foucault asserts in *Discipline and Punish*—the work that introduces the concept of penality with the most analytical precision—the force of punishment is manifested through an accumulation of signs, symbols, discourses, and material practices, one in which "the art of punishing, then, must rest on a whole technology of representation."[15] Here, the penitentiary "technique" culminates in a carceral archipelago which extends throughout the entire social body. At the heart of the carceral is a complex network, but one, importantly, which, as we have already discussed, is founded upon a juridical author- ity and legitimacy which materializes through the declaration of punish- ment. Such embeddedness explains how institutions of punishment (the prison; the sanction of death; internal technologies of control and surveil- lance) are further mapped into other, seemingly distant institutional de- signs (hospitals, factories, schools, airports) that reflect and reproduce the relationship of knowledge to power. At the foundations of the social in late modernity, penality circulates ceaselessly for Foucault, through its in- stitutions, practices, and discourses, until its disciplinary logic structures self-governance itself. Importantly, however, this power to punish and its embeddedness in modern social life and thought becomes most insidious in its naturalized appearance and legitimacy—its seeming transparency as social practice. In this way, the penal is fundamentally structured within contemporary social life in ways that are largely invisible. Penality is, thus, an important expansive rubric within which the scope of this phenom- enon may be explored. Sociologist David Garland refers to this term as "'punishment' in its wider sense," invoking "discursive frameworks of au- thority and condemnation, ritual procedures of imposing punishment, a repertoire of penal sanctions, institutions and agencies for the enforce- ment of sanctions and a rhetoric of symbols, figures, and images by means of which the penal process is represented to its various audiences . . . the network of laws, processes, discourses, representations and institutions which make up the penal realm."[16]

More significantly, penality reveals that analytical and disciplinary frames for understanding punishment often differentiate and isolate penal practice in a manner which ignores the fact that "in the penal realm these various relations are actually fused in a series of *condensed* and *complex* relations."[17] No analytical consideration of punishment is truly possible without an awareness of this complex overlapping and spiraling environ- ment. As Garland continues:

> Clearly, then, the penal sanction of imprisonment is a complex condensa-
> tion of a whole series of relations. The same is true of other penal sanctions.
> These relations are neither external nor accidental in relation to penality.
> They are part of its structure, of its significance and of its effects. Each type
> of relation at once operates through penality and at the same time links pe-
> nality into a direct connection with other social realms and institutions (the

political realm, the ideological formation, social policy, the legal system, the economy, etc.). The task of social analysis is to lay bare these connections and relations, to explain how they enter into penal practices and policies, and to explain penality in light of that knowledge. In political terms, this promotes the double effect of viewing penality in all of its complexity *and* of reconnecting penal issues with more general political struggles.[18]

In an effort to "lay bare" some of "these connections and relations" as they enter, reproduce, and alter penal patterns in cultural life, the development of better explanatory frameworks requires particular attention to grounding. Understanding the complexity of penality requires careful attention at the moment of its practice as well as attention to the ways in which that practice occurs broadly across social life. This pursuit takes on a distinct kind of contemporary imperative, particularly as this moment of practice cannot be extricated from political, moral, ethical—and ultimately, social—struggle, a transformation, as Garland calls it, of penality.

Ultimately, the emergence of penality as a structuring concept for the sociology of punishment reflects larger debates about how to access and study culture. With the emergence and rise of a cultural criminology, a community of transnational scholars has dedicated itself to the analysis of the place of culture in relation to crime and punishment in late modernity, relying heavily upon critical theoretical frameworks and qualitative methodologies (ethnography, discourse, and textual analysis) borrowed from both the social sciences and the humanities.[19] Critics like Garland, who has similarly privileged culture in his own work, have, in response, encouraged a deeper reliance upon sociology as the primary discipline through which to achieve explanatory analyses of culture.[20] Interestingly, both critiques extend beyond criminology but in a manner that is still formative in their ability to integrate successfully and persuasively the role and place of other disciplines in an examination of punishment and culture. Social scientists are inherently skeptical of many of the critical methods of cultural studies, and few criminologists are trained at the graduate level in anything other than a sociological or criminological conceptualization of the role and function of theory. Similarly, the most critical of cultural criminologists find it difficult to privilege sociology as a foundation not without its own set of limitations in explaining culture. Part of my argument in this volume is that there are profound benefits to be attained theoretically and methodologically from an integration of scholars, near and far, and not always harmonious, who have taken punishment and, more broadly, the production of pain as their research commitments. Across this volume, the work of social scientists (not only criminologists and sociologists but importantly anthropologists, historians, and political scientists) converges with the work of intellectuals whose origins are more directly related to the humanities (literary scholars, art historians, philosophers, media scholars, and cultural theorists). And the conceptual map that develops out of such convergences is one that follows our object of study, the pain of punishment, in its travels.

A discussion of punishment which begins here affords us the significant opportunity to reframe punishment in a larger narrative about the project of pain and human compassion, thus a story of the limits and potentialities of human experience and action. From this perspective, punishment becomes more than an institution or lens through which to think about social life or contemplate the dark, disciplinary underside of modernity but rather a central site from which to understand the most base and the most hopeful of social—and human—aims, the infliction of pain and its prohibition through compassion and mercy. Contemporary social theory foregrounds these questions with a new sense of urgency. As sociologist Ulrich Beck theorizes, risk follows vulnerability and these kinds of turns mark a place from which to be wary of emergent inequalities with unprecedented depth: "There is a fatal attraction between poverty, social vulnerability, corruption and the accumulation of dangers. The poorest of the poor live in the blind spots which are the most dangerous death zones of world risk society."[21] In such contexts, Beck argues that the sociological imagination must be renewed and the foundations of sociology revisited. Now more than ever, an orientation is needed, he argues, which recognizes that "learning about others" is not simply a tenet of sociology but something upon which the fate of humanity rests. Similarly, post-structuralist and feminist theorist Judith Butler, relying heavily upon French philosopher Emmanuel Levinas, insists that the future of the present depends upon the construction of a subject position in which we are capable of reflecting and responding to the suffering and vulnerability of distant others, of strangers with whom we share very little in common. Here, importantly, the concerns of social scientists and moral philosophers converge.

For all of the thinkers in this chapter, the force of punishment is always implied in the foundations of social order. Social control and regulation depend upon constructions of "order" and "norm," which, sociologist Zygmunt Bauman argues, "are sharp knives pressed against the society as it is; they are first and foremost about separation, amputation, excision, expurgation, *exclusion*," promoting "the 'proper' by sharpening the sights on the improper; they single out, circumscribe and stigmatize parts of reality denied the right to exist—destined for isolation, exile or extinction."[22] In this way, punishment always represents a collective decision to build inequalities, to respond to pain and violence through its infliction. It is,·ultimately, a violence and force particularly compelling in the way in which it extends throughout social patterns and institutions and the manner in which it intersects with social vulnerability, what anthropologist João Biehl has carefully mapped in his analyses of "zones of social abandonment."[23] In her provocative invocation of a genocide continuum, anthropologist Nancy Scheper-Hughes similarly encourages us, based on her own fieldwork experiences, to reconsider sociologist Erving Goffman's work and the "logical relations between concentration camps and mental hospitals, nursing homes, and other 'total' institutions, and between prisoners and mental patients."[24] For Scheper-Hughes, such relations include a capacity and ordinary willingness to engage in a routinized, indifferent violence that risks increasingly positioning specific kinds of groups as disposable waste or as less than fully human: "'better off dead' or even as better off never having been born."[25] These populations are defined by their vulnerability, invisibility, and exclusion: the very old, the very sick, the mentally disabled, the poor-unto-death, the imprisoned, victims of extreme violence, as well as other historically marginalized groups on the basis of race, religion, and ethnicity. Scheper-Hughes argues that such tendencies lay the foundation for "mass" killing and are active agents within the logics, languages, and practices of all social institutions, including family, health care, education, religion, and the military. Out of this confluence emerges

> an evolving social consensus toward devaluing certain forms of human life and lifeways (via pseudo-speciation, dehumanization, reification, and depersonalization); the refusal of social support and humane care to vulnerable and stigmatized social groups seen as social parasites ("nursing home elderly," "welfare queens," "illegal aliens," "Gomers," etc.); the militarization of everyday life (for example, the growth of prisons, the acceptance of capital punishment, heightened technologies of personal security, such as the house gun and gated communities); social polarization and fear (that is, the perceptions of the poor, outcast, underclass, or certain racial or ethnic groups as dangerous public enemies); reversed feelings of victimization as dominant social groups and classes demand violent policing to put offending groups in their place.[26]

Such interconnections across social life may seem stark but they point to an important and dangerous quality of embeddedness that makes the interrogation of punishment such an integral practice to democratic and inclusive processes. To engage in or talk about punishment is to pull from a nexus of meanings centered upon the nature of social support and what occurs in its absence and reflects a conscious decision to do so. To do so without this deliberate awareness positions us all in a precarious space for several reasons. First, punishment is never about inclusion. It is an institution always to be engaged in as a last resort, when all others have failed. In light of this fact, it always marks the limits of the social, the contexts and settings in which we fail. Thus, in the work of penal spectatorship, we are making decisions about the proliferation or minimization of violence by choosing how we imagine and build structures of exclusion—a choice that demands a critical mindfulness. This makes punishment the institution par excellence from which to consider how and when we will treat those who fall outside the frames of social inclusion, of how and under what conditions we will respond through the intentional invocation of pain to the weaknesses, violence, vulnerabilities, and suffering of others. It is, thus, a social practice to be thought through perpetually and interrogated relentlessly in its application. The possibility of acting outside of or otherwise to punishment's violence and the violence that drives punishment can only occur through this kind of critique.

In criminology, this kind of discussion has been given a privileged but somewhat segregated space. The major thinkers today in the sociology of punishment are certainly engaging with such concerns, but there is a mainstream, influential, and larger group of researchers, largely made up of criminologists and sociologists, who map mass incarceration, capital punishment, and its satellite sanctions mostly through methodological as opposed to theoretical frames, often privileging empirical measurement without or with narrow theoretical frames.[27] Such approaches substantively mute these dimensions through an emphasis on a technical, instrumentalist, and correctional orientation to punishment which, quite simply, is self-limiting. These efforts, although often quite valiant, restrict the important role the scholar of punishment plays in the larger, far more extensive and influential story of pain and human suffering. Work that has addressed this potentiality is largely guided from within criminology by a Foucauldian emphasis upon governmentality and a new penology.

Governmentality, with its implied rationalities, centers upon knowledges and practices that operate across and are shared between individuals, institutions, and the state. Within the framework of the new penology, a concept framed through governmentality by sociolegal scholars Malcolm Feeley and Jonathan Simon, punishment and its discourses, objectives, and techniques come to operate broadly across the social body as a form of governance. Within this new mode of governance, crime control efforts on the part of the state are defined by an abrogation of responsibilities to other kinds of social institutions that are already and historically un-dersourced and undertrained—thus governing from a distance or govern-ing the least. This mode of governance is most compelling in its ability to move out from political centers through dense, overlapping networks in which authorities, groups, institutions, and individuals all reflect a new emphasis no longer on production but on the calculation of the activities and desires of others. Such entities will direct classification via an assess-ment of risk, including where it is most likely to occur and how it might most efficiently be managed. Under the new penology, risk, in the form of "dangerous" populations, is most effectively managed, not through normalization, but via spatialization marked by a well-mapped exclusion and isolation through mechanisms of classification rather than the more disciplinary mode of segregation through social control institutions. This phenomenon is noted in the governmentality literature as governing from or at a distance, and importantly parallels the faraway subject position of the penal spectator. This pattern is most visible when social control is or-ganized in a manner that extends beyond justice agencies into families, communities, schools, churches, and other primary social institutions as well as the fabric of social life. For instance, increasing attention and debate has centered upon the mapping of sex offenders in communities through social policy and legislation as groups who remain intractably in need of management, grounded in a fundamental public pessimism about the possibility of individual reformation or change. In the clinical and jus-tice discourses surrounding that management, the vocabulary of actuari-alism through risk management models is strongly apparent. These pat-terns are significant in the manner in which they invoke penality as a way to generate fundamental changes in political culture, generate regimes of truth, exercise power, differentiate groups, classify individuals, and thus in general reorder social life. In such a context, material structures have social and political effects with life organized around the prison and a perpetual search for security.

Such patterns are strikingly similar to other emergent sociological con-cepts, including Zygmunt Bauman's paradigm of exclusion, Jock Young's exclusive society, and Loïc Wacquant's urban outcasts and "deadly symbiosis" of community and prison. In such contexts, Foucauldian disciplinary modes, with their emphasis upon normalization—and the closing of a gap between a norm and its deviation—no longer dominate. Rather, these gaps are simply accommodated and regulated largely through exclusionary practices. In contemporary social and political contexts, "it is cheaper to know and plan around people's failings than to normalize them."[28] This marks a critical site from which the study of punishment must distance itself, careful not to reproduce these exclusions and normalizations through an institutionalized myopia in its own reports and research. Rather, the place of experts is one that calls direct attention, like the authors above, to these dangerous convergences. This kind of engagement with governmentality reminds us that emergent modes of governance shape the nature of what it means to be social and risk making it more difficult for groups and individuals to build solidarity and exercise political choice. At stake is the preservation and protection of human agency from forms of regulation and classification that may, at first glance, seem all too rational, logical, and "natural." In such contexts, the privileging of actuarial techniques risks denying the moral, political, and social significance of the historical markers of vulnerability—race, class, gender, and age—instead arguing these differences are no longer problematic, closing off significant social debates a priori. Beyond this, individual and group identities are rendered flat and sterile with little critical reflexivity. As Simon argues, "Rather than making people up, actuarial practices unmake them."[29] Out of this emerges a new and dangerous kind of social collectivity, one that is defined not by a deep sense of shared bonds or experiences but by exclusion.

In such scenarios, the weakening of social welfare frameworks for governance has led to an expansion and exportation of punitive carceral strategies by the United States, a new mode from which to regulate minorities, the poor, and otherwise "urban outcasts" across the planet.[30] Importantly, these shifts are not hidden or invisible but rather prominent, naturalized features of emergent urban landscapes. Such transformations map the manner in which sovereignty is reconfigured in a broad social and global landscape with the imprint of a distinctly American mode of punishment. Citizenship in these contexts is experienced as hierarchical, determinedly and dangerously paternalistic and punitive in its reliance and reproduction of social and cultural oppositions of race and class, all of which flow into and out of insecurities surrounding criminality and dangerousness. In this sense, penal spectatorship is a distinctly dangerous way of seeing in its capacity to feed into social practices which extend globally and foundationally into social order and life.

For political theorist and philosopher Georgio Agamben, the stark nature of this emergent sociality is found in the exclusionary foundations of modern political life itself. Agamben insists upon a complete reorientation of our understandings of social and political life around the notion of the ban (exclusion), which he argues is the origin of public relations, integral to the original act of sovereignty. Here, Agamben argues, the very assertion of the state's existence depends in its production on a formative exclusion. In this process, the politicization of bare life, what he calls homo sacer—the life, under Roman law, imagined as one which may be killed by anyone—becomes the decisive event of modernity, with sociality and political life fundamentally grounded in abandonment as opposed to some semblance of consensus or inclusion idealized within the social contract. For Agamben, it is the astounding possibility of the concentration camp, as opposed to Foucault's prison, as the exemplar of modern life which makes his case so important to the reorientation of political and social life. The camps capture the place and moment in which exclusion, the state of exception that is the origin of law and sovereignty, is given permanence and visibility, unto death. The camp then serves as the limit concept for understanding all social relations when moved beyond law, politics, and the social, where its inhabitants are rendered agentless actors, the living dead. In Agamben's polis, then, we are bound to an exemplar of exclusion as opposed to a social contract of inclusion.

It is this space of the camp that is reopened when the state of exception becomes the rule, a formation that Agamben views as the fundamental biopolitical paradigm of the West and the administrative role of the United States in the war on terror.[31] Sovereignty and law then are built upon a series of contradictions: the fact that sovereignty depends upon an existence outside and inside the juridical order; the fact that ultimately the violent transgression of the law is indistinguishable from the execution of the law and the violence of the state; and the notion that the state is founded not upon a social contract which implies and depends upon a collective inclusion but rather a fundamental exclusion, an "untying" of social ties in a state of exception. In such a state, the production and reproduction of the political, of the social, of power, and of the law depend upon exclusion, a state of exception that becomes the rule, abandoning certain ones to the power of death and reopening, daily, the possibility and spaces of the camps.

This concern with the worth of human life sits center stage to debates about and beyond punishment and has emerged as a key focal point for contemporary theorists. For Judith Butler, the apprehension that lies at the heart of Agamben's state of exception is evident in her concerted attempt to point to the precariousness of life evident in U.S. practices of indefinite detention, extraordinary rendition, and the development of new war prisons, all of which depend upon the failure of contemporary "structures of address." In Butler's analysis, she insists that the recognition and response we construct in moments of address, in which other human beings demand notice and acknowledgment, are the shape of things to come. Relying heavily upon Levinas's notion of the "face," she reveals this structure to be one in which the human face, the human gesture, in pain calls out and demands a response from social actors in the midst of life's most fragile and precarious conditions. It is in the failure to recognize that look as an address, in the failure to respond, that a bleakness which marks the ends of the social begins. Similarly, real and meaningful transformation, for Agamben, does not begin "until a completely new politics—that is, a politics no longer founded on the exception of bare life—is at hand." In the meantime, "every theory and every praxis will remain imprisoned and immobile, and the 'beautiful day' of life will be given citizenship only either through blood and death or in the perfect senselessness to which the society of the spectacle condemns it."[32] Importantly, here Agamben points to the manner in which human action itself is locked into penal terms with citizenship (who "counts") defined and moderated through pain, death, violence, and spectacle. To move beyond such states, he concludes, "implies nothing less than thinking ontology and politics beyond every figure of relation, beyond even the limit relation that is the sovereign ban. Yet it is this very task that many, today, refuse to assume at any cost." Agamben's vision is most startling not simply in its assertion of exclusion as the foundational dynamic of political and social life but in the aversion of viewing, explaining, or taking up the work of rethinking this very dynamic. For contemporary social theorists, the task remains then limited in its purview, one which foregrounds exclusion in social organization—a task that many of us either expressly or inadvertently avoid in the practice of daily life.

What does such a potentiality and routine evasion mean for punishment? The punished mark in many ways the ultimate stranger, those who are criminalized within deeply individualized frameworks and thus must bear often sole responsibility for a spectrum of harmful acts, including violence. Interpretive frames that have dominated penal decision making emphasize individual responsibility and the positioning of the imprisoned as monstrous while simultaneously organizing their relocation across geographies of aggregate segregation and exclusion. These individuals and the groups we assemble them in, consequently, mark the limits of desert and worth in social life. Deciding what to do with them stands at the heart of criminology—and the social enterprise—and is directly bound up with the gaze and understandings of the penal spectator. The question of how we pursue this task at a time when penality proliferates has assumed center stage in criminological debates. Many find themselves asking what it might mean to privilege a kind of ethics and contemplative reflection, from which we might "better understand, refute and supplant the dangers of the moralism which seem to provide plausible responses to contemporary threats to global security"[33] and yet open up dangerous patterns in exclusion. Some imply that this will depend, as Ulrich Beck argues, upon a new discussion of the basic goals and categories of social scientific thinking, an opening up of disciplinary boundaries in a manner that focuses upon the very "unthinkable-ness" of a sociology or criminology in the penal places we find those we study. All of these contemporary theoretical perspectives, importantly, see in the current moment a turning point in the history of power. Out of that moment, new questions, methods, theories, and modes of writing become paramount, while simultaneously new and dangerous social and political conjunctures occur within a global framework. Such movements will depend upon new ways of looking and new understandings of punishment as work itself. In the final portion of this chapter, I turn from an admittedly dystopian penal framework to one that explores how a counter-discourse of work in penal practice might assist us in invoking punishment's limits. This cultural work of punishment is a site from which to formulate an alternative to penal spectatorship, a pursuit that underlies each of the empirical cases this volume examines.

The Work of Punishment

> Such moments of ideological rupture and transformation are never smooth; the ideological 'work' required, shows through; so do the breaks and dislocations. (Stuart Hall et al., *Policing the Crisis*, 1978)

The privileging of work in this argument marks an attempt to open up the sociological significance of the responsibility and civic burden that punishment carries with it. In late modern life, work quite often carries meanings centered upon alienation and disillusionment, including the constraining protestant ethics of productivity, the iron cages of formal, rationalized bureaucracy, and postmodern, consumerist notions of labor as empty and meaningless. This confluence marks the sociological understanding of work, a complex arena of thought largely theorized as occupational and organizational. I rely on some of these notions but also draw from intellectual theories and invocations of work that emphasize its place in culture and its role and possibility in the active construction of meaning. In contrast to the stark vision of exclusion voiced by theorists above, political theorist Michael Ignatieff argues that "a decent and humane society requires a shared language of the good," one that depends upon "a theory of human needs . . . to define what we are in terms of what we lack, to insist on the distinctive emptiness and incompleteness of humans as a species" and to insist upon our unique "capacity to create and transform our needs."[34] For these reasons he argues that "the deepest motivational springs of political involvement are to be located in this human capacity to feel needs for others."[35] In modernity, however, need may be addressed institutionally in ways that are staggering in their capacity to keep us removed from its materiality and visibility, "strangers from each other."[36] Echoing Agamben, Ignatieff invokes Shakespeare's King Lear, caught now in "the vast grey space of state confinement . . . Needs are met, but souls are dishonoured. Natural man—the 'poor, bare, forked animals'—is maintained; the social man wastes away."[37] This claim of need "has nothing to do with deserving; it rests on people's necessity, not on their merit, on their poor common humanity, not on their capacity to evoke pathos."[38] It is out of this framework that my own elaboration of a work of punishment begins.

What happens if we center the concept of work in relationship to punishment as one built around a public and collective good as opposed to a harsh retribution? What is the relationship of work to agency—what does it mean to act deliberately and with intention in order to build the world collectively as opposed to segregate it through the production of pain? What might it mean to take on collectively the pain of victims and perpetrators and to serve as arbiters and mediators in that project—a project in which both are distinctly disabled due to their proximity to pain? For political philosopher Hannah Arendt, this work in its orientation and attention toward pain and suffering, which is unlikely ever to recede fully, is a fundamental marker of our human-ness and thus a condition of the social. She writes:

[T]he human condition is such that pain and effort are not just symptoms which can be removed without changing life itself; they are rather the modes in which life itself, together with the necessity to which it is bound, makes itself felt. For mortals, the 'easy life of the gods' would be a lifeless life. . . . The fact is that the human capacity for life in the world as always implies an ability to transcend and to be alienated from the processes of life itself, while vitality and liveliness can be conserved only to the extent that men are willing to take the burden, the toil and trouble of life, upon themselves.[39]

For Arendt, our shared humanity is found not through pain's displacement or its resolution but through its experience—through our engagement, however fundamentally problematic and partial, with the suffering of others. It is, for Arendt, the capacity and willingness to take up a kind of work, the burden of toil and trouble which preserves vitality, liveliness, and potentiality. Work here is experienced not as a product but as the "sheer actuality" of living, of life's performance.

In an intellectual eulogy dedicated to philosopher Louis Marin, Jacques Derrida theorizes a similar kind of analytical framework against another end of the social, the circumstance of mourning. Here, Derrida elaborates the endless, perpetual quality of such an engagement.

Work: that which makes for a work, for an *oeuvre*, indeed that which works—and works to open: *opus* and *opening*, *oeuvre* and *overture*: the work or labor of the *oeuvre* insofar as it engenders, produces, and brings to light, but also labor or travail as suffering, as the enduring of force, as the pain of the one who gives. Of the one who gives birth, who brings to the light of day and gives something to be seen, who enables or empowers, who gives the force to know and to be able to see—and all these are powers of the image, the pain of what is given and of the one who takes the pains to help us see, read, and think.[40]

For Derrida, work marks a project with no end or closure, a labor bound up with creative expression, illumination, and possibility through the experience and witnessing of suffering and pain. In this work, closure and resolution are always false acts—as work continues perpetually. In his conceptualization, the work of mourning marks *all* work, present in any effort to bring something to light, open it up, let it be seen and made meaningful for us—a process that continues in perpetuity and is fundamentally bound up with suffering. The work of mourning is thus defined through its proximity to pain—the physical pain of another that it cannot access and the pain of lost human relationships that it cannot evade—experiences beyond communication and social exchange.

Derrida's passage is striking in the way in which it parallels fundamental aspects of punishment. For instance, both pain and punishment mark specific limits of the social. They are fundamentally about the destruction of human relationships and the failure of social institutions. Although rebirth and hope are possible within their contexts, they are always qualified possibilities, never guaranteed and dependent upon human action. As experiences, they simply cannot be closed off—there is no closure or resolution to the meanings, pains, or effects of their projects. They also mark the limits of representation, incapable of ever achieving anything more than partial expression and understanding. The work of mourning and the work of punishment in this way demand critical reflection—a conscious effort directed toward interrogation of pain and its expression. In this way, both death and punishment make demands of the collective that are unusual, pushing the possibilities of the social to extreme ends, challenging the capacities and potential of social and personal action. To be understood or rendered meaningful, they require an intimacy with suffering and travail. They require work. Here perhaps—and with finality—the similarities end.

Literary scholar Elaine Scarry, in her powerful elaboration of *The Body in Pain*, offers a related conceptualization of work when she theorizes that pain and imagination are usefully contemplated as "each other's missing intentional counterpart . . . perhaps most succinctly suggested by the fact that there is one piece of language used—in many different languages—at once as a near synonym for pain, and as a near synonym for created object; and that is the word 'work.'"[41] Scarry's application of "work," like Derrida's, captures both the degenerative and the regenerative possibilities in the experience of pain. Within this application, there is a corollary theory of punishment, one dependent upon punishment's most base intentional element: pain. She outlines below the conditions under which these potentialities are made realities through the fulcrum of work:

[T]he deep ambivalence of the meaning of 'work' in western civilization has often been commented upon, for it has tended to be perceived at once as pain's twin and as its opposite: in its Hebrew and Greek etymological origins, in our spoken myths and unspoken institutions, and in our tradition of religious and philosophic analysis, it has been repeatedly placed by the side of physical suffering yet has, at the same time and almost as often, been placed in the company of pleasure, art, imagination, civilization—phenomena that in varying degrees express man's expansive possibility, the movement out into the world that is the opposite of pain's contractive potential. Any sense that this duality is arbitrary dissolves when work is seen against the full array of intentional acts and objects; for work (like all the intentional states looked at above but to a much greater degree than was apprehensible there) conforms to this same arrangement. The more it realizes and transforms itself in its object, the closer it is to the imagination, to art, to culture; the more it is unable to bring forth an object or, bringing it forth, is then cut off from its object, the more it approaches the conditions of pain.[42]

Punishment, defined classically by its intentionality—and yet simultaneously by the failure of those intents (penitence, rehabilitation, crime control, retribution)—is remarkable in this context. It is precisely the realization of intentional acts, the transformability of objects that lends meaning to work. Punishment, primarily defined by the absence of this realization, by the impossibility of achieved intentionality, is necessarily "cut off from its object," therefore explaining its deep resonance with pain. Its force and practice in cultural life will always carry this dissolution and severance with it, as will the work of its critique.

For Scarry, work is the arbiter between pain and imagination as they become externalized events, breaking the internal boundaries of body and mind, moving out into a new framework that is "sharable," "social," "human," and, thus, to some degree, hopeful. In this process, Scarry argues, "it hurts to work," but this is also a point from which one can begin to build a grid of collective alteration: "Imagining a city, the human being 'makes' a house; imagining a political utopia, he or she instead helps to build a country; imagining the elimination of suffering from the world, the person instead nurses a friend back to health."[43] Here, pain, its experience, and its witnessing become mechanisms through which to imagine the world otherwise—and against pain. The objects of these imaginings take on the material form of artifacts, and "in the end artifice has a scale as large as that in imagining because its outcome is for the first time collective."[44] In this regard, we are able to witness the processes by which the social is born and its relationship specifically to the production and alteration of pain. But what if pain is implicated and practiced in social life in a manner distinctly disconnected from its own experience, from the processes or recording of witnessing, of thoughtful, collective deliberation?

This volume is very much about what happens in the process of pursuing the work of punishment in this manner, a work that is distinctly different from most human labors and the practices, institutions, and discourses that emerge out of them. The contemporary cultural work of punishment, I find, is necessarily directed at destruction rather than construction, a labor that has no clear or measurable contribution to the well-being of social life in the way that other social institutions, such as family, education, economy, and religion, do. For this reason, it is an institution fundamentally conflicted and one whose work is always thwarted and truncated—whose labor is always occurring at the ends of the social, cut off from its object. This makes punishment a practice of unique analytical, cultural, and practical significance. This distinctiveness of punishment as a productive and meaningful kind of work does not imply that punishment accomplishes nothing—that it does not have an extensive and complex cultural work; rather, it pursues a work that is radically disengaged from its origins (pain), startlingly unacknowledged, and, from a contemporary framework, proliferating. The futility of this work, and its exemplar, is perhaps nowhere more apparent than in the prison itself. As anthropologist Lorna Rhodes demonstrates in her carefully researched ethnography of the control prison, reason itself is projected through pain—where the infliction of pain is seen as a necessary duty in order to bring inmates forcibly to reason, to make them acknowledge their necessary identity as rational actors, in settings marked by a surplus of power: maximum security.

With the rise of maximum and now super-maximum prisons, the mass movement of the mentally ill into prison systems, the racialization of incarceration, and the sheer scale of the prison-industrial complex, prison work can no longer be separated from patterns of consumption and a prison sociology defined by game-like tensions built around exclusion and control. Here Rhodes theorizes individual choice and responsibilization strategies among inmates and staff in a manner which not only privileges the "full possession of free will," an essential and necessary maneuver in the rise of the control prison, but one which offsets and distracts from fundamental questions about the manner in which selves are positioned in relation to one another—in relation to the social. Prisoners are responsible for their crimes, their infractions, their resistance—all of which is carefully, complexly constructed as "choice" while the role of prisons, institutions, and the social goes unmarked—as do the ways in which prison workers and communities are caught in the same techniques. Such frameworks demand an ongoing public mechanism of thoughtful critique as a check on what can become dangerously insular worlds in which extreme acts that pleadingly demand social attention are misconstrued as pathological. This kind of interrogation would be one, like Rhodes's, which asks: "What are the contexts in which certain ideas about self and self-responsibility become useful? What *work* is done, in the kind of practice that engages this man, by regarding himself in such full—not to say murderous—possession of individuality and autonomy?"[45] This kind of work is problematic and distinctly different from that of other social institutions and kinds of cultural production, not in the manner in which it privileges individuality but in its distinct denial and erasure of structure in its most rigid manifestation—the prison—against individuality. As Bauman writes, "in the process of exclusion, the excluded themselves are cast as the principal, perhaps the sole, agency. Being excluded is presented as an outcome of social suicide, not a social execution."[46] In this way, "the guardians of order" are guaranteed not simply legitimacy and authority but a moral force of judgment that resists challenge. Ideas about the possible solidarity and community-building functions of punishment, the earliest of justifications in the United States, are transformed. No longer directed at human transformation for the sake of inclusion, an "aggressive solidarity"[47] develops built upon total exclusion. The control prison is exemplary in the manner in which it marks this turn. Here, prisoners who are confined nearly every hour of every day are left with few avenues to engage in sociality beyond the use of their own bodies (the throwing of excrement, blood, and urine; self-mutilation; suicide attempts). Of course, such behaviors are misconstrued by the penal spectator, who views such performance as pathology when, in fact, it is the starkest of socialities—the last line of an assertion of being and need for human relationships. In the desperate act of this labor or work, there is a clear lack of reflexivity, an inability to articulate the cultural logics which define punishment and our disconnection (let alone, our connection) to it, even as it expands. Here, we see vividly how the absence of an understanding of the relationships shared between the daily practice of punishment and larger discourses about pain and suffering materialize into radical disengagement.

Such detached conceptions of work in relationship to penality are argued by some to be characteristic of late modernity. Bauman describes work now, in the context of risk society and in the aftermath of the collapse of Enlightenment, as "labyrinthine," game-like, and fundamentally altered: "And so work has changed its character. More often than not, it is a one-off act: a ploy of a bricoleur, a trickster, aimed at what is at hand and inspired and constrained by what is at hand, more shaped than shaping, more the outcome of chasing a chance than the product of planning and design."[48] More significantly for Bauman, the transformation of work reflects a change in the social imagination of the worker: "Work can no longer offer the secure axis around which to wrap and fix self-definitions, identities and life-projects. Neither can it be easily conceived of as the ethical foundation of society, or as the ethical axis of the individual life."[49] In this context, work is missing its ability to project forward into the future, labor which outlasts the worker and benefits others besides herself and her time. Rather, Bauman argues, work is largely "aesthetic," no longer "expected to 'ennoble' its performers, to make them 'better human beings'" but "measured and evaluated by its capacity to be entertaining and amusing, satisfying not so much the ethical, Promethean vocation of the producer and creator as the aesthetical needs and desires of the consumer, the seeker of sensations and collector of experiences."[50] Cultural understandings of punishment are similar, in that the foundations of punishment have been thoroughly challenged over the last four decades, leaving contemporary and popular understandings of penal workings in a largely "aesthetic" framework, one, as I will outline throughout this volume, where punishment is more likely to be openly engaged by a democratic citizen who assumes a subjectivity built around the notion of "the seeker of sensations and the collector of experiences." What are the implications of such shifts in conceptualizations of work for the articulation and practice of punishment as a cultural labor?

The work, then, of punishment in culture marks a critical limit and case study in understanding what it means to be social, to be human and humane, and to have some agency in that project. This work extends from the deep architectures and technologies of punishment into the everyday organization of penal spectatorship. As Rhodes and the theorists of this chapter insist, a radical potentiality of the penal is embedded in such movements, embodied in the madness of the control prison. In such settings, Rhodes argues, "The only way 'rehumanizing' can happen under these conditions, as many staff and some inmates see it, is to locate and display the individual's availability for compassion, connection, and learning—to mark his accessibility to a conversation that proceeds elsewhere, without him."[51] This location and display make demands upon the penal spectator, the participant in this conversation that proceeds elsewhere. In this way, ultimately, the distinctly unique problem that punishment poses has never really been for the punished but for his punishers. Punishment then is among the ultimate tests of the social relation. Judith Butler formulates this difficulty for us another way:

> What if there is an Other who does violence to an Other? To which Other do I respond ethically? Which Other do I put before myself? Or do I stand by? Derrida claims that to try and respond to every Other can only result in a situation of radical irresponsibility. And the Spinozists, the Nietzscheans, the utilitarians, and the Freudians all ask, "Can I invoke the imperative to preserve the life of the Other even if I cannot invoke this right of self–preservation for myself?"[52]

Butler struggles with an answer to her own question but is clear in the principle that to ignore this violent Other or rid the world of him is a means by which to "consummate our own inhumanity" rather than "return us to the human."[53] Punishment in this way is profoundly linked to the ends of the social and the severing—and repairing—of every social tie. And for those of us who frame these questions on the ground, this observance is vital.

Punishment today is inseparable from an understanding of pain and exclusion, not just *in* the social world but at its very foundations. It is difficult consequently to imagine this work at this point. But certainly it begins with questioning and the power of a built-in self-sustaining critique, an interrogation that does not go away. These new questions would ask how we might empirically measure and theoretically expand upon questions of otherness, bare life, exclusion, exception, and pain in relation to punishment and its cultural meanings. The chapters and cases that follow attempt to do precisely this. In such a context, the public space we create would be loud with oppositional voices and potentially rich with substantive debate and deliberation. As it stands, social suffering in its many modes struggles not simply to achieve visibility but to lend that visibility a meaningful context from which to make sense of other people's pain. As medical anthropologists Arthur and Joan Kleinman write, such contexts will require "historical, ethnographic, and narrative studies that provide a more powerful understanding of the cultural processes through which the global regime of disordered capitalism alters the connections between collective experience and subjectivity."[54] Through these carefully theorized empirical accounts, so urgently needed, we might be better able to explore and understand how "that moral sensibility, for example, diminishes or becomes something frighteningly different: promiscuous, gratuitous, unhinged from responsibility and action."[55] In short, we might better understand penal spectatorship. Like the Kleinmans, Butler writes that it is in the realm of representation where much of this work begins, where "the task at hand is to establish modes of public seeing and hearing that might well respond to the cry of the human within the sphere of appearance," a realm currently "constituted on the exclusion of that image."[56] With that, it is to the image we turn.

3

Prison Iconography
Regarding the Pain of Others

The image, the imagined, the imaginary—these are all terms that
direct us to something critical and new in global cultural processes: the imagination as a social practice. No longer mere fantasy
(opium for the masses whose real work is elsewhere), no longer
simple escape (from a world defined principally by more concrete purposes and structures), no longer elite pastime (thus not
relevant to the lives of ordinary people), and no longer mere con-
templation (irrelevant for new forms of desire and subjectivity),
the imagination has become an organized field of social practices,
a form of work (in the sense of both labor and culturally organized
practice), and a form of negotiation between sites of agency (individuals) and globally defined fields of possibility. This unleashing
of the imagination links the play of pastiche (in some settings) to
the terror and coercion of states and their competitors. The imagination is now central to all forms of agency, is itself a social fact,
and is the key component of the new global order. But to make the
claim meaningful, we must address some other issues.
> —Arjun Appadurai, *Modernity at Large:*
> *Cultural Dimensions of Globalization*, 1996

This chapter sets out to make some of the above claims "meaningful," but with special regard to Appadurai's qualifier: That in order to
reveal the cultural work of the imagination, particularly in relationship
to punishment's pain, we must first "address some other issues." Most of
those issues pertain to our approaches and theoretical contexts for the
study of representation—for how we both pursue and explain this work.

The study of representation in criminology remains a field of thought preoccupied with its own justification and the pursuit of a clear articulation of the reasons why we should take cultural texts, images, and performances seriously—related, no doubt, to the challenge of the humanities more generally in their critical work. The notion of the imagination as an "organized field of social practices" and complex form of work, as a negotiated mode of agency embedded within intricate and dense media structures and economic conditions, points to the manner in which the production of desires, subjectivities, terror, and coercion sit center stage to issues of representation generally but also with an important specificity to criminology. In other words, it is criminology specifically which must assume certain theoretical obligations with regard to issues of representation—particularly the limits of representation where images of crime and punishment, pain and death largely proliferate. In this chapter, I explore this task through a discussion of conventional and emergent ways in which to understand the representation of punishment in relationship to penal spectatorship. I conclude with a discussion of the specific roles that both images and spectators have to play in a larger discussion of the politics of penal representation.

In the main, criminology assumes particular trajectories in its discussions and debates surrounding the justification and meaningfulness of image work. In an articulation of the classic constructionist position, criminologist Ray Surette argues, "[P]eople use knowledge they obtain from the media to construct a picture of the world, an image of reality on which they base their actions. This process, sometimes called 'the social construction of reality,' is particularly important in the realm of crime, justice, and the media."[1] Communications scholars Angela McRobbie and Sarah Thornton represent a more contemporary take, insisting

that the media is no longer something separable from society. Social reality is experienced through language, communication and imagery. Social meanings and social differences are inextricably tied up with representation. Thus when sociologists call for an account which tells how life actually is, and which deals with the real issues rather than the spectacular and exaggerated ones, the point is that these accounts of reality are already representations and sets of meanings about what they perceive the "real" issues to be. These versions of "reality" would also be impregnated with the mark of media imagery rather than somehow pure and untouched by the all-pervasive traces of contemporary communications.[2]

Such a framework emphasizes the tension within which much of the work of cultural representation in criminology is done. In the first account, reality is measured against a mediated "picture" which in turn shapes social action and crime policy—there is a discrepancy between "reality" and popular knowledge, what Stuart Hall refers to as an old view of representation, one which pursues an interrogation of the gap between an image's "true" meaning and its representation. In the second and newer view of representation, the image is no longer separable from reality. The former explains much of why the study of representation in criminology is dramatically directed at disparities between what is "real" and what is "imagined"—with special attention to the empirical manner in which crime images fail to represent what is known about crime realities yet serve to moderate public discourse on crime. Much of this work remains text-based through content-driven sampling methods or case studies which reveal and emphasize the dramatic disparity between crime, justice, and the image. These include such important contributions as Ray Surette's *Media, Crime, and Criminal Justice: Images and Realities* (1992); Philip Jenkins's *Using Murder: The Social Construction of Serial Homicide* (1994); and ground-breaking work by Stanley Cohen in *Folk Devils and Moral Panics* (1972); Hall and colleagues' *Policing the Crisis* (1978); and Mark Fishman's "Crime Waves as Ideology" (1978). These sorts of texts set the stage for complementary work that seeks to "examine the cultural life" of the institutional practices surrounding crime and punishment, including the cultural politics of criminology and the processes of social construction—how popular culture communicates specific kinds of knowledge and upholds particular ideologies.[3] Key exemplars here include Nicole Rafter's primer for the study of crime and film, *Shots in the Mirror* (2006), which systematically examines the relationships between various kinds of crime films, ideology, and culture. Similarly, writings like Austin Sarat's work on capital punishment and representations of law and death, some of which, for example, examine the hidden ideological aspects of cultural conservatism embedded in films which are popularly construed as anti–death penalty films. In an important presidential address to the Law and Society Association, Sarat pioneers a call for a "move from the study of law on the books and in action to law in the image,"[4] providing templates for ways of reading cultural performance within criminology while also soliciting the field to rise to the challenge of what it means to pursue image work in late modernity. Similarly, as Jeff Ferrell and Clinton Sanders argue in their influential formulation of cultural criminology:

It is no longer possible to retain the quaint, linear view of a world in which criminal acts and other objective happenings occur, are then observed and reported by the news media, and are finally transformed into quasi-factual stories or offered as fictionalized representations for the entertainment of the public audience. Instead, the most viable model is one in which media presentations, real-life events, personal perceptions, public policies, and individual actions spiral about each other in a complex, mutually affecting and ever-changing structure of inner-relationships.[5]

Other work insists upon an acknowledgment of the role of audiences and spectators not simply in the construction of meaning but of rationalities and subjectivities as well. Garland argues, for instance, in his elaboration and revision of the concept of moral panics, that "an implicit, unarticulated concept of the well-judged moral response is always present in such work, although rarely articulated or defended."[6] In such a way, analytic frameworks for observing and investing mediated events with meaning depend upon processes of looking which rely heavily upon moral judgment, skepticism, and vocabularies of attribution (and thus, blame)—all of which are penal in their foundations.

The contribution I wish to make to this developing legacy is one that seeks to demonstrate not simply how crime and punishment are irrevocably and intrinsically bound up with the image but also insists that certain kinds of images, specifically penal iconography, in their spiraling effects, carry their own unique sets of representational concerns, problems, and questions. Such a pursuit insists upon a much larger theoretical framework for understanding the interaction between the image and the vast variety of everyday discourses, representations, communications that they are caught up within. Simultaneously, such a framework unleashes a set of questions directed primarily at how one interrogates the nature of this relationship and, by extension, how one approaches the image, particularly the penal image, with analytical integrity. Specifically, as Judith Butler articulates it, "it would be a mistake to think that we only need to find the right and true images, and that a certain reality will then be conveyed. The reality is not conveyed by what is represented within the image, but through the challenge to representation that reality delivers."[7] In many ways, it is the latter problem that seems to be the emergent imperative for those who analyze both penal culture and its image within criminology. Claire Valier similarly directs our attention to the relationships between the artifacts and performances we examine in proximity to the imaginary of a penal spectator: "It is time to look into the changing textual, rhetorical and pictorial practices through which penal practices draw the imaginative engagement of multiple viewing and reading publics"[8] and to raise the question of what it means "for a text to be 'addressed to the contemporary,'" a question, she argues, that "is central to the legitimacy of studies in the humanities and social sciences, raising imperatives to which all must respond."[9] In addressing such imperatives, the penal image and its spectator present a special case.

What follows are the findings from having surveyed 400 prison films, defined as narratives which examine or rely upon institutional environments centered on confinement. I also extended my search by following texts which invoke prison-like environments in an effort to move intentionally beyond classical prison films whose settings are primarily built around penal institutions. I used this strategy to explore how penality and its meanings circulate more broadly in performances and representations generally perceived as removed from punishment. Similarly, I sampled a range of contemporary television programs and popular culture performances based upon their invocation and reliance upon key penal correlates: exclusion, isolation, blame, and the infliction of pain.

The Case of Punishment

> The problem is not that people remember through photographs, but that they remember only the photographs. (Susan Sontag, *Regarding the Pain of Others*, 2003)

In the emergent debates surrounding issues of representation, within and without criminology, the question of what the cultural "work" of representation may look like with specific reference to issues of penality and its signification is central. In order to understand punishment broadly and at work in culture, as David Garland insists, "we need to study not just the grandiloquent public statements which are occasionally made but also the pragmatic repetitive routines of daily practice, for these routines contain within them distinctive patterns of meaning and symbolic forms which are enacted and expressed every time a particular procedure is adopted, a technical language used, or a specific sanction imposed."[10] This attention to a penality of the everyday emphasizes the redundancy and routinization of penal architecture and social order in daily life. As a measure of this, penality—that complex term which stakes out the need for a synonym to

"Most of what the average person knows about prison life comes from pop culture: literature, history, news and most importantly television and film . . . but where do the memories come from?" (Quote from art exhibit, titled "I Always Wanted to Go to Paris," at Eastern State Penitentiary, August 2006. Photo of exhibit taken by author.)

punishment that would be markedly more complex with its "discursive frameworks of authority and condemnation, ritual procedures of imposing punishment, a repertoire of penal sanctions, institutions and agencies for the enforcement of sanctions and a rhetoric of symbols, figures, and images by means of which the penal process is represented to its various audiences"—is inextricably bound up with issues of representation.[11] Consequently, it is instrumental to the manner in which we produce subjectivities, modes of spectatorship, and social order. In short, as Garland suggests, "the ways in which we punish, and the ways in which we represent that action to ourselves, makes a difference to the way we are."[12] This kind of approach hinges upon the acknowledgment that social reality and experience are fundamentally constituted through mediated representations in late modernity—and, more specifically, that the image must always be privileged with respect to punishment in that it carries a peculiar moral authority and structure of self-governance in its representation—at a distance. Beyond this, the image remains the crucial cultural site where punishment is routinely enacted. Consequently, we know more about how we represent punishment than the official or lived act of punishment itself. We cannot think about crime or punishment outside of the image, and this complicates any kind of sociological or representational work we pursue, both scholarly and popularly. But it also marks a moment of theoretical opportunity, a chance to explore how existing classification strategies in penal representation, although useful, are only prototypical. A better understanding of the role of images in criminology will depend upon breaking down and through constraints in form and content in a manner that challenges and interrogates punishment as a social practice. It also is a moment in which we might investigate more clearly how images of crime and especially punishment, because of properties that are specific to their practice, have a very specific role to play broadly in the construction of cultural theory, in theories of social action, and in the production of a penal spectator.

Sites of entertainment and leisure, popular culture presents us with the most powerful place in which the practice of imprisonment has been re-enacted to the largest audience. In American culture, citizens are much more likely to screen the prison rather than visit it. They are consequently familiar with imprisonment not through its institutional practice but its cultural representation, and this is an important site for the construction of a cultural memory that is largely iconic. Our experiences of formal state punishment derive primarily from mediated images composed largely of celebrated prisons and prisoners. This is the space where the maps of modernity are broken up and re-navigated in a complex, often conflicting environment of images, motives, and moralities. That there is a very real interplay between these imagined worlds and the reality of imprisonment is only beginning to be acknowledged, in part because mapping this interrelationship is so difficult. The cultural imaginary is not subject to simple cause and effect models and is a nebulous, playful arena where vicarious identities and moralities are picked up and later discarded, but with consistent patterns and attractions to particular disguises. These tendencies then gradually become ideology and convention, habit and value, proper narratives of punishment. With regard to punishment, these processes render representations of imprisonment a particularly seductive site for the production of cultural scripts and classifications on the part of the spectator. Such schemes, however reductive, always hold out the rather illusory promise of patterns and predictability, rendering complex cultural practices more amenable to comprehension and containment and thus easy mechanisms of desire.

Exemplary of this process, films set within prisons or incorporating prisons into their narratives have existed from the inception of cinema, among the most economically viable and enduring celluloid environments in film history, representing thousands of films circulating across American cinema. Serving as key models for other modes of representation (television, comic books, video games, and a wide range of new media), prison movies or some derivative of them make up a persistent category within the Hollywood system, including such contemporary and wide-ranging examples as the popular award-winning musical, *Chicago* (2002); a recent remake of *The Longest Yard* (2005); the critically acclaimed *Capote* (2005); and recent post–9/11 films such as *Rendition* (2007) and *Taxi to the Dark Side* (2007), as well as work from independent and international cinemas. Prison films also routinely appear across politically alternative and experimental categories, documentary, B-movie distribution, pornography, and television (HBO's *Oz* and Fox's *Prison Break*). The prison film, thus, crosses generic boundaries with relative ease, an amalgam of conventions and intersecting tendencies assembled from film noir, social consciousness films (including social documentary and social problem cinema), gangster films, crime thrillers, police procedurals, mysteries, action/adventure films, melodrama, and women's cinema. In short, there are few, if any, genres in which films built around prisons do not exist, including comedies (*Take the Money and Run*, 1969; *Stir Crazy*, 1980; *Life*,

1999; *O Brother Where Art Thou?* 2000); westerns (*Hellgate*, 1952; *Devil's Canyon*, 1953); musicals (*20,000 Cheers for the Chain Gang*, 1933; *Jailhouse Rock*, 1957; *Chicago*, 2002); and animation (*Big House Bunny*, 1950; *Cellbound*, 1955; *Chicken Run*, 2000). The prison film is, consequently, among the most complex kinds of cinema, impossible to classify simply according to genre, period, or narrative conventions. In this respect, cinema has served as a prolific and active site for the complex cultural enactment of punishment and the prison a persistent resource for narrative drama. Although generic classifications are sometimes convenient and can sometimes "clarify relationships," as Nicole Rafter argues, "what is ultimately important is not definitional labels but rather understanding the complex relations between film and society—the ways they reflect and influence one another."[13] Rafter describes the import of this analytical process as one which permits us to "shift films around, juxtaposing and regrouping them to identify trends, detect previously unnoticed concerns, and discover new meanings."[14] This fluidity proves absolutely crucial to insightful examinations of crime and prison films but is also usefully extended as a process whereby we may track penality in its cultural uses more broadly—wherever the image may go. And the penal image in late modernity, surprisingly, is always moving.[15]

Point of Origin: Prison Cinema

In American popular culture, the work of penal representation as a formula for building narratives of punishment perhaps begins at the cinema but ends at an infinite number of points across social life, where image and practice blur. In many of these settings, we see the prison through a deeply structured cinematic legacy with specific tendencies, long-standing conventions, and its own cinematic vocabulary. For instance, "prison films" have historically operated as primers in prison sociology, introducing their viewers to the mechanical daily routines and bureaucratic processes of imprisonment typically through the entry of a central character into the overwhelming subculture of the institution. The viewer follows the new "fish," who is usually unjustly convicted or punished and therefore an easy point of audience identification, through the dehumanizing pains of imprisonment, his (or, less often, her) introduction to the convict code, and the consequent patterns of adaptation. Thus, prison films come typically with what Nicole Rafter identifies as conventional stock elements: big casts that are easily typologized, including the new fish as hero; his older, more experienced (and hardened) buddy who is often the con with standards (the "real man"); the "square john"; the rats, snitches, and squealers; the paternalistic and often impotent warden of the 1930s and '40s who transforms into the cruel, sadistic warden of more contemporary cinema; the unsophisticated, brutal guard as "smug hack"; and the psychotic inmate, proof that prisons are functional to some extent in that they always house one or two individuals beyond reclamation.[16]

In these worlds, the prison continues to serve classically as one of those "forcing houses for changing persons in our society. Each . . . a natural experiment, typically harsh, on what can be done to the self"[17] where these classic "pains of imprisonment" are to be carefully considered as "a set of threats or attacks which are directed against the very foundation of the prisoner's being."[18] Prisons and often prison films are thus best understood in cultural invocations as laboratories of the self where control is directed precisely at the regulation of individuals and individualism. These films have always astutely cued into the idea of the penitentiary as an experiment in individual transformation—a powerful element of historical and contemporary interpretations of the work of punishment. And certainly, Hollywood classical prison films have served as complex environments from which to build audience sympathy for the prisoner. However, in the prison film, the possibility of identification always runs up against a specific voyeuristic spectacle, where the film's most fundamental plot mechanisms and narrative devices are manipulative acts of personal and collective violence: torture in *Cool Hand Luke* (1967); rape in *American History X* (1998) and *American Me* (1992); riots (*Brute Force*, 1947; *Riot in Cell Block 11*, 1954);, thrilling escapes (*I Am a Fugitive from a Chain Gang*, 1932; *The Defiant Ones*, 1958; *The Shawshank Redemption*, 1994); and executions (*Angels with Dirty Faces*, 1938; *I Want to Live!* 1955; *Dead Man Walking*, 1995; *The Green Mile*, 1999).

The classic contemporary case for this phenomenon, Frank Darabont's *Shawshank Redemption*, marks a useful demonstration of these conventions but also marks the way in which such a representation is mapped by cultural desires in the reenactment of punishment. The film achieved critical acclaim during its initial release, but its box office success was moderate at best. Its legacy and intense relationship to its viewing audience are better understood through its domination of video rental charts for weeks, then months, breaking new records, and its perpetual recycling across various syndicated television networks. The film's popularity and critical acclaim are often described in terms which invoke the classical conventions of prison cinema as the key to the film's successful building of an epic narrative. Advertised as a spiritually uplifting drama about two men who forge a deep friendship across two decades within the confines of the prison, who must both break their emotional and psychological bonds before they can be free, the film expresses a deep awareness of the most commercially rewarding uses of the prison—as an existentialist metaphor for the human condition—powerful in its use of the prison to build audience identification. At the center of its themes are complex engagements of fear and hope and the struggle to set free the self. This struggle, however, depends in many ways upon the spectator's distance from the prison, now visualized, as a resource from which to build a vicarious exploration for the audience. This facilitation, which pervades prison dramas, is perhaps nowhere more clear than in the manner in which *Shawshank*, and the classic prison films it relies upon, build a kind of classic prison sociology—a careful visual and narrativized record of the "pains of imprisonment," the necessary adaptations by the inmates, their gradual reduction to dependence, quintessentially captured in the film's images of institutionalization (specifically, Brooks's hanging upon his release to the free world and the foreshadowing of this possibility for Red). As Red famously states, "These walls are funny. First you hate 'em. Then you get used to 'em. Then you depend on 'em."

Andy Dufresne (Tim Robbins) embodies in many ways the classic "real man" whose masculinity and self-identity are admired over time by the entire inmate (and staff) culture. A study in prison routine, the daily life of the "big house" is spelled out in scenes which invoke familiar codes and readings of imprisonment. Quiet, philosophical, and meditative, the plot moves by way of Red's (Morgan Freeman) resinous first-person narration and his considerations of such abstract qualities as time, patience, loyalty, and personal worth in prison. Simultaneously, the film employs many stock character and plot elements of prison cinema in its invocation of penal themes: an innocent hero, an experienced convict buddy, an evil warden, a "smug hack," a fantastic escape.[19] Pulling from a large cast of typological characters, the film pivots upon traditional axes of prison plot motivation, profiting by creating confrontational circumstances, positioning a wrongly accused man in unjust confinement, subjecting him to sexualized violence and abuse, ultimately permitting him transcendence. A simplistic interrogation of the nature of justice (in a world that is either good or bad/black or white), where authority is wholly corrupt and the fantasy and enactment of escape and transcendence border upon the surreal, the film nonetheless moves comfortably within a familiar, durable penal iconography. This symbolic space implies much about the desires of the penal subject who looks in upon such worlds. The performance of imprisonment is less about communicating any fundamental aspect of incarceration (the "real") and more about the staging of an existential framework for the spectator through a model friendship—thereby reminding us of the image's ultimate failure—a failure that at once becomes one of its most important contributions and certainly its most analytically interesting moment.

The truly amazing thing about such a production is not simply *Shawshank*'s intense level of self-reflexivity in its invocation of classical prison cinema, but the absence of any irony or commentary in such a reproduction. In this way, the "real" that *Shawshank* imitates is not real at all but a celluloid fantasy—built upon the memories and conventions of past prison films. The film's cultural resonance is most likely grounded in at least some component of this nostalgic engagement of familiar penal terrain, but it is an engagement which begs questions concerning cultural evasion. Let me carefully frame this critique about the film. Many of us, including myself, found *Shawshank* to be riveting in its ability to humanize such dystopian carceral environments and its ability to achieve an epic treatment of the human condition, of good and evil, within such isolation. But its ability to tap into those kinds of audience desires is revealing of key cultural tendencies which materialize in the film's production and interpretation. For instance, the film's apparent seamlessness is a suture that struggles to remain in place—with frequent disruptions and troubling moments that read from multiple perspectives. These disruptions begin with the replacement of Stephen King's original Irish "Red" with black actor Morgan Freeman. In the midst of an imprisonment binge whose defining contours are racial, this decision in casting rises above the fictional world to a troubling question about mass, racialized incarceration that is left unposed within the film's narrative. The film's theatrical release predates by only a few months the Sentencing Project's groundbreaking report which found that one in three black males were under some form of criminal justice supervision. The success of a nostalgic, penal retrospective film amidst the world's largest imprisonment binge in history demands consequently a certain kind of cultural contextualization. Much of the analysis of its popularity revolves around the film's ending, which materializes in a thrilling escape and what many consider to be its most amazing feature— its final scene—where Andy and Red are reunited by way of an extensive panning helicopter shot on a beautiful warm, white beach along the Pacific coastline—as Andy describes it, a place "with no memory." This finale in such a vast, open expansive space, with such spectacular closure, is so disconnected from its previous two prison-bound hours, a turn so fantastic in the narrative, that we are driven to ask: Is this a dream? The afterlife?

Such a conclusion is a marked turn from the penal conventions of prison noir and social problem films of the classical era, which rarely exceeded the walls of the prison and almost never ended happily. Darabont writes of his hesitancy to incorporate this Hollywood-ized ending, preferring instead to leave Red, as in King's novella, seated on the bus headed for the border, uttering the words "I hope" as a private monologue in his mind—thus, as producer Niki Marvin writes, "a note of hope but not fulfillment."[20] As it stands, the film ultimately ends with Andy and Red brought together again, smiling in recognition of one another, while the camera pans out, resolving all of the film's ambiguities and contradictions in one swoop. Darabont writes that his decision to include the shot is bound up with test audiences who cried, cheered, and voted the ending their favorite—a decision that is connected with cultural needs and desires of the audience as penal spectators.

> But there's a difference between pandering to an audience and giving them something they love. Besides, as I said, I'd started falling in love with it myself. . . . By ending with that final image, we've brought the viewer on a full journey that begins in tight claustrophobia defined by walls and concludes where the horizon is limitless; the movie has traveled fully from darkness to light, from coldness to warmth, from colorlessness to a place where only color exists, from physical and spiritual imprisonment to total freedom. . . . Bottom line is, I think it's a magical and uplifting place for our characters to arrive at the end of their long saga.[21]

Film critic Mark Kermode, on the other hand, writes, "this finale reduces the fantastical possibilities of the narrative, in which escapist myth and cinematic magic are splendidly conjoined, to the level of an oddly down-to-earth climax in which a beach and a boat are the greatest rewards imaginable."[22] Commentators and critics continue to explore what made *Shawshank* such a phenomenon with its audience. This final scene tells us much, however, in that its visualization of closure, no matter how utopian or escapist, is something audiences prefer over the irresolute, open,

uncertain ending—one in which the contradictions and futility of penality persist. The film's desire to rebuild hope and redemption, at a moment
in which retribution and incapacitation were to achieve unparalleled privilege in the American prison system, culminates in a message so abstract,
so fantastic, and so centered within traditional conventions that the audience is seductively encouraged to walk away from the theater deep in
metaphors about their own lives and romanticized assumptions about the
production of justice (consistent with director Darabont's second feature-
length engagement with Stephen King, addressing capital punishment
and the denial of race in *The Green Mile*). The film's gentle prodding toward what takes on meaning in the prison world—the gift of a harmonica
or movie poster, nurturing a bird that has fallen from its nest, a couple
of beers on a summer afternoon, the sound of music echoing through
the prison—gestures always toward a discussion of the human condition,
encouraging its audience of spectators to find in imprisonment a larger
universalizing message about life. When asked about his stint in solitary
confinement after subversively playing classical music across prison loud-
speakers, Andy replies, "Easiest time I ever did. Mozart—in my head. . . .
They can't get that from you. Here is where it makes the most sense. So
you don't forget that there are places in the world not made of stone—
places they can't get at—hope." Because *Shawshank* presents us with an
experience of prison where transcendence is inevitable, it too is easy time
for its audience. We easily identify with our protagonists and, in getting to
know them, suffer with them and cheer their escape and reunion. Yet in
turning back to real prisons, the logic and rhetoric of retribution persist.
We have taken no journeys with the imprisoned who remain locked in.
We know them only from a distance and less so than their celluloid coun-
terparts. It is not that what is necessary to open up a space of critique
is a better assessment of the real, some careful replica of contemporary
prison conditions, but rather penal conventions and narrative structures
which challenge the penal spectator to interrogate punishment, to leave
them with uneasy contradictions and uncertain absences in resolution—
and their place in that problematic. Instead, an important and hard shift
in the gaze of the penal spectator occurs with *Shawshank*. In the end, the
film's promise is muddled by its resort to a familiar cultural vocabulary
in its pursuit of an easy resolution, one where the only choices are always
the "simple choice(s)" of either/or discourse: "Get busy living or get busy
dying." In such a film, the moral spectator gets away . . . with a prison
daydream.

Importantly, I showcase *Shawshank Redemption* precisely because it is the kind of narrative most would consider friendly to the aims of prison reform, working meticulously to humanize prisoners on an epic scale. My critique centers upon an effort to push our best representations of punishment in a manner that encourages more thoughtful, self-aware, and informed portrayals of the complexities of punishment. Because the prison film persists across cinema as a perennial setting in which to enact primary social dramas centered upon physical, social, and psychological entrapment, because it is a site for enacting the struggle between good and evil, perpetually pitting the individual against the apparatus of the state, often through scenarios of stark injustice, these narratives remain potential sites from which to experiment with and trouble penal discourse. With their characteristic bleak and oppressive worldviews, these films have routinely served as extreme settings in which to act out the fundamental tensions of the human condition: struggles to preserve individual identity, humanity, and dignity in the face of inflexible power structures and corrupt authorities. The rigid physical structures and restricted spaces of the cinematic prison are modeled in such a way so as to mimic the constraints in social forces which lead central characters to the prison, thereby rendering this environment a powerful metaphor of structure and agency. In this manner, the prison film has always existed somewhere between social consciousness and exploitative spectacle, between a specific concern with existing social realities (specifically, the conditions of crime and imprisonment) and the institution's seductive use as ideological metaphor. These parallel but conflicting uses point to the manner in which more contemporary explorations of penality in representation prove too amorphous to be contained within the unity of medium, industry, and audience that genre often implies. Although penal meanings continue to circulate upon the basis of a shared consensus about the nature of expectations, the familiarity of key codes, the recognizableness and easy decoding of a particular configuration of conventions, these frames are no longer specific to an explicit representation of punishment, embodied in a narrative structure set inside prisons. Here, punishment moves beyond prison walls and extends outward—where the carceral becomes "not the 'centre of power,' not a network of forces, but a multiple network of diverse elements—walls, space, institution, rules, discourse . . . a strategic distribution of elements of different natures and levels."[23]

Beyond Prison Walls: Penality in the Future

> Morpheus: Let me tell you why you're here. You're here because you know some-
> thing. What you know you can't explain, but you feel it. You've felt it your
> entire life, that there's something wrong with the world. You don't know what
> it is, but it's there, like a splinter in your mind, driving you mad. It is this feel-
> ing that has brought you to me. Do you know what I'm talking about?
>
> Neo: The Matrix.
>
> Morpheus: Do you want to know what it is?
>
> Neo: Yes.
>
> Morpheus: The Matrix is everywhere. It is all around us. Even now, in this
> very room. You can see it when you look out your window or when you
> turn on your television. You can feel it when you go to work... when you
> go to church... when you pay your taxes. It is the world that has been
> pulled over your eyes to blind you from the truth.
>
> Neo: What truth?
>
> Morpheus: That you are a slave, Neo. Like everyone else you were born into
> bondage. Into a prison that you cannot taste or see or touch. A prison for
> your mind.

Another way to get at the role of penal spectatorship in relation to punishment is through the images which many of us do not at first glance conceptualize as penal. Yet the iconography of punishment in filmic discourse
converges with other kinds of representational discourses that extend
broadly into everyday life. The main correlates of this iconography are,
much like the classic prison film's sociology of imprisonment, concerned
primarily with temporal and spatial displacement—the key correlates of
discipline through insular worlds where people have been abandoned or
trapped—thereby invoking many of the key narrative devices of prison
cinema, including elements of escape, authority, and transcendence. These
settings are defined in contemporary settings both by their prolific quality
and their wide-ranging diversity across media platforms, genres, and narrative contexts. One significant thread in these treatments which historically has been underexamined is the manner in which prisons and penal
iconography circulate as narrative resources and matrices of meaning in
contexts otherwise perceived as absent of penality. The case study for this
kind of application is science fiction, with its horror underpinnings, defined by a deep penal architecture in its imagining.

Claustrophobic spaces, industrial entrapment, material exclusion, and near total isolation in some form of "outer" space or exile are typical of Hollywood prison films and television overtly and obliquely (*Escape from New York*, 1981; *Escape 2000*, 1981; *Prison Ship*, 1984; *The Running Man*, 1987; *Alien 3*, 1992; *Fortress*, 1993; *No Escape*, 1994; *Gattaca*, 1997; CBS's popular reality programming, *Survivor* and *Big Brother* as well as ABC's prime-time hit series, *Lost*; BBC's perennial *Dr. Who*; and SciFi's remade *Battlestar Galactica*). These performances have historically been defined by cultural anxieties which often focus upon the dehumanizing end of commercial capitalism in human entrapment and repression (*Outland*, 1981; *Blade Runner*, 1982; the *Alien* series: 1979, 1986, 1992, 1997; *The Matrix*, 1999; *The Island*, 2005) and have characteristically materialized within a dynamics of post-industrial power which, as film scholar Annette Kuhn argues, "is typically constituted as invisible but all-pervasive, institutional rather than personal, corporate rather than governmental."[24] Some of these more contemporary engagements, however, including *Battlestar Galactica*, *Lost*, and *Dr. Who*, invoke questions of governance, sovereignty, and power in penal landscapes. These narratives largely take place in fantasy settings, science fiction worlds which privilege secluded islands, private planets, and hidden futures. In television, these settings are increasingly invoked in order to simulate exile but within a carefully staged and choreographed economy of representation. In fact, it may be precisely this celebration of celebrity and capital that figures into the penal structures and prominence of reality television programs like *Survivor*.

These sites have historically converged in existentialist elaborations of the human condition. This metaphorical maneuver, of course, is nothing new, but a rapid proliferation of films and programming which attempt to render communities, cities, societies, entire worlds as prisons or position actors in competitive penal-like environments (islands, apartments, professional training, etc.) is unprecedented and represents an unusual engagement of the notion of a control culture or prison society. Prime examples, where individuals are caught up in an oppressive, sometimes meaningless framework with their own actions as their sole recourse, include *A Clockwork Orange* (1971); *Escape from New York* (1981); *Blade Runner* (1982); *Brazil* (1985); *Alien 3* (1992); *Fortress* (1993); *Natural Born Killers* (1994); *Dark City* (1998); *The Matrix* (1999); *A.I.* (2001); *Vanilla Sky* (2001); *Resident Evil* (2002); *I, Robot* (2004); the *X–Men* series; and *V for Vendetta* (2005).

Some of these films are concerned with panoptic surveillance and disciplinary entrapment through technology—emergent forms of techno- or cyber-confinement, reflecting acute cultural anxieties about the intensification and expansion of technological capacity and its potentially coercive uses.[25] Examples include the imprisonment of the human race through digital code (*The Matrix*, 1999); entrapment in the mind of another or one's self through techno-telepathy (*The Cell*, 2000; *The Ring*, 2002; *The Grudge*, 2004; *Eternal Sunshine of the Spotless Mind*, 2004); the complete or near-total loss of privacy through a media panopticon (*The Truman Show*, 1998; reality television); or, the ultimate end of incapacitation, technology that permits arrest before the crime is committed (*Minority Report*, 2002).

Stephen Spielberg's *Minority Report*, based on a Philip K. Dick short story, represents a useful case for understanding this extensionality in the manner in which it foregrounds the role of spectatorship through the field of vision's blind spots. The film centers upon the establishment of a "pre-crime" unit which, in its reliance upon three psychics known as "pre-cogs," is able to end homicide altogether. Because murder can now be seen before it occurs via the minds of the pre-cogs which are mapped into a televisual environment, pre-crime is able to stage arrests before the crime occurs, pinpointing the locus of danger before the act. The system is confounded, however, by the missing record of a homicide that the most sensitive of the pre-cogs, Agatha (Samantha Morton), is nonetheless able to see—the murder, ironically, of her mother by the founder of pre-crime. When police chief John Anderton (Tom Cruise) realizes that a homicide case is missing, a chain of events occurs which quickly positions him as the next forecasted murderer. As the state focuses its energies upon capturing Anderton, he attempts to resolve these contradictions, solve the missing crime, and prevent his own while submerged in a world whose surveillance is so pervasive that Anderton must go underground in search of eye transplants to avoid iris and biomedical recognition that is now inscribed in the architecture of everyday life. In this way, seeing into the absent, blind spots of pre-crime's seemingly perfect system of crime control literally requires new eyes. The film is particularly compelling in the manner in which it designates authority and legitimacy to a mode of spectatorship in which punishment, through a high-tech prison in which predetermined murderers are put into a state of unconscious sleep, occurs without a crime, only its premeditation.

In many of these films, another strand of representation appears in the phobia of identity erasure or mistaken identity, where an individual of particular import, usually a minority (often a black male) becomes the target of the state apparatus: *Ricochet* (1991); *12 Monkeys* (1995); *The Net* (1995); *Face/Off* (1997); *The Game* (1997); *Enemy of the State* (1998); *Bait* (1999); *Life* (1999); *The Hurricane* (1999); *The Green Mile* (1999). This category in its vast and overlapping trajectories extensively mobilizes various cultural anxieties of late modernity by imagining the potential ends of "emerging civic structures and spatial arrangements of the digital era" and the manner in which these new configurations will shape "our access to economic opportunities, the character and content of public discourse, the forms of cultural activity, the enaction of power, and the experiences that give shape and texture to our daily routine."[26] These films are particularly compelling in what Giovanni Tiso calls a "technophobic bias amplifying the feelings of fear and disquiet" rather than "exploring the ways in which it reflects on social structures or indeed cinema's own involvement—as a technology-intensive industry—in the surveillance process."[27] The centrality of ways of seeing and being seen anchors these kinds of films and makes surveillance the key mechanism through which penality is enacted. Structured ways of looking and the knowledge that comes with the gaze are foregrounded in films ranging from Francis Ford Coppola's *The Conversation* to the German production and Academy Award–winning *The Lives of Others*. Films like these which are reflexive about this encounter struggle with the nature of knowledge and power in such looking and our ability to make sense of realities that we can only partially piece together. To that end, the politics of penal spectatorship are foregrounded in the more complex pathways of social control in everyday life.

Penality in Everyday Life

With its intersections of power, bureaucracy, and surveillance, penal iconography is a seductively dramatic framework from which to visualize and comment upon the world in late modern life. With penal structure embedded at the foundations of all major social institutions, it is a convenient framework from which penal spectators may construct and critique social life. A few examples of this tendency include the intersection of penality with home and the workplace in representation. In late modernity, both serve to some degree as settings for a chronic kind of dysfunctionality, converging often with penal configurations. The implied failed family and its relationship to delinquency is the subject of the documentary classic heralding the rise of retribution, *Scared Straight!* (1978), in which the prison serves as the classic marker of the last resort. It is the disruption of the family through some hidden dysfunctionality which drives the violence of Thomas Harris's *Manhunter* (1986), its remake *Red Dragon* (2002), and which undergirds *The Silence of the Lambs* (1991), all of which depend upon the penal anchoring of a madman with insight into these repressed concerns. More significantly, in films like *Monster's Ball* (2001), the prison has become a site which haunts those who live in its shadow, radically disrupting and ending family ties across generations. In the Jodie Foster vehicle, *The Panic Room* (2002), it is the home itself which is reconfigured into a prison. However, as the film's title credits flash across the screen (the familiar landmarks of downtown Manhattan become endless slates of blank, empty people-less windows), there is a clear connotation that the panic room is not simply a single room in an empty institutional, oversized flat, but is somehow indicative of a certain vision of urban space itself and the accompanying fears of late modernity (aggregate anonymity, bitter isolation, lonely vulnerability, irrational claustrophobia, amidst the apparent collapse of traditional social institutions—like the family, for instance) which are feeding into the film's tensions and the production of crime, punishment, and prevention. In Fox's critically acclaimed comedy series *Arrested Development*, the hilarious treatment of family dysfunctionality centers around an "absent" but omnipresent father whose life in prison is central to the narrative structure. In *Minority Report* (2002), extreme family loss marks the drive toward incapacitation and consequent system failure. Finally, in documentaries like *Aileen: Life and Death of a Serial Killer* (2003) and *Capturing the Friedmans* (2003), penality is the troubled anchor and end in a world where truth is uncertain and the role of family in criminality opaque. Importantly, these narratives not only reflect the logic of penal configurations in representation but demonstrate the complex extension of those formations into one of the primary social institutions of late modernity, the family—where in the films themselves images and reality blur. Such relationships, although centered in other primary concerns and anxieties related to family, rely heavily upon penality to moderate, navigate, and resolve these issues.

Representations of the workplace demonstrate a similar kind of penal attention but primarily through the emergence of a penal architecture in occupational space. One particularly influential sci-fi rendition of this world is the Wachowsky Brothers' *The Matrix* (1999), a film whose narrative is driven by the main character's dissatisfaction with late modern life, embodied in a crucial scene which takes place in an office building (a frequent trope in the film) where Neo (Keanu Reeves) is first exposed to the reality of the matrix. It is out of this context that the penal imagery of *The Matrix* derives. We are told first that the Matrix is "everywhere. It's all around us, here even in this room. You can see it out your window or on your television. You feel it when you go to work, or go to church or pay your taxes. It is the world that has been pulled over your eyes to blind you from the truth." It is also the carceral archipelago, a world prison created by knowledge which assumes its own life-form (artificial intelligence)—humans caught in a machine of their own making, a virtual penal regime created by digital code and software. Penality within the matrix is structured through a false consciousness that is strikingly consistent with theoretical perceptions of the built-in constraints which reproduce social structure. This false reality is so pernicious as to force exclamations from the virtual agents themselves: "I hate this place. This zoo. This prison. This reality. Whatever you want to call it. I can't stand it any longer." The settings of both the virtual reality and the real world are claustral and confined—a city pressed in upon itself, tight corridors and alleys, overshadowed by jutting skyscrapers, cubicle work spaces (drones in hives, controlled by the transmission of data—all halograms, cyber constructs—soulless), small interrogation rooms, dank basements, and sterile ships. Lived experience, the site of salvation, occurs in a penal context of limited mobility and sensory deprivation, enclosed in a ship whose hull is reminiscent of the physical structure of the prison.

The popular television program, NBC's *The Office* (modeled after Ricky Gervais and Stephen Merchant's BBC sitcom) and the cult classic *Office Space* (1999) serve as exemplars of how penality emerges in mundane, everyday occupational contexts through institutional configurations that are largely naturalized into late modern environments. These sites are particularly compelling in the manner in which they serve to map the shared relationships and functions fundamental to prison sociology. For Goffman, total institutions—hospitals, schools, and prisons—were markedly similar in their logics and latent functions, and for Foucault, partitioning is a crucial component of the function of discipline where "each individual has his own place; and each place its individual."[28] Disciplinary space is directed then at the establishment of "presences and absences, to know where and how to locate individuals, to set up useful communications, to interrupt others, to be able at each moment to supervise the conduct of each individual, to assess it, to judge it, to calculate its qualities or merits. It [is] a procedure, therefore, aimed at knowing, mastering and using. Discipline organizes analytical space."[29] This design is reflected in the modern "open" office design which, although permeable and subject to the volition of the actors it contains, is often actually quite segregated and subject to surveillance through the somewhat apathetic routinization of workplace habit and convention, a tendency mapped into other kinds of institutions beyond the scope of this study, but characterized by Foucault's famous exclamation: "Is it surprising that prisons resemble factories, schools, barracks, hospitals, which all resemble prisons?"[30] As Joe Moran argues in his examination of office life as a new form of space, the business park increasingly is situated in a peripheral no man's land, near the boundaries of metropolitan and suburban spaces where commercial property is both affordable and conveniently placed near airports and interstates. The office design itself is defined through the insular cubicle, "quasi-offices assembled from partition panels . . . what Andrew Ross calls 'the signature footprint of alienation' for white-collar workers.[31] The cubicles are often filmed from above to highlight their boxy uniformity and the proximity they enforce between coworkers. As Moran points out, the docudrama, soap opera-ish format of popular representations of office life rely upon a slow-paced episodic structure in which very little happens, most significantly very little work, all of which tends to foreground the physical environment and arrangement of the workplace. The relationship between the physicality of office space and workplace occupational culture is foregrounded in often the most disturbingly uncomfortable and yet humorous scenes in which workers are constrained in place or coerced to participate in sluggish, useless meetings with management. This relationship is epitomized in a popular episode of *The Office* ("The Convict") where an employee is revealed to be an ex-con and is ultimately eliminated through liberal but misinformed efforts on behalf of the boss to incorporate him into the workplace. The episode explodes when, after listening to the prison experiences of their colleague, employees decide that prison is better than the workplace, and their boss then, in the midst of a misguided effort to scare them straight, locks employees in a meeting room in order to simulate the reality of incarceration.

The late modern workplace remains often envisioned as an open space that is at once a segregated and isolated world. Here relationships are imagined as strained through physical environments and conventions driven by a sheer bureaucratic repetition and inertia—an environment that is represented as entrenched and intractable in its design and meaninglessness. Although coercion and entrapment are not overt, they are structured into design—and the valuelessness of work, something everyone knows and yet maintains for their own unenthusiastic self-preservation. Here the ordinary constraints of work culture, the iron cage of rationality, carry penal overtones forward into the social control maps of everyday life and popular culture's fascination with the prevalence of these routines. Bleak, bland, institutional, and institutionalized, with their failed hierarchies and nonproduction, these spaces remain striking in their basic sociological similarities to spaces of confinement—and more significantly, the manner in which they have become popular points of representational focus *and* everyday experience. Interestingly however, penality in this space is often constructed as subversive where power and authority are routinely sabotaged and discipline actively and openly resisted, as spaces for the revitalization of sociality are carved and "struggled" out. In such space, resistance and open defiance to social control and hierarchy are definitive to what makes the programming comedy. Here, as the popularity of *The Office* demonstrates, spectators follow the constraining structures of their own everyday life, playfully mapping the irrationalities, ambiguities, and witty resistances of late modern social lives caught within emergent occupational cultures.

The Space of Judgment

Beyond this, there is a darker space in which penality circulates in many of the daily declarations that make up television's most popular daytime and prime-time programming. Within such contexts, a less reflexive, far more accusatory space emerges in which a kind of perpetual judgment and authority are given privilege. The judicial declarations and enactment of authority prevalent in programming like *Judge Judy* and *People's Court* as well as the pursuit of sanction which sits at the heart of the many versions of *C.S.I.*, *Law and Order*, and television crime docudrama anchor penality in the rituals and background noise of everyday worlds in which television is an ever-present agent.[32] Here, we are reminded of Foucault's insistence that

> the ideal point of penality today would be an indefinite discipline: an interrogation without end, an investigation that would be extended without limit to a meticulous and ever more analytical observation, a judgement that would at the same time be the constitutions of a file that was never

closed, the calculated leniency of a penalty that would be interlaced with the ruthless curiosity of an examination, a procedure that would be at the same time the permanent measure of a gap in relation to an inaccessible norm and the asymptotic movement that strives to meet in infinity.[33]

This kind of interrogation and judgment is routinized in the production of news reporting and the industry of commentary which surrounds it, epitomized in the accusatory and aggressive rhetoric of celebrity personalities like CNN/Court TV's Nancy Grace, Fox commentator Bill O'Reilly, and the angry parodies of Stephen Colbert's late night comedy program, *The Colbert Report.*

Exemplary of contemporary transformations of media journalism, the popular rise of Nancy Grace and the category of journalism which she reflects runs parallel with the rise of an outspoken executive power and assertion of a particular brand of victims' rights that Jonathan Simon maps in his examination of governance through crime. A former prosecutor and crime victim herself, Grace builds her authority through personal experience and the necessity of a voice through which to make claims for the historically maligned crime victim. Her show unabashedly assumes a moralistic framework from which to interview people actively involved in contemporary crime cases, facilitating a running discourse about guilt and innocence in the midst of active trials. In this exercise, Grace relies upon a panel of witnesses, experts, and suspects from which to create frameworks of individualized accountability. Well known for her combative accusations of guilt in connection with ongoing cases, Grace's program creates an atmosphere for the active interrogation of individuals and institutions in order to get at what she insists is the "truth." After the suicide of an individual who appeared on her show, the mother of a missing child whom Grace had implied was guilty, a discussion of the role of media scrutiny in the private lives of citizens briefly took shape. More significantly, the aura of legitimacy which popular news and legal commentary like Grace's program authoritatively claim reflect shifting ways in which penal judgment is introduced and elaborated in American culture. Here judgment is populist and summary as opposed to impartial and deliberatively democratic.

A similar kind of conventionality is manifest in documentary, the most prolific and accessible genre of penal representation. Across programming like Discovery Channel's *World's Toughest Jobs* and National Geographic's *Megastructures*, high-tech prisons and prison guards make brief, spectacular appearances; however, programming such as MSNBC's *Lock-Up* series,

A&E's *Investigative Reports*, History Channel's *Big House*, and National Geographic's *Lockdown* depend upon penal structures, with the titillating promise to take their viewers "inside" the real world of gangs, drugs, violence, women behind bars, death row, and maximum security. As documentaries, these programs privilege the notion of a normalized empirical reality, often beginning with the stark statistics of prison demographics and expansion. The spectatorial enters in as producers point to the extraordinary (which is now quite ordinary and redundant across television) circumstances under which they were able to gain access to the most hidden and dangerous institutions. With a reliance upon prison workers, inmates, and experts, producers construct a narrative that is presented in its objectives as an effort to inform its audience by revealing the realities of prison life. However, in their reliance upon ominous soundtracks against often repetitive or mundane footage of prison spaces, converted into fast-paced zooms, pans, and dissolves, producers strain to create a coherent narrative that is framed as documentary but steeped in sensationalism. Through a heavy reliance upon individualized frameworks, often following an inmate or guard through the daily routine of incarceration, the films rarely effectively create sociological connections between structure and agency, but instead pivot precariously from the mundane conditions of prison life to pure spectacle. Episodic in structure, such treatments are also discrete, brief, and emphasize the most sensational aspects of prison life—violence and its potentiality—in a manner that rarely interrogates any of the social conditions driving violence, incarceration, or its social effects. Nonetheless, such engagements prove seductive environments from which penal spectators may peek into the world of imprisonment— and simultaneously claim legitimacy and authority. Even against the new wave of critically acclaimed box office prison documentaries, including HBO's Emmy Award–winning *Ghosts of Abu Ghraib* and the Academy Award winner *Taxi to the Dark Side*, prisons are still places where disproportionate focus upon guards and victims often leads to the reproduction of these identities and a pathologization of the individual—as these settings become universalized in a manner where ordinary actors engage in extraordinary violence, thereby closing off discussions of the political, social, and cultural conditions in which violence takes startlingly specific form. Sadly, this occurs even as the story attempts to construct tales of systemic violence and corrupt government. What are rarely, if at all, invoked in these contexts are the conditions under which prison cultures and torture arise.

Importantly, in prime-time television drama, these same kinds of juridical frameworks emerge. The Emmy- and Golden Globe award–winning program 24 stars Kiefer Sutherland as Agent Jack Bauer, who heads a field operations unit of the Los Angeles Counter Terrorist Unit. The show, famed for its real-time episodic structure, remains one of television's most popular action dramas, syndicated worldwide, and is a classic rendition of the ticking time bomb scenario. Moving at a fast pace, the show requires that its viewers, like its characters, engage in split second decisions under imagined extreme duress as to whether or not to engage in lesser evils for larger social goods and public safety, such as when terrorists plan to release nerve gas in busy malls. Yet, the program has been critiqued for its resort to and popularization of torture and the manner in which it lends such practices credibility and effectiveness. Both Amnesty International and U.S. military and intelligence agencies have critiqued 24's presentation of torture as effective, averaging a torture sequence roughly every other week, including high-tech sensory deprivation, stun-guns, electrocution, and physical torture. The pedagogical functions of this imagery make ironic appearance in one particular account of interactions between the show's producers and the U.S. government. Famously, the show's creator, Joel Surnow, was approached by brigadier general Patrick Finnegan, dean of West Point military academy, and top military and FBI agents, who explained to Surnow that the show was having a "toxic" effect upon efforts to recruit and train military interrogators.[34] They requested alternative points of view, including those which depict torture as problematic and ineffective, based on evidence of torture's unreliability. Surnow's response is embedded in media commentary below:

> For all its fictional liberties, "24" depicts the fight against Islamist extremism much as the Bush Administration has defined it: as an all-consuming struggle for America's survival that demands the toughest of tactics. Not long after September 11th, Vice-President Dick Cheney alluded vaguely to the fact that America must begin working through the "dark side" in countering terrorism. On "24," the dark side is on full view. Surnow, who has jokingly called himself a "right-wing nut job," shares his show's hard-line perspective. Speaking of torture, he said, "Isn't it obvious that if there was a nuke in New York City that was about to blow—or any other city in this country—that, even if you were going to go to jail, it would be the right thing to do?"[35]

In this way, frameworks of accusation and judgment are anchored in riveting, imaginary spaces of popular culture where spectators play with scenarios they later interpolate into real-world discussions and contexts. Beyond this, complex assessments of accountability, retribution, and confinement pop up in other popular penal spaces, including popular crime drama and the majority of reality television with its competitive frameworks of game-like desert. One of television's most popular programs, ABC's *Lost*, involves a storyline where plane crash survivors stranded on a desert island individually and collectively attempt to make sense of their past, present, and future amid fragments of information and mysterious incidents and entities in their newfound setting. With its emphasis upon isolation and entrapment, the series positions its characters and its audience in complex hermeneutic spaces, where various themes, often bound up with faith and science, encourage viewers to construct complex theories about the nature of the show's premise, including how the characters came to be "lost," and the possibility of escape/rescue. Such a framework necessarily carries with it a subtext of guilt and accountability not uncommon in constructions of disaster. The series consequently relies heavily upon conventions in which the moral certitude of one character is pitted against another through a recurrent politics of blame and judgment in an environment where authority and legitimacy, albeit perpetually shifting, are paramount. Thus, characters, in the uncertainty of their environs and against bursts of collective good will, are chronically suspicious, accusatory, and divided—in a manner that is strikingly evocative of similar conventional structures in reality television and crime drama. In such a manner, *Lost*'s large ensemble cast and its dependence upon a juridical framework parallels the dynamics and proclivities of penal spectatorship.

In all of these instances, representation is envisioned not as a passive space, but as a provocative one. This media world is also a space characterized in many ways precisely by its recursiveness—its "interrogation without end." This kind of television programming as well as classic prison films (most infamously, *The Shawshank Redemption*) can be seen routinely, in cycles, due to the advent of cable/satellite television. In such media worlds, directed toward niche audiences and streamed through repetition and syndication, penality circulates and recurs across visual culture prolifically. Penal iconography is so much a part of the fabric of everyday life that it can no longer be extricated in a manner that is easily categorized. It is simply too voluminous in its embeddedness. The stuff of the everyday with regard to punishment, beyond the institutions themselves and their celebrated cinematic representations, includes as well the advertisements, novels, magazines, news, television, cartoons, video games, webcam images, photographs, postcards, art, government reports, public campaigns, political slogans, institutional architecture, professional and trade journals, and conversational chat and gossip that make up the quotidian world that is the public sphere.[36] In this world, image is perpetually poached, re-invented, reclaimed, and reaffirmed in complex networks of penal usage. Consequently, in late modernity, the image is social life. For this reason, penality's place must be interrogated within this complex usage, not to insist on its predominance alone but rather, and more productively, to develop new ways of reading, understanding, and altering the penal. If penal spectatorship allows certain tendencies that are less likely to problematize punishment, then the structures of that viewing and the depth of their organization within and across social life must be interrogated and critiqued. As John Bender argues in *Imagining the Penitentiary*, the idea of art and representation as solely effects of social institutions is "precisely the theory of reflection I wish to avoid."[37] Rather, these representations, interpretations, and experiences and practices of the everyday enable and reinvent punishment as much as reflect it by "formulating, and thereby giving conscious access to, a real texture of attitudes, a structure of feeling, that I call the 'penitentiary idea.'"[38] It is this "idea" and, more certainly, this "structure of feeling," that can at least partially explain, as penal spectators, where "our memories come from."

The Spectacle of Suffering

> Such images cannot be more than an invitation to pay attention, to reflect, to learn, to examine the rationalizations for mass suffering offered by established powers. Who caused what the picture shows? Who is responsible? Is it excusable? Was it inevitable? Is there some state of affairs which we have accepted up to now that ought to be challenged? All this, with the understanding that moral indignation, like compassion, cannot dictate a course of action. (Susan Sontag, *Regarding the Pain of Others*, 2003)

One of the most important implications of the extensionality of penality across and through social life is the nature of its relationship to intentionality—that core set of properties and meanings that define punishment. As the primary social institution which privileges the infliction of pain, punishment sits at the intersection of the body and the social, the private and the public, and insists upon attention to the transgression of these boundaries in its practice and its study, even as it permeates daily life in dense but largely naturalized carceral formations. In this regard, punishment, by virtue of its explicit dependence upon representation, is most analytically useful and influential when invoked, as it often is, through the extreme case or exemplar of penal patterns—the penal icon: those images, due to the manner in which they are privileged and circumscribed with power, are in turn linked to a positionality of the spectator that implies or necessitates action and judgment. These images are easy to reference culturally, visual memories: the postcard lynchings of the American South, the point-blank shooting execution of a Vietnamese man in the streets of Saigon, the prison photos of Abu Ghraib, the survivors in the barracks at Auschwitz. In this manner, the penal gaze is ultimately one which pivots upon the issue of responsiblilization, a decision that is always implied in the manner in which one looks at these images.

To articulate the nature of this "structure of feeling" with a bit more specificity, Bender asserts that the "powerful expository system" of punishment is, in fact, dependent in its significance upon the fact that the "penitentiary regime" is identical to other forms and institutions of social life such as the spatialized, segregated metropolis with its grids, classifications, and supervisions, the partitioned workspace, the cellular home as fortress. But the nature of this dependence is grounded more significantly in the idea that the penitentiary is "the extreme case—the 'total' instance, to use Goffman's term" of these forms and ways of living and representing.[39] Because of the prominence of the penal icon in this working cultural logic (an intentionality sustained through extensionality), "the penitentiary does not need to be accessible to visitors, or even physically present to view . . . because its rules are one and the same as those that govern consciousness itself. Citizens at large function, in imagination, as the beholders of penitentiary punishment, picturing themselves at once as the objects of supervision and as impartial spectators enforcing reformation of character on the isolated other."[40]

It is this particularly complex bifurcated mode of penal consciousness that a number of contemporary social theorists elaborate, alluding to or directly commenting upon its peculiar "structure of feeling," that pain of punishment which epitomizes the processes of spectatorship when regarding punishment. Here, the key actor is not the prisoner nor his or her custodian but the moral spectator invested with juridical authority, imagining punishment. Punishment is then most often, in late modernity, an imagined exercise of judgment. Recent discourse on the representation of pain increasingly insists that from this imagining must emerge some consideration of the nature of responsibilization implicated in the gaze. Consequently, part of the peculiarity of punishment as a cultural form derives from the relationship of this very specific kind of looking with a politics of affect. Recent work on penal representation claims there is a power to prison film in its ability to reveal, benchmark, defend, keep alive, and humanize prisoners as people.[41] Cinema remains, from this perspective, a viable resource in the pursuit of penal reform. Austin Sarat argues similarly that cinema has an ethical pedagogy to it, one in which the viewer may actively choose positions in that "Film gives testimony to the fact that, as Morson . . . says about narrative, time is always 'a field of possibilities, (and that) each moment has a set of possible events . . . that could take place in it.' It quite literally restores vision and brings the field of possibility into view. It 'recreates the fullness of time . . .' When we watch the moving image, we have the chance to confront what was, what is, what might be, multiply, fluidly, and often in ways that are hard for us to grasp."[42]

Similarly, in *Punishment and Culture*, sociologist Philip Smith gives us a powerful account of how complex and multiple our viewings and interpretations of punishment are, where "messages from the center generate readings that are often distorted, unintended, or unexpected. Sometimes explicit struggles can ensue over frames of interpretation, at others 'sleeper' critiques slowly chip away at dominant discourses as messages are persistently misunderstood or resisted on the societal periphery."[43] In his analysis, we can rely upon cultural meanings, particularly in relation to punishment, and at historically configured moments to be excessive, unruly, and surplus. Efforts to congeal or control the meanings of punishment through ritualistic practice (the public execution, for instance) may also misfire, what Smith calls a vulnerability to "cultural failure," forcing cultural response (the consequent movement of the execution behind prison walls) and a new effort to realign cultural codes in a more predictable manner.

From our perspective we might consider it fortunate that, as Smith writes, "There are possibilities for contested action and failed performance, for faulty or obstinate counter-readings, for the deliberate or unintentional production of unwanted signs."[44] In such a way, spectators may rescript, recode, revise, and return meanings in ultimately influential ways—what Smith ironically refers to as evidence of a "failure to communicate."[45] Penal failures in cultural transmission demand cultural solutions, and part of what Smith emphasizes is the manner in which historical shifts and reforms in punishment are indicative of struggles to cultivate meaning in social control. This may be a starting point from which to think through strategies for disrupting cultural codes and complicating dominant ideologies on punishment. Importantly, all the texts and performances examined in this chapter are open to multiple readings (certainly not just my own, which are designed to be oppositional) and reflect in the complexities of audience response these very contests. For instance, certainly the films *Shawshank Redemption, Minority Report,* and *Taxi to the Dark Side* ask us to consider the problematic pathways of punishment and their effects upon individuals. Even here, however, I have intentionally and strategically pointed to how such texts undercut their own narratives by limiting their engagement with larger questions about punishment. Beyond this, it is incredibly difficult to find a popular, mainstream representation of prisons which privileges, over spectacle, the kinds of complex narratives necessary to challenge our presumptions about prisons, a finding that I would argue indicates something profound about efforts to represent punishment and the viewing culture we have created around such penal predicaments.

Such limits point to how, within penal frameworks, elements of uncertainty and precariousness, to borrow Judith Butler's term, predominate. In these spaces, we are reminded of Sontag's warning of the taken-for-granted collective subjectivity, the "we" which looks at other people's pain.[46] Claire Valier writes likewise:

> Images make possible a kind of imagination that might prompt viewers towards critical engagement with punitive displays. According to Sartre, the imagination embodies the capacity to refuse the present and visualize what is not now the case. Imagination, he believed, possesses an ability to open a space for choice and for action. Images might, then, permit a revisionist imagination of justice and injustice, through those "magical transformations of the world" . . . that the emotions bring. Perhaps viewing events can be encounters within which an affective force, in a certain enchantment, might propel an ethical generosity. There are, however, no guarantees. [47]

The penal spectator with juridical powers is consequently a figure fraught with the potential for an intense "ethical generosity," moved to action, but also may be only a passive bystander framed by denial or apathy. Sontag outlines how "Images have been reproached for being a way of watching suffering at a distance, as if there were some other way of watching," but much like the representation of punishment, "watching up close—without the mediation of an image—is still just watching."[48] And the problem with watching remains one where "to speak of reality becoming a spectacle is a breathtaking provincialism," one that denies the power of looking and the juridical spectator implied as "It assumes that everyone is a spectator. It suggests, perversely, unseriously, that there is no real suffering in the world."[49] Both the power and the danger of the penal image are the privileging of the spectator alone, outside of the province of pain—and specifically, other people's pain, a looking, again, which is already positioned in its own extensive penal architecture of everyday life.

In a post–9/11 context, this reworking of the gaze is a significant point of intellectual assertion, a rare site at which configurations of the gaze converge at brief penal intersections in a politics of affect. These theories imply a reworking not simply of looking at pain but of pain itself, largely rejecting notions of psychological desensitization, brutalization, and compassion fatigue in the process of looking in late modernity. Rather, various thinkers emphasize the vitality and prominence of pain, no matter how repetitive, in human experience. The potentiality for mobilization, action, and social change is bound up in these moments with cultural and social distance as well as absent mechanisms for meaningful action, all of which depend upon mediation and representation. As Stanley Cohen argues, "'wanting to do something'" is most likely a widely shared aspect of humanity and if we witness a moment in which "everyone's responses become dimmer" in this respect, then arguably this has "little to do with fatigue or the sheer repetition of images."[50] Rather, it is more likely to be bound up with some overarching assumption "that nothing, nothing after all, can be done about problems like these or people like this."[51] Angela McRobbie writes similarly of the cultural implications of the governmentality expressed in the new offshore, off-limits American prison: "The new war prison thus figures as a mode of incarceration reflecting this informal, managerial form of power. The 'capricious proceduralism' outside the law' . . . also has ramifications which are more broadly cultural. If sovereignty inside governmentality informally licenses the intensification of aggression in and across everyday life, there is an even greater need for an ethical vocabulary which might provide the terms for opposing everyday cultures of aggression."[52] Penality, historically prominent in its absent cultural vocabularies, in the sites

(execution, incarceration) which mark the ends of speech, becomes a critical site from which, at least, to insist upon the necessity of speech, of coun-
ter-discourses, of witnessing what is concealed.

As Alison Young insists, much of the intellectual work on representation in criminology and certainly in penology is bound up with the act of
witnessing—"a response to a trauma buried in the crimino-legal condition" where "each event demands that we read it and attempt to witness
its meaning" through a "process of repression and representation that is
contingent and continuous."[53] This is to say, then, that for penal representation to do its work, it must open up a set of questions which it cannot
close off. It must open up a space that requires work, rather than resolution. As Judith Butler writes, "For representation to convey the human,
then, representation must not only fail, but it must *show* its failure. There
is something unrepresentable that we nevertheless seek to represent, and
that paradox must be retained in the representation we give."[54] In this
conceptualization, it is the field of vision that must be disrupted—and the
identities which depend upon that structure. Images that ignite, provoke,
and mobilize are often both penal and disruptive—historically they are
images that have "pointed somewhere else, beyond themselves, to a life
and to a precariousness that they could not show."[55] It is here, as Young
argues, that "we might begin to imagine an otherwise, an elsewhere,
a scarcely heard whisper in a conversation that has been going on and
is ongoing and cannot yet be understood. At that moment of imagination, eyes . . . might begin to blink, unfix themselves and look beyond the
frame. Until then, our eyes will be frozen in a never-ending gaze, fearfully
seeking the criminal, imagining her crimes."[56] This kind of penal spectator is one which will have difficulty seeing the "other" as well as her own
embeddedness in penal frameworks.

The activation of a moral account implies a dependence also upon the
existence and circulation of various kinds of images, but especially the
disruptive kind, which is, frankly, the absence to which most of these authors are writing in the first place. As Butler virtually cries out in the last
few lines of *Precarious Life*, "But what media will let us know and feel that
frailty, know and feel at the limits of representation as it is currently cultivated and maintained?"[57] The irony then is that the position of critique,
challenge, and interrogation, that perpetual "structure of address" which
must be struggled for, depends, in the end, upon representation.

•   •   •

The question of the image's functions remains a site of development and, in Sarat's terms, a point of productive "restlessness." Many continue to theorize the image as a testing ground, a place to think through and try out various theories and models of crime, law, and punishment. This approach often merges with an effort to read cultural texts historically and sociopolitically as ideological markers, reflecting dominant perspectives and the cultural contests which undergird them at particular junctures in time and space. Beyond this, there is a clear self-awareness within the field of a pedagogy of the image, reflecting the manner in which visual culture is instructive in its application and seductive in its accessibility to discussion. Sarat insists that a close reading of the film as text or case "reminds us of the contingencies of our legal and social arrangements . . . not just a mirror in which we see legal and social realities reflected back in some more or less distorted way," but "Instead, it always projects alternative realities that are made different by their filmic invention or by the editing and framing on which the film image always depends."[58] For Sarat, these contingencies, these alternate possibilities, permit "both greater analytic clarity and political sensibility in our treatments of law."[59] Rafter points out how recent trends in alternative cinema, the most viable source of disruptive images, "tend to decenter criminality, interweaving it with larger patterns of daily life" while moving toward "genre dissolution," patterns consistent with the contemporary popular mapping of penality.[60] All of these discussions also factor into a larger debate centered upon the image as a tool for social reform—an aspect of representation that takes on heightened salience in the context of penal iconography against the backdrop of a violent and volatile late modernity.

In such worlds, we are encouraged perpetually to move with the image into the real world of embedded and spiraling complexity. This is a world in which, to return to Arjun Appadurai's passage which opened this chapter, the penal image is inextricably bound up with "the terror and coercion of states," where images in general are "the key component of the new global order," and which, most significantly, reminds us that images are now "central to all forms of agency."[61] The work of punishment in representation then is one which forever traces the everyday configurations of penality to their most overt instance: the infliction of pain in order to remind all that with every look, we have a choice.

"Open For Tours"—Eastern State Penitentiary, John Haviland's model for the Pennsylvania Penitentiary solitary confinement system and widely considered to be the world's first true penitentiary, officially opened in 1829 and closed in 1970. It has been re-opened to visitors in downtown Philadelphia since 1994 when over 10,000 people visited. Now annual visits exceed 100,000 people (Photo by author).

4

Prison Tourism
The Cultural Work and Play of Punishment

Tourism is such a substitute, a substitute satisfaction of a genuine
need—that could otherwise prove creative and deeply ethical: The
need to top up the proximity of otherness with recognition of
shared humanity and enrichment of its contents.
> —Adrian Franklin, "The Tourist Syndrome:
> An Interview with Zygmunt Bauman," 2003

Preserved prisons are stony silent witnesses to the things former
regimes were prepared to do to people who violated laws or who
seemed threatening or suspicious. The murkiest project of all
would be to close them to tourists rather than to confront the
ongoing challenge of interpreting incarceration, punishment, and
forced isolation.
> —Carolyn Strange and Michael Kempa,
> "Shades of Dark Tourism: Alcatraz and Robben Island," 2003

Another cultural arena in which penal spectatorship is achieving new and unprecedented possibility lies in the realm of prison tourism. Across the United States, commercialized tours of defunct prisons
are gaining popularity, attracting hundreds of thousands of visitors annually. These sites include such recognizable institutions as Alcatraz and
Eastern State Penitentiary, but also a wide range of lesser known former
penitentiaries, reformatories, and jails in West Virginia, Ohio, Massachusetts, Colorado, Montana, Wyoming, Arizona, New Jersey, Hawaii, Indiana, South Carolina, California, Pennsylvania, and beyond. This chapter
explores the kind of cultural work that these sites and practices perform,

including the penal discourses and mythologies they invoke, through an examination of the social construction of the prison as tourist site. Based upon an assessment of institutional advertising, Internet descriptions, media representations, interviews, and the experience and design of the tours themselves, I map the manner in which a peculiar kind of penal spectator is produced as new life is given to dead prisons in a society which imprisons on an unprecedented scale.

One kind of penitentiary tour in particular has achieved unusual levels of popularity—the overnight prison ghost hunt. Groups arrive late in the evening, are given a quick tour of the premises, with special attention to "haunted" sites—spaces where assaults, murders, and executions occurred. Along the way, some experience the thrill of being locked into cells. Late in the course of one evening tour, huddled in an old gatehouse, the guide begins to describe the place visitors are standing as the former site for the state's executions. The building now serves as a back entrance to the facility but had been the setting for the hanging scaffold where 85 men were executed when the state still had death penalty statutes in place. The scaffold still exists high in the rafters where inmates were dropped through a trapdoor in the ceiling. As the guide moves toward the completion of his story, he directs everyone's attention to the still existing trapdoor which suddenly bursts open, with a dummy dropping and then dangling from a noose suspended above the group. Tourists scream, jump, gasp, and then burst into laughter. Everyone is then left alone, locked in with only flashlights and curiosity, allowed complete freedom to roam the dilapidated premises on their own, searching for ghosts, exploring the empty space, and periodically scaring one another. In the early morning hours, tired and cold, participants assemble in the souvenir shop, make their purchases, and begin the long trek home.

Across prison tours, day and night, the question of how groups develop at sites of prisons arises. What brings people, children, students, families, the disabled, the elderly, and researchers to the gates of old, dilapidated prisons day and night? How do these sites create constellations of meaning in which education, history, and spectacle merge? And finally, what is to be done with the role of pain in this construction of meaning? Importantly, night tours are organized fundamentally around the idea of prisoners' past violence, pain, and death—via their ghosts. In general, tours depend in their sociality upon moments in which strangers collectively bond around the replication of the infliction of pain and death. In this way, prison tours produce fascinating spectrums of sociality, built fundamentally around the prison's past as lived and remembered experience and the spectacle of cruel cultural fantasy. The frames of the tours themselves rarely provide an opportunity to reconcile these tensions in any meaningful way but rather leave participants suspended in the context of vast omissions even as they encourage their audience to participate vicariously in past judgments. The imprisoned voices of the past and present are largely missing, but we experiment with their fates in the present, knowingly, often disapprovingly, sometimes sympathetically. In this kind of setting, the meanings of prisons are left circulating within narratives which struggle to make any account for power and instead speak only partially, selectively to biography and history, while rarely interrogating the relationship between the two—the sociological narrative that would provide an account for how punishment is socially structured. What would it take to devise a framework for this kind of work—one in which citizens and prisoners might encounter one another in a meaningful context and confrontation of imprisonment, built neither purely upon history or spectacle?

This question takes on an interesting precedence as the original fortress prisons age and are abandoned for new ones. A question that looms for local and regional government is what to do with the monstrous spaces of the penitentiary, the asylum, and other total institutions. Carrying conflicting sentiments with regard to cultural heritage and how and why we remember, these places remain strategic research sites in that complex, and far-ranging responses to them and the manner in which they change across time are bound up with underlying social tensions and the ambivalence present in attitudes toward pain, violence, and tragedy. These complex associations leave some committed to their erasure through demolition and new development while others fight to preserve these institutions for equally complex reasons—education, historical conservation, architectural and artistic purposes, and commercial profit. The question of how to use such spaces constructively within the fiscal constraints of local budgets produces profound tensions and heated debate, bringing competing interpretations of the proper meanings of prisons to the fore. Eastern State Penitentiary, argued to be the first American penitentiary, transforming the way we think about and implement punishment in a democracy, is a prime example. The penitentiary officially closed in 1971, after nearly 150 years of operation, with no clear plan for its future. The site remained intact for the next two decades, not because of any clear directive but because its demolition was simply too costly. After being purchased by the city of Philadelphia in 1980, proposals began to circulate for converting the site into condominiums or a shopping mall. In response to these proposals, a task force formed in an effort to save the prison. Volunteer and task force lobbying efforts took over ten years to convert the prison into an operational tourist site. Their argument centered upon the idea that Eastern was the architectural centerpiece for how the United States as an emergent democracy would punish and had served as a massive force in the history of prisons worldwide, with over 300 prisons on five continents modeled after it. Efforts to salvage the prison were successful, but even now the most lucrative event remains a haunted house that runs nightly during the fall, enticing visitors with the possibility of a "massive haunted house in a real prison."

At the other end of the spectrum, in New York, Massachusetts, Michigan, and Oregon, old state asylums and prisons are being converted into condominiums with little or no mention of their previous functions. Preservationists have been unsuccessful in legal efforts to prevent the rise of commercial development. There is consequently no single meaning or outcome which predominates in the outcomes of defunct prisons but rather a confluence of discourses held in tension, marked by a desire to look—and not look—at these spaces through particular kinds of cultural frames.

Prisons in particular, consequently, are sites "in process," as geographer Kenneth Foote puts it, sites which "await the development of interpretive traditions within which they can be assessed, framed, and promoted."[1] Many of them have existed without purpose for years. And all have quickly, without use, descended into costly, dilapidated ruins. Due to their historical function and sheer scale, they remain nonetheless formidable markers in the community landscape. The island prison of Alcatraz, opened by the National Park Service for tourists in 1971 and operating under a five-year contract at that time, assumed that interest would simply dwindle away. It now has over a million visitors a year. Nearly 150,000 people visited Eastern State Penitentiary in Philadelphia in 2006. Other lesser known prisons (more than three dozen across the United States) are going from a few hundred visitors their opening year to thousands across time. Others are completely erased from the cultural landscape, demolished as condominiums, shopping malls, and commercial development rise up in their place. And then there are the hybrid cases, where prisons and economic redevelopment converge as hotels in Boston, Amsterdam, Istanbul, and Oxford maintain the structural framework and stylistic

Terror Behind the Walls, a haunted prison running nightly across the month of October and through Halloween, is the most profitable tourist event at Philadelphia's Eastern State Penitentiary (Graphic provided by Eastern State Penitentiary Historic Site, Inc.).

features of the prison, marketing the building's former status as a reason to stay there. Beyond this, the idea of building tourism more overtly into working prisons is under discussion at sites like Sing Sing, where prisons might serve as living museums. This type of commemoration colludes with consumption in ways that are increasingly difficult to disentangle or prevent with the most rigorous of respectful preservationist frameworks. And while social responses to sites of violence may range from sanctification, commodification, and preservation to outright obliteration, little analysis of these places and their historical fate has occurred.[2]

Significantly, prison tourism exists within a set of larger sociological patterns in relation to late modern tourism, one which demonstrates a growing interest among tourists with death, disaster, and atrocity. Visitors arrive at the gates of closed prisons for many reasons—to retrace history, to search for ghosts, and to view otherwise prohibited places. Still, most have trouble articulating why they are visiting at all. One tour administrator argues that many tourists are "simply enamored of the disintegration of the place. It's hard to say why people come. We just know they come and it's getting bigger and bigger."[3] This notion of a "dark tourism"[4] has historical antecedents in the form of pilgrimages and visits to battle sites and graveyards. However, now, such sites are mapped into larger institutional forces created and mapped by international development, consumption, and mass media. In such contexts, dark tourism researchers argue that local murders, celebrity overdoses, nuclear accidents, and death camps come to exist on level playing fields in tourist projects where fatality and fatalism converge. Such sites and visits depend clearly upon a convergence of mass media with a marked commercial ethic, one which necessarily relies upon tragedy as a complex mechanism of both preservation/sanctification and profit, amid a newfound capacity for immediate and mass popularity. The relationship between "the sad and the bad"[5] then is one which generates anxiety and ethical debate about the role of recreation, leisure, and pleasure in proximity to pain. Dark tourism is directed at assessing the manner in which these kinds of limit experiences have become patterned into consumption, how such a phenomenon is a product itself of late modernity, and how social life in turn is transformed by such economies. These bodies of literature include Seaton's thanatourism, Rojeck's "black spot" tourism,[6] and even "grief tourism," where individuals and groups travel to and bear witness at the site of terrible events.[7] The spectator in these circumstances, the "dark tourist," is not someone who comes because of some sort of specialized interest—a personal historical connection, a research or informational project (significantly, this group is argued to be the minority of most tourists at these sites)—but rather shows up out of serendipity, the direction of the tourism industry, or simple curiosity on a cursory outing. They are then the otherwise distanced spectators who are just passing through. Among these tours, "former sites of incarceration—places where the intentional state-sanctioned infliction of punishment, pain, and privation took place—are among the most popular."[8]

Contemporary popular intersections with penality structure prison tours in ways that are defined by the ambiguity and volatility of penal discourse. Here, the scripts that actors are most likely to invoke and improvise depend heavily upon a cultural ambivalence toward punishment. This occurs in part as the prison tour inverts many of punishment's fundamental properties. Culturally invisible, the institution is now rendered visible. Fundamentally closed and exclusionary, it serves now as a border that is open and accessible but also "dead," a remnant of institutional failure, implied as a marker of national history. In these contexts, penal engagements are at once historical and informative, voyeuristic and spectacular, and, consequently, contradictory—and thus, of distinct analytical interest. This complex cultural attraction to sites of trauma importantly marks a turn not simply in popular taste or cultural sensibilities, but in conceptualizations of the social, including the self and the collective. Inevitably, these processes reveal something important about the late modern subject and her preoccupation with pain, trauma, and violence. The ways in which this fascination with the crossing of public and private is built and sustained indicates much about the fleeting manner in which cultural attention looks at and observes others in contexts, like the penal, that are inseparable from violence and pain. In this regard, the structure of prison tours foregrounds the manner in which this ephemeral glance can be conflated with the more complex, prolonged, and engaged act of memory and witnessing—of deliberately questioning and demanding accountability of the project of punishment.

This foregrounding of the traumatic—and how we choose to imagine penal history as trauma—is a primary mechanism of the prison tour. The politics of the penal gaze here are inevitably embedded in spectacle and thrill-seeking. However, these tours also serve as experiences that, once completed, can be claimed as exemplary and authentic, grounded in institutional and historical experience. Although commodification and even trivialization of death and pain sites do not mean that counter-hegemonic stories and accounts are not possible, most stories of the prison nonethe-less tend toward a penal progressivism, which may emerge as a result of various competing interest groups. This tension, I argue, is rarely fore-grounded; rather, any distinction between the spectacle of trauma and the authority of the tour as a genuine engagement of punishment is not simply ignored but structurally denied. Contradictions are concealed and the ambiguous and volatile conditions of punishment carefully narrated over. I follow the implications of this way of looking through data drawn from a series of popular tours at several American penitentiaries, but with special emphasis on tours of Eastern State Penitentiary in Philadelphia, the central remaining artifact of the original Pennsylvania penitentiary system which launched the project of American punishment; the former Ohio State Reformatory, a massive Auburn-style tier prison most famous as the site for the filming of *The Shawshank Redemption*; and the former West Virginia Penitentiary at Moundsville, a developing tourist site at-tempting to model and publicize itself in a manner that brings financial incentive to an economically depressed region. In the concluding pages of this chapter, I explore how these dynamics shift within the context of educational or classroom tours of functioning prisons, where the poli-tics of representation are similar but complicated by the live exhibition of the incarcerated. Here, the precise dynamics that shape popular tours are foregrounded again through contradictions embedded in claims about penal knowledge, legitimacy, and authenticity. Across these contexts, I ar-gue that the politics of the gaze intersects with the production of penality in ways that proliferate with little impetus for thoughtful consideration or interrogation of what punishment may mean; rather, the structure of the prison tour maps cultural fascinations and imaginings of punishment, doing much to reveal the kind of fleeting and surface cultural work we would prefer to do when visiting or "seeing" prisons. Consequently, prison tourism affords us a site from which to interrogate how penal spectator-ship assumes legitimacy and authenticity even as it distances its observers from a deeper interrogation of the work of punishment.

Visitors at the Birth of the Penitentiary

Tours of the American penitentiary are present at its inception. These kinds of visits reflect the widespread and public appeal of institutional observations at the burgeoning onset of democratization and industrial-ization. Asylums, factories, slaughterhouses, and slums were, like prisons,

Plaque above guest book at Eastern State Penitentiary (Photo by author).

part of modernity's open display of the changing conditions and capacities of social life. These institutions and the violence at the core of their internal processes were marked by the idea of mass production and destruction at the heart of modern enterprise. Such institutions also marked the rise of social documentary in its effort to get at the problem and possibility of any meaningful witnessing of the new urban center, its deep inequalities and poverty, world war, and emergent global spectacles of personal, now public individual/mass suffering and death.[9] With the appearance of an affluent class of people willing to pay to visit these hidden zones, suffering and death were conjoined with commerce and bureaucratization as well as the arrival of inherently problematic attempts to document this context of human pain and experience. Out of this pursuit, a kind of spectatorship emerged which permitted privileged glimpses of a world that both defined and distanced the observer. These troubled performances, the historical vestiges of a popular misery tourism, carry forward into dark tourism contexts—where a new wave of reality tours is directed at brief observations of disaster (New Orleans post–Hurricane Katrina; Chernobyl post–nuclear meltdown), hot spots, war zones, and the most intensely poor regions of the world, including the slums of Dharavi[10] and the notorious *favelas* of Rio de Janeiro.[11] These touring contexts are built upon foundational ironies that cannot be evaded, through structured ways of viewing which profoundly challenge any possible distinguishing of spectacle from efforts directed at consciousness-raising. Dark tourists find themselves instead caught and complicit in complex viewing environments that are structured fundamentally through the inevitable reproduction of unequal gazes.

Prisons are similar kinds of contexts. In the earliest days of the republic, penitentiaries were some of the most visible and important testaments to the democratic commitment to public works, fundamentally bound up with the project of modernity. The nature of their design, scale, and missions was hotly debated across public and political discourse and, as a result, all the more grandiose.[12] The early American Pennsylvania and Auburn systems were points of international attention and commentary, a fascination grounded in the political experiment in self-governance that the United States posed. The celebrated and oft-cited visits of French ambassadors Alexis de Tocqueville and Gustave de Beaumont to Sing-Sing, Auburn, and Eastern State penitentiaries, as well as Charles Dickens's deeply critical account of his own visit to Eastern State in *American Notes*, are revisited across historical studies of the penitentiary, popular documentary, and built self-reflexively into contemporary tours of the prisons themselves. These early ambassadors and diplomats spent days and sometimes weeks in the study of the prisons they visited, talking openly with administrators, staff, and inmates, observing daily operations, and writing about the experience in correspondence, notes, and eventually key works, citing the American prison project as a crucial democratic experiment in governance and the production of civic life.

As part of this test of democracy, the structure of these early tours was open in design, eager to display the penitentiary and its vision of social order as an American invention to foreign guests. Charles Dickens wrote of his time at Eastern State:

> I was accompanied to this prison by two gentlemen officially connected with its management, and passed the day in going from cell to cell, and talking with inmates. Every facility was afforded me, that the utmost courtesy could suggest. Nothing was concealed or hidden from my view, and every piece of information that I sought, was openly and frankly given. The perfect order of the building cannot be praised too highly, and of the excellent motives of all who are immediately concerned in the administration of the system, there can be no kind of question.[13]

Dickens outlines nicely the routine of the prison tour: official accompaniment, administrative effort to depict openly and realistically the daily life of the institution, receptivity to questions, perfect order. More famously,

Dickens is noted for having observed and analyzed in his day-long excursion at Eastern State the effects of the Pennsylvania system's defining feature, solitary confinement:

> The system here, is rigid, strict, and hopeless solitary confinement. I believe it, in its effects, to be cruel and wrong. In its intention, I am well convinced that it is kind, humane, and meant for reformation; but I am persuaded that those who devised this system of Prison Discipline, and those benevolent gentlemen who carry it into execution, do not know what it is that they are doing. I believe that very few men are capable of estimating the immense amount of torture and agony which this dreadful punishment, prolonged for years, inflicts upon the sufferers; and in guessing at it myself, and in reasoning from what I have seen written upon their faces, and what to my certain knowledge they feel within, I am only the more convinced that there is a depth of terrible endurance in it which none but the sufferers themselves can fathom, and which no man has a right to inflict upon his fellow-creature. I hold this slow and daily tampering with the mysteries of the brain, to be immeasurably worse than any torture of the body: and because its ghastly signs and tokens are not so palpable to the eye and sense of touch as scars upon the flesh; because its wounds are not upon the surface, and it extorts few cries that human ears can hear; therefore I the more denounce it, as a secret punishment which slumbering humanity is not roused up to stay. [14]

Dickens foregrounds a complex and crucial tension in prison tourism by positioning the benevolent intentions of the system's implementers against the uncanny sense that something remains dreadfully wrong with the practice of punishment itself. What seems especially disturbing to him is not simply the effects of solitary confinement, its fundamental perversion of the social, but the manner in which it is institutionally and culturally hidden—"a secret punishment" which leaves observers and non-observers alike relatively unmoved. In this regard, it is a social practice unlikely to engage the social—or the civic-minded—and the structure of the tour itself is defined by this absence in recognition on the part of others. Similar kinds of tensions undergird Beaumont and Tocqueville's observations in *On the Penitentiary System*, when they write: "But when the day is finished, and the prisoners have retired to their cells, the silence within these vast walls, which contain so many prisoners, is that of death. We have often trod during night those monotonous and dumb galleries, where a lamp is always burning: we felt as if we traversed catacombs; there were a thousand living beings, and yet it was a desert solitude."[15] Here, in the solitary and silent systems of the early penitentiaries, the contradiction of American punishment is openly observed—the reliance upon an institution defined by its severing of the social in order to produce precisely that—the well-disciplined, normalized, socially integrated citizen. Not surprisingly, upon evidence of the perennial problems of incarceration—high recidivism and, in the case of solitary confinement, madness, Beaumont and Tocqueville write: "To sum up the whole on this point, it must be acknowledged that the penitentiary system in America is severe. While society in the United States gives the example of the most extended liberty, the prisons of the same country offer the spectacle of the most complete despotism."[16] The descriptive work of these early observers is particularly fascinating in its foregrounding of the disturbing manner in which fundamental aspects of prison sociology, in the institution's foundational distortion of the social, remained invisible to its designers and supporters and depended, in its critique, precisely upon the presence of outside observers. Their notes also demonstrate a level of rigor in observations and interpretations that is dramatically distinct from the processes that comprise prison tourism today. The purposes of such nascent visits and the publications that emerged out of them (Dickens's *American Notes*; Tocqueville's masterpiece, *Democracy in America*) serve as crucial historical reminders that the stakes of these visits were openly acknowledged as bound up with international diplomacy and discussions of state-building. Prisons were, thus, in ways deeply disconnected from contemporary practices, recognized by both visitor and host to be a project framed in the interrogation and assessment of strategies and critiques of governance, sovereignty, and citizenry.

The project of tourism, however, is embedded more deeply than this in the birth and institutional design of the penitentiary which, although closed off from society, has always depended upon a power structure defined through the presence of a penal spectator. As elaborated by Foucault in his discussion of the birth of the prison, ways of looking define the prison as a project of modernity. In its ceaseless inspection and supervision, the prison ideally held out the promise, through calibration, regulation, and discipline, of normalization. Within these "laboratories of virtue," inspection and surveillance constituted key factors in the penitentiary's design, lending it a unique "architecture parlante." John Haviland, chief architect of Eastern State Penitentiary, described the selection of the institution's famous hub-and-spoke design as a means of promoting a confluence of penal terms grounded in the distribution of power and people, including "watching, convenience, economy, and ventilation."[17] According to this design and others, exemplified in one of the penitentiary's most celebrated forms—Bentham's panopticon—the idea of an outside perspective was fundamental, embodied in the prison structure as an "invisible omniscience" and "external conscience" for the inmates, a presence that could oversee both prisoners and their custodians.[18] This gazing presence could be multiple and diverse, as Foucault demonstrates, in the seemingly limitless potentiality of interpretation and motive at the center of the panoptic tower: "the curiosity of the indiscreet, the malice of a child, the thirst for knowledge of a philosopher who wishes to visit this museum of human nature, or the perversity of those who take pleasure in spying and punishing."[19] Although other kinds of prison designs are far more widespread and prominent in practice, technologies of confinement and processes of looking have always maintained a complex relationship to one another in prison settings, an association that is argued to be central not simply to the blueprint and organization of the penitentiary, but to modern social life itself.

According to sociologist John Urry, the tourist gaze is similarly socially, expertly, and institutionally organized.[20] Like the penal gaze, the look of the tourist is always constructed through the axis of difference. Tourism, in Urry's account, organizes around the pursuit of an experience that is not one's own, usually by voyeuristic observation of what is considered other, alien, and unfamiliar. The pleasure in this looking is framed through patterns and structures of consumption and culture that are careful to avoid destabilizing the hierarchy of the gaze—and thus work to ensure that the look returned—the possibility of being looked back at—is discouraged, if not overtly prohibited. This way of looking often depends upon a controlling and sadistic gaze that distances and objectifies the subject of that gaze. The power of this mode of observation is found at its limits in its production of hierarchy, denial, distance, and other people's pain as pleasure. Prison tours are further complicated in this regard as distance—and difference—is institutionally structured into the hierarchies of prison design already, thus creating a complex set of intersecting power differentials. Also, because the tour is framed by punishment, the voyeuristic gaze is given greater legitimacy in its observation of other people's pain as it carries with it authority and judgment. The idea of pain is thus reworked into a context of leisure and entertainment with very little, if any, interaction with those largely imagined "others."

Popular prison tours occur in institutional contexts that are emptied of inmates, where the past is given a spatial dimension and historical narrative that is selective and staged. These stories depend upon particular codes of penal representation, including not simply what is known about prisons but what is desired by a consuming public. Such "emptiness" and historical silence provide a setting in which fantasy is privileged and culturally sustained. As Urry argues:

> Places are chosen to be gazed upon because there is an anticipation, especially through daydreaming and fantasy, of intense pleasures, either on a different scale or involving different senses from those customarily encountered. Such anticipation is constructed and sustained through a variety of non-tourist practices, such as film, TV, literature, magazines, records and videos, which construct and reinforce the gaze.[21]

Satisfaction in these contexts, the successful achievement of entertainment, depends upon an alignment of expectations with the actual tourism experience. There are shifts in practice as well. When people assume the roles of tourists, their viewing habits change and become more sensitive to external and visual environments, in efforts to read, decode, preserve, and collect this unusual moment: "People linger over such a gaze which is then normally visually objectified or captured through photographs, postcards, films, models and so on. These enable the gaze to be endlessly reproduced and recaptured."[22] The authenticity of punishment then is rendered further dependent upon cultural imaginings, souvenirs, and representations of "going to prison." The structure and design of tours then stretches toward an accurate historical record, but one which appeals to the punishment myths of the tourist. In order to subject this theoretical framework to a greater degree of rigor, I wish to lay out, through a description of a particular set of prison tours, how this way of structuring cultural practice through penality works. In such contexts, we see how the penal gaze lays claim to particular effects of truth, how it produces and disciplines particular kinds of subjectivities and subjects— and finally, how, through this work, it conceals key contradictions, uncertainties, and alternatives that might otherwise challenge the current practice of punishment.

Architecture Parlante—How institutions speak: Arrival at the Ohio State Reformatory (above) and Eastern State Penitentiary (below) (Photos by author).

Day Tours

Driving up to a prison for the first time is a visually defining moment. Looking becomes an outright compulsion. In the midst of downtown, as with Eastern State Penitentiary, or in the case of rural settings in the middle of fields beside highways, as with the Ohio State Reformatory, "ideal" prison structures rise up out of the landscape, monolithic and anachronistic vestiges of earlier prison systems in which punishment's effects were bound up with the public display of the institution. At tour times, groups congregate in the parking lots or line up outside the institution, gazing upward and around, pointing and snapping photos, marking the momentousness and transgressiveness of the penal encounter, where culturally prohibited space is suddenly open, accessible, and recordable.

At the gates of the prison, sally ports and administrative offices are converted into ticket desks and souvenir shops. This staging area is carefully arranged with both historical materials—signs, brochures, pamphlets, photos, posters, books, and plaques describing and commemorating the history and function of the institution as well as consumer spectacle—magnets, key chains, coffee mugs, shot glasses, T-shirts, playing cards, postcards, Hollywood souvenirs, disposable cameras, and ghost hunting equipment (flashlights, dowsing rods, etc.). At the Ohio State Reformatory and the former West Virginia Penitentiary, these discourses intersect as friends and families take photos of one another standing beside the electric chair or weapons display cases of homemade prisoner shanks and shivs. At West Virginia Penitentiary, some pose for the camera in areas designed to simulate mug shots. The entrance to prison tours consequently sets the stage for how to treat the event, emphasizing the tour as both museum and theme park—an experience to be carefully documented through the accumulation of a visual record (photos/postcards) and the purchase of souvenirs. The tension for the penal spectator embedded in this structure is rarely foregrounded by staff and preservationists; rather, when analyzed at all by tour organizers, it is presented as a losing battle. The program director at Eastern State Penitentiary comments on the decision to include a depiction of one of their celebrity inmates, Al Capone, on a T-shirt in the souvenir shop:

> And we also spend a bit of time thinking about, less than we should, what we carry in the store but we really did talk a lot about the Capone t-shirt. You know, what does this mean to print a t-shirt with a murderer

"Authentic" bowls from the "hole" next to *Shawshank* scripts (Photo by author).

on it, that people are going to wear and what are they thinking when they wear it and does it matter—do you care? I've been resisting the shot glass thing forever and finally gave up and it's one of our best sellers . . . We should get rid of all the books. The books are just a complete loss except for the . . . ghost books.[23]

Such tensions echo Philip Smith's argument about the problem of meaning-making generated by prison tourism when he writes, "Prison tourism is itself prone to a second-order renarration as voyeuristic and morally suspect, as the exercise of a polluted gaze. Trying to control this can present severe problems of genre management."[24] He then describes how efforts at Alcatraz to design tours that inform visitors about the natural history of the island, its political past in relationship to Native Americans, or the role of shifting visions of crime and punishment in the history of Alcatraz are all overlooked in favor of tours built upon Hollywood sensationalism and the role of a popular imaginary in the mythos of Alcatraz. Here, Smith argues that prison tourism constitutes one of those compelling sites in which we see "expert knowledge fighting a losing battle against popular culture . . . Propelled by the seductions of evil, the experience of visiting a sacred space," Smith writes, "is one that celebrates myth and rejects institutionally sanctioned but rather unexciting forms of knowledge. By encouraging visitors to the island of Alcatraz, the National Parks Service has unwittingly perpetuated what it wished to eliminate."[25]

The commercial aspects of prison tourism, then—tour fees and profits from souvenir sales—although always mapped into some sort of preservation effort, depend upon a popular imaginary which defies historical and educational efforts, culminating in deep and perhaps inescapable contradictions. The preservationist aims of the prison, consequently, are inevitably embedded in their economics and strategies to avoid or invoke commercialism. For instance, Eastern State Penitentiary takes pride in the fact that the majority of its operating costs (including payroll, utilities, renovation, and insurance) are not covered by endowments but rather by ticket sales. The Penitentiary also actively recruits a substantial membership which has led to over $3 million in preservation, restoration, and programming funds from charitable foundations and government agencies.

Although most sites offer a range of tour options, they are often similar in structural design, framed historically and directed at particular wings of the prison or critical events. At the Ohio State Reformatory, for instance, day visitors choose from a West Tower Tour (with emphasis upon the guard tower, the inmate cemetery, and an underground tunnel system), the East Cell Block Tour (the world's largest freestanding steel cell block), and the Hollywood tour (which covers key set sites from films like *The Shawshank Redemption* and *Air Force One*). Across prisons, these guided sessions are often topical, focused upon such subjects as prison riots, escapes, special exhibits or collections, and daily life in the institution. They are often brief, lasting only 45 minutes to an hour, and are usually conducted in groups with an expert guide, including volunteers, students, retired community members, preservationists, historians, and former guards and inmates. Additional kinds of tours are consistently being developed and serve as key mechanisms for expanding commercial profit and developing further preservation efforts. Some places, such as Eastern State Penitentiary, offer audio tours where you may traverse the prison grounds alone, engaging and disengaging the tour structure as you choose. West Virginia offers a 90-minute tour that "will allow you to hear the eerie sounds of cell blocks slamming shut behind you, as you experience life on the inside of a penitentiary."[26] Eastern State Penitentiary has recently added a summer "Twilight Tour," allowing access to the penitentiary at dusk, and a "Winter Adventure Tour," a general tour designed to bring in visitors during the off season.

Eastern State Penitentiary also offers a series of art installations and history exhibits. These displays are among some of the most interesting features of their tour structure in the ways in which they engage prison spaces and functions. Historical exhibits have included restoration projects of the prison greenhouse, hospital, synagogue, and an escape tunnel as well as the establishment of an oral history project collecting the experiences of still living prisoners and guards recording stories of their time at Eastern State Penitentiary. Art installations include a replica of a cell from Camp Delta at Guantánamo (contained within an Eastern State Penitentiary cell), a series of miniature dioramas that meticulously recreate the daily lives of prisoners across time, and an installation of televisions placed in a shower, cell, and tier corridor, running montage sequences of prison film depictions of the same spaces. These exhibits are compelling in the manner in which they encourage visitors to rethink prison spaces and make broader reflective connections than a tour of empty prison space alone invokes. In this regard, Eastern State, like Alcatraz, is unusual in its ability and commitment to creating a context in which visitors are challenged to think through their understandings of prison life at various moments in tour structures. The prisons also serve as sites for cultural festivals, including a Bastille Day celebration at Eastern State Penitentiary and a heritage craft festival at West Virginia Penitentiary.

In contrast to Eastern State Penitentiary, Ohio State Reformatory and West Virginia Penitentiary have relied upon other kinds of financial planning to facilitate preservation. For instance, West Virginia Penitentiary houses the National Corrections and Law Enforcement Training and Technology Center's mock riot and disaster training, in which the prison serves as an experiential classroom and trade show. In the course of multiple training scenarios and workshops—including staged inmate disturbances, hostage situations, refusals to comply, food fights, etc.—members of law enforcement from across the United States play the roles of guards and prisoners. The mock riot has become a significant economic force at West Virginia Penitentiary, increasing from just over 100 participants in its first year to now over 1,000. In 2000, it was estimated that the mock riot brought in over half a million dollars to the local economy.[27] At the Reformatory in Mansfield, Ohio, a recently renovated guard room, surrounded by steel bars and extensive tier systems, may be rented for $500 and has been booked for weddings, birthday and anniversary parties, class reunions, and bar mitzvahs. At West Virginia Penitentiary, classes from local schools are periodic visitors where associations with deterrence and scared straight programs are foregrounded within the informal functions of the tours. As one administrator declared, "I mean, a sixteen-year-old boy comes in here and gets the history and listens to the tour guides, he knows that he does not want to end up in this place." West Virginia Penitentiary also includes a prominently displayed search engine on their website which allows visitors to access a database of West Virginian sex offenders, where visitors are encouraged to "find predators in your area."[28]

In this way, radically different purposes for prison spaces develop at these sites, with varying degrees of challenge and engagement structured into visits and institutional uses, some directed at a critique of punishment and others oriented toward spectacle or the reproduction of punishment. These fundamental tensions are evident in the main advertisements for each site, largely found on websites and in brochures.[29] In its publicity materials, West Virginia Penitentiary headlines "Do Hard Time," and a description of the prison found on one of its brochures mixes history and spectacle, foregrounding precedent and then violence: "The Former West Virginia Penitentiary is a Gothic-Style prison situated at the heart of historic Moundsville. This 10-acre structure was the second public building constructed by the newly formed state of West Virginia after the Civil War in 1866. It housed some of the most violent criminals in the United States." Similarly, the Mansfield Reformatory Preservation Society, the nonprofit group presently managing the former Ohio State Reformatory, publicizes as its mission a mandate "to restore the reformatory and bring back to the Mansfield community, through adaptive reuse, a similar economic contribution that was Ohio State Reformatory's in 1896. A restored reformatory will provide a civic meeting location and many historical and educational opportunities as well as an increase in the current number of visiting tourists."[30] Here, the group publicizes the prison as a "civic meeting" space directed at historical and educational purposes but also seeks to mirror the prison's past economy through a new one built upon tourism. In its educational mission, the preservation society promotes largely architectural and restoration feats, including restoration of the warden's quarters and the central guard room and an accumulation of antique museum collections. There is also the assertion that with economic commitment the prison "can become a Mecca for criminal justice and penology researchers."[31] To date, however, most of the public uses, outside of tours, have revolved around reserving the renovated central guard tower as an unusual site for parties and celebrations.

Eastern State Penitentiary marks a deep contrast to both Ohio State Reformatory and West Virginia Penitentiary in the development, elaboration, and critical challenge of its mission:

> Eastern State Penitentiary Historic Site, Inc. works to preserve and restore the architecture of Eastern State Penitentiary; to make the Penitentiary accessible to the public; to explain and interpret its complex history; to place current issues of corrections and justice in an historical framework; and to provide a public forum where these issues are discussed. Eastern State Penitentiary Historic Site, Inc. carries out these activities using the highest standards in educational and public programming, and in conservation. While the interpretive program advocates no specific position on the state of American prisons, the program is built on the belief that the problems facing Eastern State Penitentiary's founders have not yet been solved, and that the issues these early prison reformers addressed remain of central importance to our nation.[32]

At Eastern, the mission statement is explicitly linked to current debates about incarceration and a self-conscious awareness of the tensions embedded in prison tourism. Because of their location and history, they mark an unusual and original prison tourist site, with more resources in terms of community support, endowments, and available expertise than the many emergent rural prison tour sites. Even so, Eastern cannot evade foundational tensions bound up with spectacle and education.

These missions reflect key tensions, features, as well as similarities and distinctions in each of the various kinds of tours available at these sites. Within their differences, elements of preservation and entertainment are strains fundamentally structured into the institutional design of all of the tours. This is in part bound up with the simple reality that tours are largely forced to do one thing: map the physical spaces of an empty penitentiary. This primacy of empty institutional space lends the visit a fundamental focus on the daily/historical operations of the prison. Tourists walk through tier blocks, casually exploring the decaying remains of the cells, wandering in and out of them and sometimes being locked up for a few titillating seconds. They stand in empty mess halls, explore medical equipment in hospital wards, gaze into showers, climb up into guard towers, stroll through the exercise yard, and linger at death row. Their wanderings take them through former cafeterias, libraries, classrooms, and industrial quarters. Stops are made along the way at various points where stabbings, assaults, rapes, and murders occurred. These are some of the most descriptive and prolonged moments of the guided tours where escorts engage in complex narrative constructions, much like a good ghost story, emphasizing at the conclusion that all of this took place "right where we are standing." These flashpoints are also highlighted in publicity materials. At West Virginia Penitentiary, tourists are encouraged to "visit North Hall, where the most violent criminals spent 22 out of 24 hours," to "witness 'Old-Sparky' which was built by an inmate, to execute inmates," and to "see Charlie Mason's letter requesting transfer to Moundsville."[33] This format lends legitimacy and authenticity to the experience, acting not only as a basic primer in institutional functions, in how inmates were housed and processed on a daily basis, but also engaging in and reproducing popular constructions and stereotypes of criminality, deviance, and danger. In the specific case of West Virginia Penitentiary, it also speaks to a marketing effort directed at achieving regional and national recognition for a prison that is otherwise relatively unknown.

The emphasis across the basic tours, however, is always upon the penitentiary regime—its sheer scale and mass volume in the number of people historically confined. Individuals enter into the description generally only by way of celebrity or notoriety, scandal or spectacle. Technologies of display—photos, showcases, reconstructions placed intermittently throughout the tours—all largely revolve around these historical parameters and tensions. It remains, as with the early penitentiary, the architecture and structure of imprisonment that dominates the tours. As touring is very much about imagining what life in such an institution might be like, visitors are encouraged to observe what it is or was to live in monstrous worlds of concrete and steel—and especially amidst monstrous situations—assaults, murders, riots, executions. For this reason, tours generally focus on the massive physicality of penal place (the uniform extensiveness of tier blocks), penal number (the incarcerated), as well as the scale of daily life and operations—what it was—or might have been—to eat, sleep, work, live and, especially, die in such worlds—all amidst a strong emphasis upon the most disturbing, yet anecdotal, aspects of incarcerated life.

In this way, the analysis of penal regimes on these day tours is intensely bound up with the navigation of both the spectacular and the mundane. Prison tours are about the practical concrete details as well as the most sensational aspects of incarceration. As such, they constitute a kind of cultural formation without a clear logic or coherence. The tours are more constellations rather than narratives but with routine points of emphasis: the mundane but awesome world of concrete and steel against the spectacular backdrop of thrilling escapes, the walk from death row to the execution chamber, the geographic flashpoints of riots, brutal assaults and murders. The tours are consequently shot through with contradiction—the kinds of contradiction that are always difficult to maintain culturally—the boring, ordinary reality of the daily life of punishment splattered episodically with instances of violence and often macabre celebrity. These tensions again reveal less about the institutional practice and more about the volatile nature of discourses on punishment, including the manner in which punishment as a practice is invested with meaning through complex, contradictory rhetorical scripts.

One factor is unavoidable in the tours of historic prisons. The construction of meaning depends upon a key feature of prison tourism: the emptiness and silence of institutional space—or the removal of the punished. The precise point of the tourist experience is to purchase an experience that is removed from ordinary life. Thus, tourism depends upon spatial change and temporal dislocation. This dislocation, however, is problematized by the fact that commercial tourism largely occurs through observations from positions of relative isolation, distance, and security—with no real danger or challenge in looking or of that look returned. For that challenge to occur, the engagement would morph into a practice more like ethnography or residency and community membership—a prolonged engagement with what it is to live in that part of the world. The long-standing historical fascination with observing the "dangerous class" depends consequently upon a search for difference, but a brief, ephemeral search in which living inhabitants are transformed into faceless and disembodied objects or spectacle. The prison tour in even its most thoughtful manifestations always reproduces this objectification. In most prison touring contexts, all human life with any direct connection to the practice of punishment is omitted. It is only empty, vacant, dilapidated space which remains—as Eastern State Penitentiary frames it: a "stabilized ruin" with echoes of the past, wired into headsets. The question arises then as to what happens in institutional spaces that are defined historically by their capacity to contain and control masses of people and are now, as tourist sites, absent or emptied of their humanity. In such instances, place becomes slowed, static, easily attached to the popular projections of imagined history and cultural memory. This silent absence sustains a perpetual practice of cultural fantasizing.

Empty place as tour space (Photo by Bruce Hoffman).

The role of this imaginary in empty space lends some explanatory power to the prevalence of other kinds of tours. These include "Hollywood" tours, engagements which center specifically upon a fictive account of prison life, framed by the use and portrayal of the institution in popular culture. The Ohio State Reformatory, for instance, like Alcatraz, structures several kinds of·tours and displays around the institution's use as a location site for the filming of *The Shawshank Redemption, Air Force One,* and *Tango and Cash.* Commemorative editions of *The Shawshank Redemption* on DVD include documentary extras focused upon the response to the prison by actors and production staff upon arrival, adding layers of myth to the representation of punishment. Tour guides point to places in the institution where famous movie scenes, music videos, or television programs were shot as visitors snap photos. In such moments, empty space is quite literally imagined space, deeply disconnected from the concrete origins upon which visitors stand. This vacant imaginary defines in many ways the most successful prison tour context of all—the haunted prison.

Night Tours

> We are in real danger of being known as a haunted house that has a daytime history tour. (Program Director, Eastern State Penitentiary)

> It is hardly an exaggeration to suggest that in the midst of many tourism forms of life, we are in death. (A.V. Seaton, "War and Thanatourism: Waterloo 1815–1914," 1999)

Prison haunted houses and ghost hunts now run annually throughout the United States from spring into late fall. These tours are unique in a variety of ways but also simply convert conventional aspects of the basic group tour into what Eastern State describes in its promotional ads as "cellblocks of terror." In the case of the prison haunted house, the penitentiary tour takes on many theme park characteristics, modeling the event after the most stereotypical and, of course, frightening aspects of imprisonment in a carefully controlled setting. Across the Halloween haunted prison sites, tourists enter and initially take on the role of prisoners with tour staff posing as guards in a simulation of intake processes, yelling and playfully harassing visitors, forcing them into lines and dark corridors of the prison. As visitors wind their way through reconstructed blocks of the prison, they are surrounded by prisoner-actors, all of whom take on a stereotyped portrayal of mental illness, reaching out from cells and jumping out of hidden corners. Medical wards are peopled with "mad" doctors who are performing experiments upon "volunteers." Physical space is depicted as an industrial ruin: toxic, damp, mist-enshrouded, and electrified. The prison again is configured as empty historical and haunted space, informed vaguely by the design of institutional daily life, where you are "abandoned, but you may not be alone. Scared straight?"[34]

This event, invoking, intermingling, and unreflexively playing off of a wide range of positivist and post-rehabilitation punitive discourses on punishment, is the single largest and most important source for historical preservation revenue at the prisons that offer them. Eastern State Penitentiary's version of this event has achieved enough popularity in just over a decade to bring in over 100,000 visitors in the weeks before Halloween.[35] As the exemplar of this phenomenon, some analysis of their planning and publicizing of the event is worthwhile.

A publicity still from Eastern State Penitentiary's Terror Behind the Walls, one of the United States' most popular haunted houses (Photo provided by Eastern State Penitentiary Historic Site, Inc.).

The challenge for Eastern State Penitentiary administrators has been finding ways to use the haunted house to promote and expand the day tours and the educational component of the preservation effort, while at the same time creating a structure that attempts to distinguish the aims of the two different tours. For instance, the website makes you choose—between the daytime historic tour and nighttime haunted house. And yet, the Halloween event at Eastern State Penitentiary inaugurated the tour program at the penitentiary and predates the day tour. As administrators concede, "The two have always had a hand in glove relationship," resulting in "a devil's bargain."[36]

> I mean, we're aware that we're definitely undermining, we're tapping into clichés and sort of unraveling a little bit of our mission for the daytime tour at night . . . .You know we tried for years to tell the building's history through Halloween. It seems like a real easy solution—that you talk about Eastern State's history at night with theatrical lighting and make it scary.

It was horrible. I mean when we were trying to do that it was just—it was completely misguided and I'm embarrassed that it took us so long to pick up on it. But it was inherently sensationalizing the building's history . . . I mean so much of what happened here was just mundane, you know. And then beyond that . . . we didn't really have a training program set up to get [guides] to understand what we were trying to accomplish and that it wasn't scary. It could be depressing but it wasn't scary.

The haunted house is only one aspect of a growing commercialism attached to prison tours. Ghost hunts are also among the most popular and most expensive of contemporary prison tour options and specialize in the construction of a uniquely prolonged tourism experience. At West Virginia Penitentiary, visitors are encouraged to "spend the night with experienced ghost hunters seeking scientific proof of the afterlife. Bring along cameras, flashlights, and recorders . . . visit the chatroom and talk with other paranormal investigators . . . upload your latest pictures in the image gallery."[37] Because openings are limited, visitors book months ahead to reserve spots for all-night access to the prison. The tours begin late— anywhere between eight o'clock and midnight—and close at dawn. Upon arrival, visitors are entered into the attendance record, gates are closed, and everyone is locked in for the evening (although free to leave at any point but not return). A short tour is conducted in which visitors are informed of the prison hot spots—places most likely to be haunted and where strange sightings are claimed to have occurred. These are, of course, sites defined by violence, containing some sort of historical trauma, most often a brutal murder that is elaborated by our guide (and tour regulars— the "repeat visitor") in detail. At the end of the tour, the lights in the facility are turned off and visitors are left in small groups or alone with their flashlight and other personal equipment to explore the prison until dawn.

Visitors on these tours often are much different from the average prison tourist in that they are all adults who come well-prepared and take ghost-hunting seriously. Upon arrival, in the parking lot and entrance areas, it becomes apparent that people have traveled from across the United States in small groups, wearing T-shirts that are home-made or branded (For instance, SciFi's *Ghosthunters TAPS*—The Atlantic Paranormal Society), reflecting their paranormal interests and commitments. Many have undergone a ghost-hunting certification process. Others have come specifically to learn the process of ghost hunting itself. Digital cameras, night vision, micro-recorders, dowsing rods, electromagnetic field detectors,

Ghostly orb in the WVP gymnasium (Photo by Ashley Demyan).

thermal imagers, walkie-talkies, notebooks, extra batteries (experienced ghost hunters cite numerous examples of energy drains as signs of spirit activity), and a deep attentiveness to intuition and the basic senses guide visitors through the night. For most ghost hunters, the best indicator of a ghostly presence remains sensational and intuitive—hair standing on end, a shiver down one's spine, a cold patch or a simple but relentless feeling that one is not alone.

The most relied upon and accessible piece of equipment in this event is the digital camera. Visitors leave the prison with hundreds of photos that are later carefully analyzed for anomalies and disruptions. The spirit "orb" is among the most visible and contested pieces of evidence accumulated in this process. Considered by skeptics to be dust, moisture, or flaws in the photo, the documentation of round, spherical objects, among believers, is a well-known measure of potential spiritual presence. Orbs are defined by paranormal investigators as spirit energy—often as either a developing (recently birthed) ghost or an old ghost whose energy is dissipating. In both cases, the spherical shape of the orb represents the easiest form for energy to take. These are spirits who, either voluntarily or through coercion, are tied to the earthly plane by some unresolved issue—a loved one who is not ready to leave family or children behind, perhaps a violent death. Thus, these are sites of uncertainty and rupture in the social order, creating important connections to punishment and why prisons might serve as key cultural sites for staging this encounter. Websites and the tours themselves have created impressive archives of these kinds of photo collections. Visitors often browse through their albums and share photos with other visitors at the main entrances on breaks from ghost hunting, producing a sociality which often extends across time through Internet exchange. Importantly, this process results in a prodigious image-making tourism. Here, the production of the visual proliferates in a space where once, when living and functional, it was strictly prohibited. In this context, the penal gaze is suddenly and surprisingly committed to a radical empiricism, one predicated upon scientific proof of the supernatural. Visitors are often meticulous in their scientific protocol, setting up controlled experiments, spending hours at one particular site within the prison, avoiding crowds and any kind of noise contamination. And of course, ghost hunters gravitate toward locations of death and violence. In this regard, spectacle again predominates.

One of the questions that emerges from these uses of prisons is bound up with the manner in which they seem so profoundly disconnected from the most significant concerns of punishment—at a time when the scale and force of punishment in the United States begs a direct, deliberate address. Something about the spectacle of haunting in these environments expresses a certain and indirect cultural discomfort with the project of imprisonment. In *Ghostly Matters*, sociologist Avery Gordon theorizes the importance of haunting to the sociological imagination as "one of the most important places where meaning—comprehension—and force intersect," where the demystification and "coming alive" of phantasmatic objects and subjects depend on rendering visible the labor, the cultural work that made and obscured them.[38] It is a space, consequently, in which the work that people do, the absences they pursue, are bound up with the "way systematic compulsions work on and through people in everyday life." For Gordon, hauntings are encounters revealed through "the ghostly matter of things: the ambiguities, the complexities of power and personhood, the violence and the hope, the looming and receding actualities, the shadows of our selves and our society."[39]

In this regard, haunting is itself an analytical device that can procure an alternative future precisely because of the terrifying space of the present—and in particular the penal present.

> To be in the seemingly old story now scared and not wishing to be there but not having anywhere else you can go that feels like a place you can belong is to be haunted. And haunting is exactly what causes declarative repudiations and voluntaristic identifications eventually to fail, although it may be said that they can be sustained for quite some time. Reckoning with ghosts is not like deciding to read a book: you cannot simply choose the ghosts with which you are willing to engage. To be haunted is to make choices within those spiraling determinations that make the present waver. To be haunted is to be tied to historical and social effects. To be haunted is to experience the glue of the "If you were me and I were you" logic come undone. (190)

Clearly, tourist spaces are not particular cognizant spaces for this kind of reckoning or engagement with penality. But their very existence also speaks to a kind of cultural fumbling with this commitment—a certain vague unease with the project of punishment and its relationship to trauma, pain, and violence. The spectral assumptions that pull visitors into defunct prisons, their fascination with the prison's massive empty institutional space and its troubled history, carry traces of contemporary punishment with them—as a failed project defined by a deep chasm between the public and the punished. As Avery points out, "change begins slowly with individuals who are unsettled and haunted by forces that are much greater than themselves and barely visible," out of a developing sense that something must be done—that something must be addressed.[40] This evolving structure of address—of engagement—begs the question of what kind of sociality we envision within the frameworks of penality. Gordon anticipates the kind that demands and depends upon the inevitability of what she calls a "reckoning" and defines as "knowing what kind of effort is required to change ourselves and the conditions that make us who we are, that set limits on what is acceptable and unacceptable, on what is possible and impossible" . . . "of reckoning with the structure of feeling of a haunting, of reckoning with the fundamentally animistic mode by which worldly power is making itself felt in our lives, *even if that feeling is vague, even if we feel nothing*" (emphasis added).[41] In this reckoning, hauntings are most analytically useful when the ghosts are brought in among us—and recognized as part of the collective structure of the social. That possibility within a growing popular tourism around prison ghost hunts remains an open question.

The cultural uses of the defunct tour prison are many and extend well beyond what I have documented here. These tours and penitentiaries have become important sites for structuring reality television—as viewers vicariously travel with program narrators and guests into these same spaces for many of the same spectacular purposes. Eastern State Penitentiary, the Ohio State Reformatory, and the West Virginia Penitentiary have all been visited by various paranormal, investigative, and reality television programs, including SciFi Channel's *Ghost Hunters*, Fox's *Scariest Places on Earth*, MTV's *Fear*, as well as documentaries produced by the Travel channel, Discovery, National Geographic, A&E, and the History channel. These mass-mediated sites converge with strange patterns of consumption in connection with penality which reflect again the tension between spectacle and preservation. In Boston, the Charles Street Jail was recently renovated at a cost of $150 million into a luxury hotel, the Liberty, while maintaining much of the original jail architecture, including the sally port and prison bars. In the hotel restaurant, named "Clink," servers wear prison numbers on their uniforms.

Incarceration Live

> I took my students on visits to places that, either as prosecutors they might be sending people, or as defence attorneys their clients might end up. (Frederick Wiseman, director of Titicut Follies, in interview with Toby Miller, "Historical Citizenship and the Fremantle Prison Follies: Frederick Wiseman comes to Western Australia," 1994)

> Natasha and I had seen men, women, and a child in those cells that day, people whose names we did not know, whose crimes we had no knowledge of, who may have committed no crimes, whose pasts and futures will be forever blank for us, to whom we did not speak—and whom we had managed to acknowledge personally only by looking away. I would not wish to be misunderstood: This is not an ethnographic method. It is a confession." (Carol Greenhouse, "Solidarity and Objectivity: Re-reading Durkheim," 2003)

The commercial prison tour is perhaps of ultimate analytical interest as it bends inevitably toward another kind of prison tour, one in which citizens are brought into close proximity with prisoners. When compared to the educational tour of working prisons, key variations emerge which result in fundamental shifts in the construction of the penal gaze and its attendant moral judgment. These "live" visits, most often conducted for professionals and students, continue to follow commercial tour conventions in that they are brief (one or two hours), mapped by the physical design and functions of the prison, and marked again by a scripted blend of the spectacular and the mundane. However, now these narrations take place in contexts where inmates are living and thus visible, passing, watching—where the look may be partially returned. These environments quickly escalate into heightened visual contexts where everyone, in differing degrees, is uncomfortably placed on display with the potentiality of interaction, of engagement arising precariously across our visit. Institutional procedures for hosting these tours are built rigorously around this possibility. Students, like staff and visitors, go through a detailed screening process, including insistence upon a strict dress code adherence; removal of all belongings, including money, jewelry, phones, etc.; passage through a metal detector; a physical frisk; and a hand stamp for identification purposes. Before entering general population quarters, students are given firm instructions, often justified in frightening ways, to stay on the opposite side of the hall as inmates and to avoid eye or verbal contact. The penal gaze then is rendered silent and constrained and thus, furtive and brief, fundamentally lacking in depth and engagement—again, premised in voyeurism. In an environment in which the whole purpose of the visit is to see, visitors are ironically asked to look away. Beyond this, as Carol Greenhouse so eloquently attests, this looking away is often precisely what one feels compelled to do in the face of so much difference, such dramatic inequality, on display.

Something significant happens, however, the moment the tour is directed away from prisoners, into prison geographies where looking is no longer observed. The power and authority of seeing returns—and with a vengeance. The place where this is most likely to occur is again in empty space. On vacant tiers, subject to renovation or simply shut down, students become more confident and assertive. They step into cells, lie on beds, sit at desks, exploring—experiencing—the space of incarceration, suddenly chatty and often amused. The site in which this performance is most troubled and most prolific is always the death house, a space defined by its absolute off-limits secrecy. On a class tour of one Midwestern prison, students are invited to get a view from the lethal injection gurney. At another, they are invited to sit in the electric chair. A few always accept.

It is hard to predict how students will react to a tour like this. As the instructor, I imagine and present it as an introduction to the daily administration and operations of prisons, a chance to lend a concreteness to course concepts and discussions. I structure it as an opportunity for them to be confronted with the stark realities of today's system and their visual apparentness, including the seemingly undeniable image of racial disproportionality, the sheer scale and volume implicit in the warehousing of human bodies, the distinct smells and incessant echoing of pent up human life across tiers, out of barred doors and through smoked windows, the profound distortion of the social. These justifications, however, I suspect inevitably fail in the overpowering framework of spectacle. Many students confirm that the tours are more often than not simply templates to be applied to whatever preexisting worldview with which one enters; still others are significantly challenged in ways that leave them more troubled by the project of punishment in its perceived harshness or leniency. Ultimately, I conduct educational tours of functioning, active prisons for a variety of purposes—and will continue to do so, although I find myself increasingly unable to create a coherent justification for these pursuits. Whatever the reason, it is tied to the possibility that the penal gaze might be interrupted—that it might be altered in some manner, some way that leads toward different ways of looking, different ways of understanding the project of punishment. That look, whatever it may be, I believe, will always require primary contact—a direct engagement, eye to eye.

The closest approximation that I have seen of this kind of engagement occurred in a service learning setting that itself was not without an inevitable sense of spectacle in its practice. Borrowing from Lori Pompa's powerful and transformative Inside Out Prisoner Exchange Model, I offered a course in which students were brought together with the incarcerated in a prison classroom.[42] Before the course commenced, outside (university) students were taken on a routine tour of the facility which incorporated many of the same kinds of components described above and was organized by facility staff. Later, midway through the course, students were taken on another tour of the facility, this time led by their inside, imprisoned classmates. The tour was far more extensive, took much longer than the average tour, and created a number of situations that I had never seen before. There was persistent dialogue between the course members as we moved through medical units, cafeterias, libraries, and living quarters. The inside students were able to develop deep explanations for the ways in which their environment and contexts shaped who they were and the role of dehumanization in the most basic institutional environments of the prison. Along the way, staff and other inmates became involved in the tour and our discussions. A certain synergy developed as we moved throughout the prison that created a commonality between those inside and out that I had never previously witnessed. We had become a familiar presence at the facility and it seemed that a primary barrier in the anonymity of tour structures had been at least partially lifted. Still ambiguities persisted, a critical reminder of the profound inability to create equal spaces from which to see and be inside prisons. For instance, several of the inside students described this experience as making them feel more human, of giving them a sense of freedom of expression and a rare ability to engage in an honest, two-way discussion where they could participate in the creation of outside perspectives. But others were self-conscious of the space in which they existed. They hoped that the prison looked better than it actually was to outsiders and found themselves in the midst of their insecurities, joking about their dehumanizing living conditions. One student later stated explicitly that he was embarrassed. The outside students clearly felt more at ease than they ordinarily do on prison tours. They described feelings of relief, glad that they were finally not simply outsiders, with the tour itself more personalized, interesting, and less anonymous than other tours.

Such experiences speak to the complexity of any alternative structure of engagement for prison tours. Clearly, such performances must be actively and rigorously designed at every turn to counter the distance of the penal spectator and instead connect visitors not simply to the conditions and experience of imprisonment but to their own complicity in current penal practices and their own agency in altering those trajectories. Tours might incorporate, for instance, audio, fact sheets, reports, and informed tour guides who comment explicitly on contemporary patterns in incarceration locally, nationally, and globally. They might provide key placements and exhibits on the tour which self-consciously encourage visitors to reflect upon the popular myths that guide their own assumptions (such as the prison film exhibit at Eastern State Penitentiary). They might conclude their most popular tours with the very question of why these tours are more popular than those grounded historically and institutionally.

There are models and strategies as well to be borrowed from museums and exhibitions which are centered upon informing citizens about the most difficult moments of their history: slavery, lynching, genocide, the Holocaust—and point specifically to the role of ordinary actors and citizens in those formations. More broadly, a tour experience that incorporated an insightful historical discussion of the shared penal character of these world events and their relationship to the foundations, forms, and contemporary practice of punishment might be staggering in its ability to disrupt popular discourses.

For all of these reasons and from a contemporary framework, characterized by the removal of the spectacle of punishment from modern life, prison tours constitute a significant point of primary contact between institutional processes of punishment and those who are largely disconnected from these practices. Here, key cultural tensions are played out in the spectacle of looking from within one of the most hidden institutions in the world. These kinds of penal encounters raise key issues related to democratic oversight and civic attention and become spaces in which punishment is rarely owned up to as a practice whose legitimacy depends upon deliberative and informed debate. Part of the lesson of prison tourism is that this kind of rational deliberation must account for a more primary and culturally seductive volatility in imagining prisons, an imagination that actively shapes the history and present of punishment as discourses are cultivated across primary penal engagements where "public" often simply merges with "popular." This imaginary speaks in complex ways, but at the site of the prison tour, it speaks most often to the limits of the social: It speaks alongside public and policy discourse in a manner marked not just by the absence of others but by an absent attempt to understand the humanity of those others who are the targets of punishment, including offenders, their family and supporters, and the communities and social contexts from which they come. Rather, at most tourist sites, cultural scripts and rhetorics that diminish and debase prisoners intermingle with history and the proper place of the penal spectator. This interpretation is admittedly overdetermined and impositional, much like my reading of mainstream media representations of prisons in the previous chapter. But it is again intentionally and strategically so. It is no doubt true that some tourists and visitors leave prisons feeling challenged, disturbed, suddenly and acutely aware of critical impasses in the practice of punishment historically and from the contemporary framework with its defining forms, mass incarceration, and capital punishment. But the majority of evidence indicates that this is a cultural matrix of meaning that is struggled for at every point, with consumers more often choosing their prison experience through preexisting, highly sensational discourses about crime and punishment, refusing the frames and tours that might undercut or challenge such assumptions. This highly patterned consumer ethic then plays a significant shaping role in the emergent commercial industry of prison tourism.

This complex intersection of popularity and penality deserves careful theoretical interrogation and empirical attention as new life is given to dead prisons in a society which imprisons on an unprecedented scale with unforeseeable long-term consequences. As tempting as it is to disregard sites of penal leisure and entertainment as pure or morbid spectacle, such practices must be taken seriously as important sources of evidence about how citizens attempt, or fail to attempt, to understand and process the meanings surrounding punishment. Even more significantly, because they function often as primary engagements by citizens with punishment, the nature of this engagement—its distance, its easy comfort, its sustenance of cultural fantasy—demands a deeper consideration of the ways in which punishers are linked to the punished. Connections exist—but they are connections dependent upon a deep cultural imaginary that actively shapes any sociality or solidarity derived from penal practice. In the context of the prison tour, distance from the project of punishment is key— and belies the manner in which emptiness, absence, and silence are fundamental to its unchallenged practice. Looking away from punishment's present to its imagined, ghostly past is one possible cultural strategy, dependent perhaps upon cultural sensibilities and a preferred distance to any acknowledgment of the violence of punishment itself. But as David Garland argues, these sensibilities are real and alterable social forces— situational, contingent, ambivalent, frail.[43] Thus, the prison haunts us.

In this haunting, we learn how space is imagined as place, how associations of place with memory, nostalgia, and popular consciousness play across everyday life and have important implications on lived space as well. Dead prisons reconfigure living prisons, not in a clear chain of direct institutional transformation but in a larger cultural imaginary and its ability to justify the pursuit of a proper "dream of order" and the proper place of prisons, punishment, and their targets in that chain of signs. The work of punishment in this context foregrounds the necessity of not simply interrogation but the very need for a critical space of interrogation, for the possibility of something more than a popular spectator, something closer

to a civically engaged critical actor. Certain kinds of institutional locations, premised in penality, because of their history, function, and practice, foreclose these kinds of possibilities and the questions they raise even
as they increasingly open their doors to visitors. Others remain off-limits
and yet subject to this same dangerous kind of imaginary. For instance,
new war prisons, like the detention facility at Guantánamo, offer only
highly controlled tours for journalists and human rights organizations
(many of whom have had no access to detainees) with only occasional
video material released by the U.S. Department of Defense to supplement
public oversight. The next chapter takes up this visual problematic and its
relation both to law and to one of punishment's extreme ends: torture.

Sociologist John Urry writes, "There has been a proliferation of objects
on which to gaze, including the media. What now is tourism and what
is more generally culture is relatively unclear. Pleasures and pain are everywhere, not spatially concentrated in particular sites."[44] Strangely, this
fluidity typifies one of the most fixed and impermeable of social institutions. Prisons may now be visited visually through television and filmic
tours, virtually through cyberspace, and in person on historical day and
recreational overnight tours of now defunct prisons with both popular
and historical appeal. These diverse kinds of interactions with institutions
of punishment mark another crucial intersection of the public and the
penal. Here, configurations emerge which mark again how citizens engage
penality and the nature of that cultural work. To return to this chapter's
opening epigraph, as Bauman reads it, tourism is a moment framed both
by the conditional and by "genuine need"—an opportunity to pursue a
"creative" and "ethical" obligation based upon a "shared humanity"—but
one that is more often typically something less, something temporary,
framed by consumption and fundamentally voyeuristic. For this reason,
on the great American prison tour, the possibility of producing "a visitor
capable of critique" remains of profound and vital consequences.[45]

5

Prison Portents

*Guantánamo, Abu Ghraib,
and the War on Terror*

I guess we weren't really thinking, "Hey, this guy has family, or,
Hey, this guy was just murdered," Harman said. "It was just—Hey,
it's a dead guy, it'd be cool to get a photo next to a dead person."
I know it looks bad. I mean, even when I look at them, I go, "Oh
Jesus, that does look pretty bad." But when we're in that situation it
wasn't as bad as it looks coming out on the media, I guess, because
people have photos of all kinds of things. Like, if a soldier sees
somebody dead, normally they'll take photos of it.
> —Philip Gourevitch and Erroll Morris, quoting
> Sabrina Harman, in *Standard Operating Procedure*, 2008

Woe betide any man who depends on the abstract humanity of
another for his food and protection. Woe betide any person who
has no state, no family, no neighborhood, no community that can
stand behind to enforce his claim of need.
> —Michael Ignatieff, *The Needs of Strangers*, 1984

To imagine the individual caught outside of the safety and security of history and society seems impossible, a resolute fiction. However,
human rights law, in its very establishment, requires us to acknowledge
such a reality—as do prisons. As political philosopher Michael Ignatieff
insists, "Beneath the social there ought to be the natural. Beneath the duties that tie us to individuals, there ought to be a duty that ties us to all
men and women whatever their relation to us. In fact, beneath the social,
the historical, there is nothing at all." Prisons and their spectators exist in

the precarious space where this "nothingness" risks perpetual disclosure but strangely rarely achieves such visibility. Punishment always carries within it the distinct ability to sever the most fundamental of social bonds and deny individuals the legal status that might not ensure but at least invoke their needs, their rights, and their lives. It is a rare case where the limits of punishment are exposed, but in the midst of the war on terror, the United States not only created such sites but actively invoked them as authoritative and legitimate spaces from which to punish.

Public discussions about imprisonment in a post–9/11 context have been structured by a small set of seemingly anomalous U.S. war prisons—detention sites like those at Guantánamo Bay and Abu Ghraib, just outside of Baghdad. In the war on terror, these prisons, in a manner distinct from any other, have predominated American media as well as public and legal discourse on punishment and pain. Their invocations across legal documents, government hearings, human rights documents, news, comedy, television, and film are common. They have become, in their routine invocation since the establishment of their operation, normalized, familiar aspects of American and global culture. As sites in which spectacle is symbiotically joined with suffering, they represent not simply another primary way in which prisons have pulled our attention and popular consciousness but a place from which to investigate the relationship of social response to the production of pain. In these spaces, the meaning and possibility of penal spectatorship, particularly in its ability to achieve any kind of meaningful witnessing, is sorely tested.

Popular engagement with these new war prisons is complex, marked by troubling gaps and silences in cultural vocabularies and an ephemeral, fleeting quality in the duration and depth of public attention. Guantánamo as the epicenter of the legal architecture of the war on terror has been commonly cited in public discourse due to its ambiguous legal and political origins, but as a site of ongoing indefinite detention and interrogation since the first prisoners were moved there in January 2002 remained largely closed off and invisible to public oversight. Abu Ghraib, on the other hand, materialized through a spectacular visual display of torture, creating an immediate popular and juridical debate about oversight with little resolution, and then dropped away quickly from popular discussions. Nevertheless, even as these prisons deny public oversight and eventually are closed, they refuse to go away, becoming instead the subjects of a wave of recent war documentaries,[2] legal and political exemplars of the Bush administration's legacy, and penal portents of the role of prisons amid shifting rules of engagement in the war on terror. Other war prisons (Camp Bucca, Camp Cropper, and detention centers in Mosual, Samrra, Baghdad, Tikrit, Bagram,[3] and Kandahar) have struggled to materialize at all, although they too were revealed as sites in which similar kinds of questionable penal practices were occurring before Abu Ghraib and after. Across the war zone, prison "abuse" has been documented officially and in a manner that speaks to its widespread, systemic quality.[4] But while certain prisons and penal practices achieve visibility, others have never been rendered popularly, and even with intensive coverage, few have had any impact upon the construction of legal frameworks by which states and individuals might be reasonably held accountable. Rather, U.S. foreign policy under the Bush administration consistently moved in the opposite direction, expanding the powers of the state to rely upon torture as a deepening mechanism in the war on terror, thereby establishing dangerous penal precedents.[5] These war prisons continue to persist in the popular forum, as do periodic attempts to explain and render visible the kind of punishment and claims to rights that characterize these institutions, specifically in relation to torture. For this reason, we find Michael Moore with a megaphone in Guantánamo Bay, pitting the rights of terrorists against 9/11 first responders in *Sicko*, and filmmakers continue to interrogate repeatedly the same set of Abu Ghraib actors who were present, torturing, and photographing at Abu Ghraib in documentaries like Rory Kennedy's *The Road to Abu Ghraib*, the Academy Award–winning *Taxi to the Dark Side*, and Erroll Morris's *Standard Operating Procedure*.

The shifting visibility and invisibility of these prisons are emblematic of penality's relationship to the law's deepest secret, its own violence. Punishment necessarily is the embodiment of the force of law and the state, but it is precisely this relationship which the law always seeks both to contain and dismiss. As various internal memos and reports have made clear, the Bush administration relied heavily upon ambiguities and interpretive aspects of constitutional and international law in order to open up new war spaces with a distinctly penal character. Through indefinite detention, the practice of extraordinary rendition, and new legal categories, such as that of the unlawful enemy combatant, a penal architecture was established which resulted in practices intended to be clandestine, invisible, and, simultaneously, common, acceptable, and global. This very normalization ironically undercuts the visibility of these penal intersections. While we focus on Guantánamo and Abu Ghraib, other prisons (undisclosed black sites and torture prisons; domestic prisons at home; immigrant detention facilities) and their inhabitants recede from or never enter public discourse. Because of this structuring relationship to law's violence, these prisons in many ways reflect a series of deeply dangerous legal and extra-legal intersections, unleashing spaces in which to remove people from the protection of international and human rights law. This tendency of course reveals something fundamental about the law itself, the ways in which its contradictions and its suspension materialize in loopholes and cracks that ultimately work to undermine the worth of human life. In these contexts, it is not surprising that both a legal and a public space emerge within democratic contexts from which to enlarge categories and applications of torture and abuse. For penal spectators, such spaces are intensely crucial sites from which to reflect upon one's own relationship to punishment and its most extreme practices up close (as in the case of the ordinary actors and soldiers at work in the wings of Abu Ghraib prison) and afar (citizens and officials who watched these events unfold with the convenience of distance).

These developments raise key questions about how and under what conditions these practices and their effects become visible, what the unanticipated consequences and potentialities of such penal developments might be, and finally what the role of the penal spectator is in such formations. What must occur for images of torture and abuse at Abu Ghraib to rip, however briefly, into the daily lives of millions globally? What makes the cultural outrage at such events so sporadic and ephemeral and how might a more sustained critique and intervention be maintained? The new war prisons are in this way harbingers—and will remain so well after their final closures and dismantlings—of new gaps and aporias in legal and penal practice. After Guantánamo and Abu Ghraib, the law is exposed as the vague arbiter it is in the regulation of pain. The future of punishment in increasingly transnational settings will be defined by how we ultimately choose to live within and without this legal ambiguity. Because these modes of punishment originate in liberal self-governing contexts, they expose as well fundamental fissures in the practice and meanings of democracy. For such reasons, the presence of new war prisons insists upon a deeper interrogation of the theorization of punishment in contexts where contemporary flows of people, technology, crimes, and punishment defy historical understandings of borders and states. Because of their international and extra-legal position between borders and states, these American prisons constitute key sites from which to interrogate the role of difference (specifically race, ethnicity, gender, and nationality), sovereignty, and citizenship in the infliction of pain in punishment abroad and at home.

The New War Prison and Torture

> It will gradually become apparent that at particular moments when
> there is within a society a crisis of belief—that is, when some
> central idea or ideology or cultural construct has ceased to elicit
> a population's belief either because it is manifestly fictitious or
> because it has for some reason been divested of ordinary forms of
> substantiation—the sheer material factualness of the human body
> will be borrowed to lend that cultural construct the aura of "real-
> ness" and "certainty." (Elaine Scarry, *The Body in Pain*, 1985)

At particular moments and in particular contexts, the infliction of pain
achieves startling visibility. Often, this image also includes crowds of on-
lookers, who stand by neither apathetic nor appalled but with an apparent
moral righteousness and visceral pleasure. As implied above in Scarry's
formulation, such moments are marked by cultural insecurities and uncertainties. These moments are historically defined by crisis, where social
institutions and norms are in flux, the fiction of law and power revealed,
and the consequent demand for its ideological re-inscription upon physical bodies an increased probability. One condition, consequently, under
which the infliction of pain may achieve visibility is in contexts where
sovereignty weakens and social orders shift, where force, as opposed to
more effective forms of social control, is deemed necessary in reestablish-
ing that order. Of course, the invocation of that force always reveals one
of the key problems of law, the fact that, as legal scholar Robert Cover
famously asserted, the law and "legal interpretation takes place in a field
of pain and death."[6] These then are always contexts defined by illegitimacy
which nonetheless seek to reassert authority through the infliction of pain
upon the body. As Susan Sontag writes, "It is, of course, precisely because
the reality of that power is so highly contestable, the regime so unstable,
that torture is being used."[7] In wartime, where sovereignty is rendered
highly precarious, pain is to be expected—covertly and from a distance.
Military police who were interviewed at various detention facilities across
the war zone routinely describe the normalcy of abuse—and how, because
it could not be visually documented, such practices never materialized in
public debates and yet were treated within military contexts as otherwise
ordinary events. What is surprising then is for such violence to achieve
representation at all and on a global scale. As Reed Brody writes, "the
only exceptional aspect of the abuse at Abu Ghraib may have been that

it was photographed."[8] Because these acts were photographed, the possibility at least of a larger narrative materializes—one about penal projects in wartime and the manner in which torture's ordinariness is dependent upon penal conditions.

Soldiers entering Abu Ghraib were struck first by its notoriety as a torture and death chamber. Under the rule of Saddam Hussein, the prison stood as the site where thousands of political dissidents were incarcerated, tortured, and executed. The execution scaffold, with its double openings in the floor and hanging hooks, remained visible. Ovens which served as incinerators were part of the barracks' living environment. Suspected to have contained as many as 50,000 people at once, it was a site from which thousands never returned, and was also home, as described above, to some of Hussein's most ingenious torture devices, a national symbol of brute oppression. In the aftermath of the fall of the Hussein regime in April 2003, Coalition Forces took over the then deserted and stripped prison, renovating and retrofitting the facility for military use. The visual quality of the site as a torture chamber was immediately apparent. Portraits and murals of Hussein remained visible across the site, as did scratches from fingernails on the wall, blood spatter, and various torture devices. Wild dogs periodically appeared on the premises, digging up human remains buried throughout the prison. Its dark halls, intense heat, and distinct prison odor of sweat, garbage, urine, and feces added to its troubling atmosphere. Thus, entry itself into the prison was marked by an iconography of pain which hung in the air and on the material surface. Soldiers described it as "haunted," "surreal," a "desert bowl of misery," "like a dream" where "*Apocalypse Now* meets *The Shining*."[9] In the heart of the arena of combat, alongside some of the most dangerous roads in the world, soldiers and detainees moved into the cells of Abu Ghraib prison, a site that would quickly become known as the most frequently attacked American base in the war zone.

In the days and months that followed, under mortar barrage and a burgeoning insurgency, in the midst of prisoner overcrowding and insurrections, particular wings of the Abu Ghraib prison were designated to hold what were considered high-value detainees, individuals who might have important information regarding al-Qaeda and other insurgent activities. In the aftermath, all were revealed to be of low intelligence value. The activities and interrogation methods at the "hard site," as this unit would come to be called, were built around new and unusual visual possibilities in connection with penality. Here, soldiers, caught in their own precarious position as penal spectators, engaged in "sadistic, blatant, and wanton criminal abuses" against prisoners.[10] These documented acts include shooting and beating detainees, acts of sodomy and rape, forcing detainees into sexually explicit postures and sexual performances, arranging detainees in human piles and jumping and sitting on them, simulating electrocution, using dogs to intimidate and in some instance injure detainees, keeping detainees naked and awake for days at a time, holding detainees in isolation cells without recourse to running water, toilet, ventilation, or windows, exposing detainees to extremes of heat and cold, pouring chemicals and cold water on detainees, and posing with dead detainees. Many of these acts were photographed extensively. Poorly trained, inexperienced, understaffed, and facing limited resources and extensive service in prisons (not unlike correctional officers at home) and war zones, soldiers were being asked to "provide a safe, secure, and humane environment" that simultaneously supported "the expeditious collection of intelligence" by "setting the conditions for successful exploitation of the detainees.'"[11]

Soldiers describe this world as one in which a gradual arc toward behavior that would otherwise prove unacceptable developed, a convergence of power and moral authority, premised in some distant notion of procuring global security and safety that was regularly promulgated by military hierarchy. Importantly, such frames are consistent with aspects of penal spectatorship where distant discourses and cultural logics have direct and powerful influences on penal practice on the ground. Abu Ghraib was not a place to question orders or put others at risk. As fellow soldiers were dying, frameworks of retribution and hierarchy reigned supreme, leaving soldiers, at war, "numb," "zoned out," where abuse and torture "just became something that you had to do."[12] As one soldier recounts, it "blew my mind how it was normal."[13] Javal Davis, one of the soldiers present at the hard site who was eventually charged and convicted, states that although he was wary of what he was being asked to do, "it was reaffirmed and reassured through the leadership: We're at war. This is Military Intelligence. This is what they do. And it's just a job . . . so, over time, you become numb to it, and it's nothing. It just became the norm. You see it— that sucks. It sucks to be him. And that's it. You move on."[14] Abu Ghraib then emerges as a place where detainees and soldiers, concurrently, experience a shift in their sensibilities, one which mutes empathy and compassion and instead devolves into a setting where all are simply, in the words of one soldier, "lost." It was also a world in which the patterns of punishment in the United States, including a highly punitive and retributive cultural and political context, an emphasis on indefinite detention of illegal aliens, and the popular and increasingly pervasive implementation of supermax levels of confinement, were more broadly applied in the extralegal setting of Guantánamo and then exported to Iraq. In making the terrible decisions to perform acts of torture, the 372nd Military Police Company found themselves in an ill-defined world with ambiguous expectations in a setting inherently designed to be retributive and loosely regulated enough for torture to be seen as permissible and desirable. In negotiating that ambiguity, they committed crimes, acts that depended upon their cultural beliefs and values, their work experience and ideologies, all of which led to particular assumptions about the meaning of war, the rule of law, the worth of human life, and the routine use of a particular mode of punishment: torture. And they recorded it visually.

Post-Nuremberg, social psychological explanations, framed by the Milgram obedience experiments and the Stanford prison experiment, have long insisted that this could be any one of us—that ordinary actors, not monsters, commit the seemingly incomprehensible. Such accounts have experienced a popular resurgence in explaining events at Abu Ghraib.[15] As valuable as such a frame may be, particularly as a counter-discourse to dominant political and legal frames where individual responsibility is privileged well beyond the systemic structure of the crimes, such an account avoids the cultural conditions that undergird and render unique these events—including the distinctly visual character of the conditions at Abu Ghraib, the reframing of law's violence by the Bush administration, and the role of penal spectatorship at a moment when the United States practiced mass incarceration on a scale without precedent. Social psychological accounts also risk the unanticipated effect of privileging individual and psychological accounts, again to the point of pathologizing the prison and the culture it derives from. In short, this explanation is not enough.

Visions of Suffering, Spectacles of Power

> Everyone in theatre had a digital camera. Everyone was taking pictures of everything, from detainees to death. (Philip Gourevitch and Erroll Morris, *Standard Operating Procedure*, 2008)

The Abu Ghraib scandal remains a study in penal spectatorship—a media event unlike any other due to its immediate and archival international visual record of torture and abuse in wartime by a democratic superpower.

The nature of the scandal and its emergence marks the unprecedented importance of technology and communications in a variety of capacities but first and foremost at the level of meaning-making. In such a context, the role of the penal spectator and the dimensions of engagement and intervention which attend him or her are placed in high relief. First, technology facilitated the act of whistle-blowing in the scandal, lending a facticity visually to the acts. Visibility of the torture and its investigation were only possible in some ways because, roughly six months after Abu Ghraib became operational again, specialist Joseph Darby placed an anonymous note and a compact disc, given to him by Specialist Charles Graner, under the door of a division officer in the U.S. Army Criminal Investigation Command. The disc was filled with photographs depicting members of the 372nd, including Graner, widely considered to be a ringleader in the scandal, engaged in acts of abuse and torture against detainees. Darby's act, although complex in terms of its own set of interpersonal dynamics, triggered the investigation which led to the implication and ultimate conviction of the infamous seven soldiers of the 372nd. Most commentators and actors in the scandal concede that should this act be omitted, there is no Abu Ghraib—its troubling place in the cultural repertoire recedes and disappears. The organized way in which this structure of omission is maintained is manifested in the acts and comments of senior administrators and chain of command who, in the days just after the scandal broke, promised amnesty to those who turned in similar photos. Across the war zone, soldiers wiped their hard drives and memory sticks clean. In this way, early on, the crimes of Abu Ghraib were configured as visual, a problem of spectatorship and record-keeping, as opposed to the physical and psychological acts themselves.

The eventual materialization of Abu Ghraib in this way depends upon the rise of digital communications and the democratization of its use. The idea that soldiers now carry cameras, phones, and personal computers which render their records immediate, accessible, and capable of global distribution marks a key shift in the representation, reporting, and understanding of war. At Abu Ghraib, soldiers' photos of key landmarks and antiquities, images of themselves, smiling, surrounded by playful Iraqi children, and standard tourism shots exist alongside of images of the war dead and of torture in a nondescript, flat equalization. Importantly, photography at Abu Ghraib also reflected a wider shift in the use of visualized abuse in and of itself in increasingly global conflicts. Soldiers on the hard site employed photos to threaten detainees in interrogation contexts in new and innovative ways. They first employed the photos as mechanisms of threat—of what might be done to them if they did not cooperate. Detainees could be shown photos of tortured individuals at the same site and realize the limits to which their interrogators were willing to go. Because wives, children, and family members were also detained at the site—often by sheer association—the photos could also be employed to terrorize loved ones. Finally, another threat involved the circulation of photos to family and friends beyond the prison in a culture in which photographed sexualized acts and poses would be perceived as shameful and devastating. Such staged sexualized performances promised to remove these individuals from the community which sustained them, marking the pursuit of a social or living death by way of this record.

Beyond this, the very fact that the acts were visibly documented not only changed processes of interrogation and torture, but changed the role of the torturers as well—from spectators to exhibitionists to torturers. In the photos, soldiers participating in these scenes clearly take on self-conscious exhibitionist styles of display—proudly, playfully going to extremes. Posing behind human pyramids of naked detainees hooded in sandbags, on the backs of detainees, and with dead bodies, they take on a patriotic pose, with thumbs up, inevitably parodying and reproducing a "mission accomplished" posture. In these configurations, we are witness to a kind of public authority which manifests within the group or the crowd and, within the contingencies and ambiguities of the prison setting, allows actors to improvise distinctly penal acts. Not surprisingly, the soldiers are strangely inarticulate about why they engaged in these practices. Sabrina Harman, popularized as "the woman behind the camera" at Abu Ghraib, mixes frameworks and discourses in her explanatory accounts. On the one hand, she says that she took them "just to show what was going on, what was allowed to be done." But she also struggles with explanation, stating of her photo of the human pyramid: "They were stripped one by one and then stuck into a pyramid. If I saw something, I took a photo of it. The first thing I think of is to take photos. That probably sounds really sick but I'm always taking photos. I mean that's just me. I've always taken photos." While she is taking such photos, Graner turns and asks her to participate in the shot. And she does.

Harman is particularly fascinating, as her photographic interests reflect a contemporary cultural fascination with crime, death, and a culture of visibility. She had enlisted in order to pay for college, after which she planned to pursue a career in law enforcement as a forensic photographer. Philip Gourevitch and Errol Morris write of Harman's photographic tendencies that

> pictures had always fascinated her. . . . She liked to look. She might recoil from violence, but she was drawn to its aftermath. When others wanted to look away, she'd want to look more closely. Wounded and dead bodies fascinated her . . . "Even if somebody is hurt, the first thing I think about is taking photos of that injury," Harman said. "Of course, I'm going to help them first, but the first reaction is to take a photo." In July, she wrote to her father, "On June 23 I saw my first dead body I took pictures! The other day I heard my first grenade go off. Fun!" Later, she paid a visit to an Al Hillah morgue and took pictures: mummified bodies, smoked by decay; extreme close-ups of their faces, their lifeless hands, the torn flesh and bone of their wounds; a punctured chest, a severed foot. The photos are ripe with forensic information. Harman also had her picture taken at the morgue, leaning over one of the blackened corpses, her sun-flushed cheek inches from its crusted eye sockets. She is smiling—a forced but lovely smile—and her right hand is raised in a fist, giving the thumbs-up, as she usually did when the camera was pointed at her.[16]

Harman would later participate in a photo where, once again, with thumb extended and a bright smile, she poses with a dead detainee whom, she was told, as he was placed on ice in storage, had died of natural causes. Here the spectatorial intervenes in a manner where, inured to pain and death, the penal spectator actively engages in the production and reproduction of pain. What is relatively unknown by those outraged by the photo is the manner in which contradictions pervade this and other war prison image-making contexts. For instance, not widely publicized in the press is the fact that Harman, with her forensic and documentarian impulses, stayed behind, reopened the body bag, and proceeded to take photos of bruises, cuts, blood, and restraint marks across the man's body, thereby, and not without irony, exposing the lie told to her by her supervisors and CIA interrogators. This contradiction is complex in that Harman, like others interviewed at the hard site, engages in explanatory discourses which offer no explanation at all. She is read as both victim and victimizer, contemptible and interventionist. There is no dominant interpretation, only unstable, volatile representations, which both challenge and reproduce relations of power framed by the American state.

The most obsessive aspect of media coverage revolved around another gendered visualization, the presence and use of female soldiers in the sexualized dehumanization of male detainees in a manner directed at cultural humiliation. Cultural commentators compared the photos focused on sexual degradation to the contemporary media staples of reality television and violent pornography in combination.[17] The focus on gender and sexuality is particularly compelling in the aftermath of the event as popular attention tended to center predominately and disproportionately upon one particular member of the 372nd, Lynndie England. Images of her at Abu Ghraib have achieved iconic status, where, cigarette dangling, she points at the genitalia of hooded, naked detainees who appear to be masturbating in one photo and in a pose similar to that of a sado-masochistic dominatrix constraining a prisoner on a dog leash in another photo. Imitations of both poses have appeared on some of television's most popular comedy programming, including Comedy Central's *South Park* and *The Daily Show* as well as Fox's *The Simpsons* and *Arrested Development*. In fact, an entire website dedicated to "doing a Lynndie" (http://badgas.co.uk/lynndie/) achieved widespread popularity—where visitors to the site are given instructions on how to perform the pose and are then encouraged to submit photos of themselves imposing the gesture upon "victims" who are "unaware, bemused, or angry" and thus, "in keeping with the original." At this site, photos from around the world document individuals performing the pose while pointing at drunks, celebrities, the homeless, animals, and numerous photo-shopped fictional and living characters. Such contexts importantly demonstrate a continuum across which the practices at Abu Ghraib are parodized, simulated, and engaged with popularly and globally. They also demonstrate the manner in which publicly available scripts about penality circulate in a manner that is dependent upon dehumanization with a disproportionate focus not upon those who are necessarily dangerous but who are defined instead by a peculiar but distinctly recognizable human vulnerability.

Beyond these uses, the photos themselves were similar to war trophies and souvenirs, objects to be shared across the prison and war zone as well as with family and friends back home. To develop a point made earlier in this chapter, the proliferation of the technology and capability to record violence by the ordinary person has been, consequently, cause for concern in the war effort. Soldiers now carry digital cameras, laptops, gaming devices, as well as cell phones with cameras which can document acts occurring virtually anywhere at any time. They then can be distributed widely and immediately via phone, email, and the Internet. Efforts by the U.S. Army to censor soldier's web logs, personal email, and use of digital technology, particularly cell phones with cameras, have circulated widely. Ultimately, the U.S. military has relied heavily upon the encryption of wireless data through the distribution of standardized devices as a means of regulation; however, cultural commentators have been quick to point out that the radical burst of new technology in its scope and scale is simply too ubiquitous to be effectively prohibited or censored in any total way. Such new and global technological contexts challenge the ways in which information in wartime has historically been regulated and closed off, opening up state violence to public display, a breach that was interpreted by the Bush administration as being against the law. When the Abu Ghraib photos first appeared, Susan Sontag wrote in an article in *The Guardian* that the key differences between the horror of Abu Ghraib and war atrocity or American lynching photos was found in the "increasing ubiquity of photographic actions": "The pictures taken by American soldiers in Abu Ghraib reflect a shift in the use made of pictures—less objects to be saved than evanescent messages to be disseminated, circulated."[18] Furthermore, these practices reflect the democratization of photography—the fact that nearly everyone can now participate in the documentation of social life and control to some extent its distribution on a massive, digital, online scale. Such possibilities are deeply disturbing for the secrecy of sovereignty. In statements before the Senate Armed Services Committee on May 7, 2004, in its investigation of Abu Ghraib, Secretary of Defense Donald Rumsfeld declared:

> To those Iraqis who were mistreated by members of the U.S. armed forces, I offer my deepest apology. We're functioning in a—with peacetime restraints, with legal requirements in a war-time situation—in the information age, where people are running around with digital cameras and taking these unbelievable photographs and then passing them off, against the law, to the media, to our surprise, when they had not even arrived in the Pentagon.[19]

This interpretation of visual information as something to be regulated and rendered invisible through state channels points to the centrality of the visualization of pain, punishment, and torture in any effort to achieve transparency—and, more significantly, the overt admission of how such transparency in violent, penal contexts is opposed to state interests, again revealing the law's own or acceptance of its own violence. The international scale of the scandal as such is only possible by way of the immediate and global circulation of the disturbing digital photos, collected for a variety of reasons, including degradation, humiliation, and sheer boredom that were then circulated across the Internet and various media outlets in a manner that supersedes law, borders, and oversight—thus leaving the American government and public surprised, exposed, and ashamed, caught in multilayered contexts of penal spectatorship.

These global mechanisms of circulation and access permitted an intense albeit relatively short-lived round of cultural commentary by a broad and international audience. Such interpretational frames offer a variety of perspectives into how meaning was made of such acts and how these acts were ultimately opened up or closed off discursively. Across web logs, news commentary, alternative media outlets, scientific journals, and intellectual debate, many argued that events at Abu Ghraib reflected a darker side of American culture and history with its emphasis upon a sexualized and racialized violence. Numerous comparisons were made to the historical practice and popularization of racial lynchings in the American South by the Ku Klux Klan and specifically the manner in which these lynchings, similar to Abu Ghraib, were carefully and proudly documented through a clear historical record of souvenir postcards, drawings, and photographs.[20] Numerous connections were made between Abu Ghraib and James Allen's *Without Sanctuary* exhibition (http://www.withoutsanctuary.org) which had been the topic of much discussion between 2000 and 2005. This discourse converged popularly with negative stereotypical depictions of the soldiers at the center of the scandal as rural, lower-class, and uneducated. In many of these discussions, events at Abu Ghraib were interpreted as retrograde and primitive, a barbarism and cruelty that is conceived popularly as uncharacteristic of current practices in punishment. As David Garland argues, however, something larger undergirds these events, and we must explore more deeply the conditions and structures through which "somehow the torture and killing of a man by a mob was experienced as a 'a good day out,' as a conversation piece to pass on to friends and family, as fitting material for that most benign communication, the picture postcard."[21] In this regard, Garland writes of racialized torture lynchings in the American South that a more sociologically informed account would view these kinds of penal events as "constituting a self-consciously *reactionary* development, a penal institution (albeit a minor, localized, temporary one) shaped by a self-conscious opposition to the trajectory of penal change."[22]

This framework of interpretation reveals something more fundamental about the process of punishment. Although the new war prison marks configurations of imprisonment in novel ways and with new potentialities, it is not without precedent or logic, although that logic is distinctly and disturbingly penal in its formation. The sense of outrage and spectacle invoked by the photos of Abu Ghraib, for instance, immediately marked them as anachronistic, barbaric, and uncivilized—a parallel discourse to much of the way in which enemies of the war on terror have been framed by the Bush administration. Such significations imply some sense of historical progress in punishment—of what is inappropriate or unacceptable in the infliction of pain. But as David Garland explains, this frame of progress lacks a thorough, sociological understanding of the ways in which contradictory discourses and practices define punishment and may emerge under particular historical conditions. The infliction of pain, in its "penal excess," permits the expression of precisely what modernity seemingly holds back—the literal inscription of punishment into the bodies of individuals through sheer force and unlimited violence in an effort to demonstrate the moral authority of unrestrained and unchecked dominance. In such boundless assertions of power, the complete and total lack of worth of individuals—as citizens and human beings—is disclosed.

For Garland, conventional histories have exaggerated assumptions of civilized sensibilities in modern life, thereby preventing us from recognizing the potential pleasure or indifference that citizens ordinarily experience in the violence of punishment. Although an important body of research has examined the role of the ordinary actor in the production of pain, a more sociological account will seek to explain the political and cultural conditions in which this kind of penal formation emerges.[23] This pleasure and the authority that comes from punishing are quite often experienced through perceptions of a need or structure for the assertion of sovereignty and difference. In instances where the state is perceived as weak or in crisis—moments where social groups form around deeply aroused emotional sentiments defined by insecurity, hatred, repugnance, and disgust of another, where the bonds between the punisher and the punished are weak and distanced. As anthropologist Lesley Gill demonstrates, impunity, a prominent feature of post–9/11 American empire-building, emerges when power is defined through inequality and social differentiation in a manner that "allows perpetrators to harm others without suffering consequences themselves, and when endured from below, it restricts the ability of people to limit violence—political, economic, and cultural—and hold perpetrators accountable."[24] Such contexts, like those qualities that lie at the heart of punishment, destroy social-building possibilities, instead displacing people, severing social bonds, generating insecurities, and damaging social trust and state credibility.

Similarly, the distinct visual quality of Abu Ghraib in popular consciousness has been argued to reflect an ancient pathos built upon "beautiful suffering." Here pain is visually inscribed historically in patterns of dominance and conquest, a formula art historian Stephen Eisenman argues has "structured the vision of a considerable portion of the U.S. public rendering them largely mute before the spectacle of officially sanctioned torture at Abu Ghraib and elsewhere."[25] Beautiful suffering is interpreted in this context as aesthetically pleasing precisely because pain and torture are depicted as sanctioned by the victims themselves for the pleasure of the oppressor. Eisenman argues that the photos at Abu Ghraib prison follow this formula as "they are the expression of a malevolent vision in which military victors are not just powerful, but omnipotent, and the conquered are not just subordinate, but abject and even inhuman. The presence of the latter, according to this brutal perspective, gives justification to the former; the supposed bestiality of the victim justifies the crushing violence of the oppressor."[26] These reminders serve as crucial cues to the larger relevance of new war prisons in our understanding of punishment and social life. Such acts of openly visible violence like those at Abu Ghraib invoke the possibility of a public and collective consensus in their infliction and their prohibition. They depend, thus, in their trajectory upon social relations. Second, they emerge sporadically and seemingly unpredictably due to the fact that so much of state violence historically evades the field of vision. Although these kinds of acts are ongoing, when they do enter the light of day, they do so through a convergence of social conditions, which include technology, agency, and culture. Third, for those who oppose these actions, those whose response is defined by moral outrage, their attitudes are consequently marked by a deliberate blindness and cultural denial: in other words, "we" do not torture in the United States—when clearly we do. These points culminate in the absence of a critical and substantive discussion not just about torture but about its relationship to pain, punishment, and social and cultural orientations toward them. As the photographs mobilize outrage and sentiment, in that engagement, they also reproduce suffering through the very act of representation, a tension that, although not inescapable, tends, uncritically, toward predominance.

As images of exclusion, the Abu Ghraib photos direct our attention toward extreme otherness. They are indicative of many of the primary ways in which punishment serves as a space in which to differentiate according to race, ethnicity, and citizenship. They have produced a voluminous public commentary on the nature of blame and accusation—one that will achieve no closure. Such contexts require theories of vindictiveness, irrational hatred and aggression and the punitive modes they assume. How these impulses and emotions culminate in sadistic acts and sadistic readings of those acts, including the infliction of pain and exclusion from human rights protections, is key in understanding shifting potentialities of the penal. As criminologists Chris Greer and Yvonne Jewkes argue, "although many of the crimes célèbre of recent years (especially those involving violent and/or sexual crimes against children) have been described as the unthinkable and the unknowable, it is perhaps more accurate to suggest that they simply alert us to the collective unwillingness to think and to know."[27] Sociologist Stanley Cohen writes similarly, "This is the essence of denial: an active looking away, a sense of a situation so utterly hopeless and incomprehensible that we cannot stand to think about it."[28] And with every appearance of these kinds of images, outrage emerges and then diminishes in some cyclical ebb and flow and the normalization of such practices extends globally. The infliction of pain becomes a distant image we have all seen, denied, and not thought about before. Ritualized viewing readily approximates apathy and such habits lead to cultural logics in which, as we see, like the main actors at Abu Ghraib, both high and low, no one can articulate an explanation for their own behavior. As anthropologists João Biehl and his colleagues write:

> These photographs . . . mark a shift in the ways people publicly organize their subjectivities vis-à-vis the suffering of others. The Abu Ghraib artifacts expose the range of moral sensibility operating in the interstices of political and legal domains. The images thus materialize a "culture of shamelessness" and the "reigning admiration for unapologetic brutaility" (29). The pictures will not go away—but will be further covered-up by our "infinite digital self-reproduction and self-dissemination," writes Sontag (42). At stake here are no longer processes of memorialization or forgetfulness but rather the normalization of the Other's dehumanization and the creation of a moral complicity that destabilizes public discussion, making clarification and eventual resolution ever more unattainable.[29]

How then do we direct ourselves and our representations toward other modes of engagement, toward a deeper understanding of ourselves and others and the pain we inflict? Such a critique, I argue, must originate at a deeper level, in the foundational dark spots of the modern state, as these vacant vocabularies of accountability risk permanent codification into the legal and constitutional framework of democracy.

Law and the State of Exception

Although the Abu Ghraib scandal shook the world in the aftermath of its immediate exposure, serving perhaps as a critical turning point in mounting opposition to the war on terror, the direct political impacts, strangely, were short-lived. The scandal did not figure prominently in the 2004 presidential election and upon reelection, President Bush promoted the controversial Alberto Gonzales to the post of Attorney General and systematically supported harsher treatment of detainees across the war zone. Reports continued to circulate of questionable detention practices, including the existence of undisclosed "secret" CIA prisons, extraordinary rendition tactics (the transporting of prisoners by the United States to undisclosed locations in other countries, where torture is less prohibited), and patterns of abuse in other off-limits war prisons. Abu Ghraib ultimately was politically and legally resolved in the short term as little more than an anomaly in wartime. The scandal resulted in at least eight major investigations, thousands of interviews, 15,000 plus pages of reports, a series of congressional hearings, the release of classified Department of Defense files, the continued emergence of new photos depicting abuse across the war zone, and a suspended general (the only female general in the war zone), all documenting patterns of abuse internationally across American military prisons as well as the presence of CIA, FBI, and private contractors and civilian interrogators at Abu Ghraib. No one above the rank of staff sergeant was convicted.

This ephemerality in accountability, explanation, and visibility is not unusual. In fact, the appearance of events at Abu Ghraib in the public register more likely is the real anomaly. Guantánamo serves as a useful comparison site in that, as the central detention facility in the war on terror, the one that has by and large achieved the most international attention, and was central in shaping interrogations and detention at Abu Ghraib, the prison camp still remains largely invisible. The images that have originated there are iconic but largely built around a central event:

the arrival of the first wave of detainees to the site. Images of detainees kneeling below razor wire fence lines are exemplary in their communication of the closed off, secretive nature of the camp. Most of these pictures are shot through the fence, physically detailing the removal of external oversight. Prisoners being transferred in the belly of a transport plane, shown beneath an American flag, wearing orange jumpsuits, hoods, goggles, and ear muffs upon arrival at Guantánamo, and positioned in outside cages essentially mark the extent of visual coverage of this site, beyond a few sterile newscasts from inside Camp X-Ray and Delta, where journalists are only permitted to have official tours. Much of the visualization of Guantánamo has occurred from a distance and via the cultural imaginary. In the fictionalized British account, *The Road to Guantánamo*, based on a true story of three detainees held there, the prison is perhaps the most fascinating aspect of the film, precisely because it portrays through news images, documentary footage, and dramatic recreation what is otherwise off-limits space. The film invokes numerous penal practices from within the United States in its visualization of segregation in solitary confinement units, cell extractions, deteriorating mental states of prisoners, and the use of technologies of confinement in controlling individual will.

In this regard, visibility at Guantánamo has primarily materialized through legal frameworks. Discussions surrounding the new war prisons in media and public discourse have centered largely upon human rights concerns, particularly the meaning of torture, and are thus dominated by juridical debates and legal commentary. Even here, this popular discussion is limited in its depth of analysis. Regardless of the frequent bursts of outrage at various aspects of their operation, including indefinite detention without trial, questionable interrogation practices, extraordinary rendition, human rights abuses, and torture, public response in the United States has been missing, defined by apathy. In tracing the documents and "torture memos" which led to Abu Ghraib, legal scholar Karen Greenberg points out how the torture debate has largely taken place out of public view, leaving citizens confused, misinformed, and relatively complacent about the role of torture in the United States. Greenberg writes of torture's unique secrecy, its "subtle relationship to the rule of law; it is the unspoken realm of the forbidden, the unnamed that law represses. It is, in many ways, the ghost in the closet."[30] Art historian Stephen Eisenman has coined this absence of attention the "Abu Ghraib effect," what he refers to as a "moral blindness . . . that allows [us] to ignore, or even to justify, however partially or provisionally, the facts of degradation and brutality manifest in the pictures."³¹ Similarly, criminologist Mark Hamm marks how Abu Ghraib has been an event largely avoided by social scientists.³² This absence of attention to pain and penality, even in the face of visual spectacle, reveals important things about the practice of punishment.

At the foundations of the new war prisons and the practices they support rests a fundamental principle: spatial confinement is always fundamentally directed at a kind of erasure—through the prohibition and suspension of the social—of human interaction and communication. This same principle is embedded in torture where, as Scarry writes, the false spectacle of power supersedes the processes bound up with the infliction of pain.

> In the very processes it uses to produce pain within the body of the prisoner, it bestows visibility on the structure and enormity of what is usually private and incommunicable, contained within the boundaries of the sufferer's body. It then goes on to deny, to falsify, the reality of the very thing it has itself objectified by a perceptual shift which converts the vision of suffering into the wholly illusory but, to the torturers and the regime they represent, wholly convincing spectacle of power.³³

Guantánamo epitomizes such space in its legal jurisdiction within and without the law, its geopolitical placement within and without the state, and its global, borderless distribution of human lives through the mechanisms of confinement. The offshore prison represents in many ways, for instance, what political theorist Giorgio Agamben argues to be the originary (in that it is both original and originating) and true nature of the political: the ban. For Agamben, the ban is the foundational political structure, a zone of indistinction between outside and inside, marking exclusion and inclusion. The ban, or abandonment, clearly sits at the heart of any project to punish, but Agamben's theoretical perspective is important in a consideration of the new war prison as it importantly points to the carceral foundations which belie democracy, a process that links democracy and totalitarianism through a new emphasis on biopolitics. For Agamben, it is this state of exception which reveals the way in which the exemplar of power and biopolitics, the concentration camp, comes to be the "hidden matrix" or "nomos" of political space, no longer delimited by time and space, by historical moment, but coextensive with political life itself. Punishment is specifically related to a state of exception or political emergency in that it always renders visible the state's violence as

foundational. Both the law and the political thus originate in the infliction of pain, the deprivation of liberty or life, in order to assert sovereignty. Because the space of exception is a border zone, it risks destabilizing sovereignty by exposing it as a question, a conscious act of will and
deliberation in its suspension or adherence. Punishment's precariousness
is apparent in the fact that states of exception, as the foundation of the
modern state, will continue to emerge so long as the ban remains the
original condition of sovereignty. In such contexts, the necessity of assert-
ing exception through executive authority and suspending the law will be
a primary way in which to moderate late modernity's most fundamental
aspect, uncertainty. Rights claims are fundamentally bound to this contradiction. Human rights and protection of life claims, as modern pro-
liferations, are, from Agamben's perspective, not successful in purported
efforts to close the space of exception but rather lay the foundation for a
new set of politics built upon exception. Here, "[i]t is almost as if, starting
from a certain point, every decisive political event were double-sided: the
spaces, the liberties, and the rights won by individuals in their conflicts
with central powers always simultaneously prepared a tacit but increasing
inscription of individuals' lives within the state order, thus offering a new
and more dreadful foundation for the very sovereign power from which
they wanted to liberate themselves."[34] From this perspective, the modern
order is irrevocably based upon exclusion and a propensity to inflict pain.
As Agamben argues, with the birth of a distinctly modern totalitarianism,
a civil war is established through law's exception, permitting the mass
elimination, politically and biologically, of entire groups and categories of
citizens by way of a permanent state of emergency. Recent assertions of
sovereignty by the United States, coded in penal terms, set the conditions
for the new war prison, where "the current configuration of state power,
in relation both to the management of populations (the hallmark of governmentality) and the exercise of sovereignty in the acts that suspend and
limit the jurisdiction of law itself, are reconfigured," a context rife with
possibilities for the violation of human rights.[35] In penal settings such as
Guantánamo and Abu Ghraib which depend upon the ambiguity of law
and legal jurisdiction, it is not surprising to find the resurgence of the implementation of torture. And even as these sites are permanently closed,
they are critical reminders of the potentiality of normalization that lies at
the heart of executive power, sovereignty, and exception in their intersection with punishment. In commentary and debates surrounding this phenomenon, scholars worry that sites like Guantánamo could "become the

norm rather than an anomaly, that homeland security will increasingly depend on proliferating these mobile, ambiguous spaces between the domestic and foreign"[36]—a kind of penality, similar to the new actuarial penology, which risks permanence.

With these new modes of punishment, a new penal subject emerges as well, one which invokes Agamben's notion of bare life. He writes, "in the detainee at Guantánamo, bare life reaches its maximum indeterminacy."[37] The detained then constitutes a crucial kind of subjectivity and the newness of this identity, Agamben argues, is based upon its radical erasure of "any legal status of the individual, thus producing a legally unnamable and unclassifiable being."[38] Here we encounter bare life and its correlates: the life that is moved outside of the juridical order in that it is the life deemed unworthy of living—and in that movement, those who mark the limits between life and death, between the human and the non-human, become foundational to political and juridical orders. Bare life speaks to the categories of humanity which render types of individuals and groups foundationally excluded from the political and social, those who are exposed to an ever-present vulnerability of being killed as they exist in exile but continue to live biologically within the law, yet with no political rights. For Agamben, it is this potentiality that all citizens carry within them, while others, such as political refugees, illegal combatants, the terminally ill, the overcomatose, actually exist in now.

Consequently, contemporary scholars argue Camp Delta at Guantánamo to be the natural "analogue" of Auschwitz and the tortured bodies at Abu Ghraib to be emblematic of "bare life," all phenomena whose appearance potentially mark exception as the rule. However, as Joshua Comaroff suggests, what really separates extra-judicial from judicial violence—Abu Ghraib from the state of Texas's Death Row? The isolation and violence of the new war prison is indistinguishable in many ways from the daily practices of supermax prisons and segregation units, where inmates are often held indeterminately in solitary confinement for 24 hours a day. In the case of Abu Ghraib, as Nicholas Mirzoeff has observed, "it now seems that the driving force behind global visuality was not an emancipatory digital culture but a mode of permanent war based on full spectrum dominance. . . . In the state of permanent war, the object of surveillance enters an interstitial state between being and nonbeing, epitomized by the camps at Guantánamo Bay, Bagram, and Abu Ghraib."[39] Here, even as state violence is given legal and visual form, through unprecedented levels of visibility, torture nonetheless recedes from our view.

These emergent penal zones carry with them an element of drift, where we encounter ethical dilemmas amid penal climates that are legally questionable, if not outright exceptions, and yet carry with them the proclivity and authority to avoid challenge and oversight. Nowhere is this more apparent than in the "torture memos" exchanged between the Bush administration and its legal counsel, an exchange which laid the architecture of exception, fundamentally rewriting much of international human rights law post-Geneva in an effort to wage a new war beyond old rules. As legal commentators have discussed extensively, these documents mark a shift in the duties and organization of legal counsel, one which, instead of testing a case deliberatively and through the lens of the constitution, pursues an argument that justifies the client's desired goal, in this case, the Bush administration. Here, the law simply becomes a malleable resource designed to give the advice needed to whatever aim is desired, thereby predicated in a framework primarily and reductively of legal liability. In this respect, constitutional and international laws and treaties are scrutinized for gaps and loopholes that might sustain the establishment of a new category of legal subject, the enemy or unlawful combatant, and carve out transnational spaces for inflicting pain with impunity, outside of war crime frameworks. In such contexts, uncertainty, with its textbook scenarios, such as the "ticking time bomb," is used to justify penal frameworks of necessity and self-defense—indefinite detention, interrogation, torture—through what David Luban argues is the "liberal fiction of the conscientious interrogator."[40] At Guantánamo, being caught in the conditional state of being either a threat (potential danger) or of intelligence value maintains one's detention. Because both are open to the imaginary, they are especially susceptible to abuse. For those detainees who have little intelligence value but are banned by their home states, their detention extends indefinitely as the United States attempts to find countries to which to return them—even as some fear torture and death upon their return. Even death at Guantánamo, in the form of suicide, is defined as asymmetrical warfare—an attack on the state via the denial of one's personal existence.

Choices to pursue this legal framework provide little transparency, protection against pain, or democratic checks and balances. Rather, as Dratel argues, such contexts succor a "torture culture" where law is utilized to structure pain through artificial, stylized justifications that are deemed necessary, regretfully, for security, protection, and the promise of certainty. The fiction implied here is one of regret, when what is really occurring is the foregrounding and privileging of law's violence. A shadow world opens up, revealing practices which are and always have been happening anyway but now can occur in daylight with impunity. In this positioning, the morality and penality of the spectator allows individuals to express a sense of disgust and moral outrage while never questioning one's core decency or complicity. In such roles, little effort is required to distinguish the self from torturers, or spectatorship from action. Such judgment borders on Baudrillard's assertions of the Abu Ghraib photos as "war porn"—"a parody of violence . . . a power which, reaching its extreme point, no longer knows what to do with itself—a power henceforth without aim, without purpose, without a plausible enemy, and in total impunity."[41] Such contexts promise an inability to limit pain's use—and the use of violence. As decriers of the ticking bomb theory argue, once we start down that road, there is no turning back—and no ability to distinguish victim and oppressor. Sadly, such justifications are not enough. We have to work through precisely what the social ramifications of such a pursuit might be, of how the consent of the governed might be reshaped in such a way as to lead to the destruction of minorities everywhere. For Garland, the prohibition of penal excess depends upon effective, responsive states, a sense of social security as opposed to insecurity, and "a degree of intra-group identification or solidarity that links punishers to punished."[42] Thus, "when government power is weak, when elites experience insecurity or have material interests inimical to the civilized treatment of other groups, or when outgroups are regarded as less than fully human, the force of such sensibilities is quite limited."[43]

Forced disappearances are one way in which this kind of penality is given form, as detainees are forcibly relocated to sites not disclosed by the U.S. government, cutting off access and knowledge about these individuals to their families, attorneys, and human rights organizations. Extraordinary rendition is particularly pernicious due to its secrecy and the manner in which it reflects a decision to place detainees in positions in which the infliction of more pain is both possible and likely, including near drowning, beatings with cables, blows to the feet, suspension of handcuffed individuals for hours from a post, electrical shocks to body parts, including genitalia, use of dog attacks, etc.—much of which was simulated or occurred in the Abu Ghraib photos. These policies are, of course, antithetical to democratic governance, and in their orchestration by a major democracy open up zones and possibilities globally for states and organizations to engage in torture. In these spaces, those who govern make a conscious decision to keep a prison's population off record and out of reach of human rights organizations. These "ghost detainees" are acknowledged by administration and detention facility staffers but denied in terms of whereabouts and fate. President Bush is famously cited as having informed the CIA that he did not want to know where these detainees were. The denial of knowledge is one thing but the desire to not know is indicative of another kind of process, including a distancing that is deliberate and with intent—one of the most dangerous aspects of penal spectatorship. Prolonged isolation and incommunication constitute, under international human rights conventions, cruel and inhuman practices, while disappearances are under an absolute ban. Ironically, at the heart of democracy, deep in the military prison at Leavenworth, Charles Graner, a former corrections officer and the alleged "ringleader" of the abuse and torture at Abu Ghraib, is the only remaining military actor still being sanctioned. His punishment—solitary confinement for over four years now in a cell as big as a bathroom where the lights are always on—what Graner describes in letters home as "torture."[44]

The Conditions of Critique

> Let us begin with some photographs that one cannot see—for, as a response to suffering, the refusal to picture may pose the most basic problem of all. (Mark Reinhardt, "Picturing Violence: Aesthetics and the Anxiety of Critique," 2007)

Numerous theories have circulated in efforts to render the story of the new war prison and its torture comprehensible. Most accounts argue that the assignment of individuals with no training, experience, or understanding of the role of pain in interrogation was, from the beginning, ill-fated. In this context, under new rules of war, a high degree of ambiguity and vagueness entered into the war zone through an emergent legal architecture designed to challenge existing human rights law. From inexperienced military police to hidden CIA interrogators to an inexperienced general, torture is argued to have occurred in settings without clear lines of oversight or, more significantly, was simply and readily embraced. In either case, it was also visually documented. These practices raise questions about a deeper, more fundamental role of penal excess. Most accounts of these events argue that the culmination of new, vague, ambiguous expectations, pushing inexperienced and unprepared actors past the borders of the law, in settings defined by war and dehumanization, led to unspeakable, only partially representable acts. But what this explanation then asserts is that the average, ordinary citizen is incapable of recognizing or setting limits to the infliction of pain. It implies that the baseline for acts in interrogation settings is one of penal excess—where again, we hear echoes of Sarat and Kearns's vision of human nature turned cruelly against itself, ceaselessly doing battle amid a world of scarcity and insecurity—the dark fantasy of law's necessity. The absence of such deliberation, of alternative frameworks from which to understand new war penal contexts, marks an important extension from sites at home in which punishment is experienced as leisure and recreation or a distant, invisible practice at the edges or hidden centers of the polis. As Mark Reinhardt suggests above, one way in which to begin to alter such orientations is by attempting to picture precisely what we cannot or rarely see in relationship to punishment. By thinking through this predicament visually, we simultaneously open up new theoretical and empirical possibilities. As Stanley Cohen suggests, "Instead of agonizing about why denial occurs, we should take this state for granted. The theoretical problem is not 'why do we shut out?' but 'why do we ever not shut out?' The empirical problem is not to uncover yet more evidence of denial, but to discover the conditions under which information is acknowledged and acted upon."[45]

A critique of such conditions in this way depends upon new questions in our theorization of punishment, including the following: Where is the location of punishment now? In other words, how can we understand state power and nationalism at its key points of articulation, its nodes of action, which include punishment, in increasingly global, transnational settings? What kinds of practices and pains constitute or borrow from punishment in these settings? What are their effects? Most crucially, what happens when practices that are distinctly penal become the means by which the world is interlinked? What happens when fragmentation and exclusion become the basis of the new world order? If punishment and specifically imprisonment comes to be a primary mechanism for regulating the flow and circulation of borders, then the question of what happens to people who are rendered inert and stationary at these boundaries, the people who inhabit sites like Guantánamo and Abu Ghraib and more importantly the people who are incarcerated at sites unknown, are crucial to any future theorizing of punishment. Because pain is artfully reconfigured in these contexts not as above but as the *face* of law, so much that low-level soldiers and ordinary actors have no reservations or hesitancies in visually recording these acts, then how shall it be prohibited or even altered? In such contexts, it will be very difficult to protect the penal subject produced in these contexts. It will be even more difficult perhaps to prove to the penal spectator that the ways in which these subjects achieve or fail to achieve acknowledgment or legal recognition has vast consequences for the movements of individuals and entire populations within and without the law. The question then is ultimately relative to empirical method and social inquiry: How may we better interrogate and study legal borderlands—these sites of punishment where material and political geographies overlap and collide with local, global, national, and transnational jurisdictions, sites that are defined precisely by their lack of access—their "off-limits" status? What does it take to achieve a meaningful visibility? A claim for address?

Such transformations in penal settings insist that it is now the state and the nation whose position, function, territories must be interrogated. There is an assumption in much of contemporary work that the state is overshadowed by emergent configurations that are transnational over international, subnational, or even global. This perspective does not imply that the state has been superseded or eclipsed by globalization but rather that the sovereign state's actions and discourses cannot be understood outside of a larger, globalizing frame. The global, with its emphasis upon flows, circulations, migrations, motion, and mobility, certainly expresses the possibility of solidarities, communities, and social action but it is also about building communities and empires through the establishment of "fortress continents," new modes of the carceral, and correlates of segregation, isolation, and exclusion to the point of death. Thus, penality in global settings is always also about the limits as much as the possibilities of the social, lending the transnational its unevenness and embedded contradictions. Punishment as a practice, discourse, and institution is critical to understanding this problematic as it speaks specifically to the logics of containment that undergird both globalization and the war on terror.

The move toward incapacitation in the United States with its consequent prison expansion and mass incarceration has positioned it as a "global archetype" for imprisonment throughout the world.[46] In both its managerialist, populist, and punitive proclivities, the United States has positioned imprisonment as a primary practice through which to regulate a variety of international insecurities built upon class, race, economy, immigration, and nationalism. In these contexts, security justifications and actuarial methods become arbiters for the use of incarceration in response to marginal actors and cultural minorities, with a massive and growing economic investment. In this manner, new modes of penality are not simply distinctly related to practices of othering but instead speak to how othering has become a primary function of incarceration. This takes on a distinctly racialized form in contemporary world settings. Criminologist Mary Bosworth writes of a "worrying relationship between imprisonment and race" but frames this more powerfully when she asks: "What if ideas of 'race' which are historically contingent and constructed, are necessary for the prison . . . .what if race has simply been written into the entire notion of punishment itself?"[47] This racialization and larger dynamics of social humiliation are evidenced in the Abu Ghraib photos which have been read against the highly racialized contexts of lynching photographs and souvenirs, Vietnam war photos, and a discourse of orientalism that fetishizes and feminizes the sexuality of subjects as a strategy of domination, invoking as well the broader framework of hard-core pornography. Such sexualized and gendered contexts are reminiscent of anthropologist Veena Das's meditation on violence against women in India, where she asks, "How is it that the imaging of the project of nationalism in India came to include the appropriation of bodies of women as objects on which the desire for nationalism could be brutally inscribed and a memory for the future made?"[48] Here, similarly, male and female bodies are appropriated for the playful, torturous aims of empire. She goes on:

> In this movement between bodies, the sentence "I am in pain" becomes the conduit through which I may move out of an inexpressible privacy and suffocation of my pain. This does not mean that I am understood. Wittgenstein uses the route of a philosophical grammar to say that this is not an indicative statement, although it may have the formal appearance of one. It is the beginning of a language game. Pain, in this rendering, is not that inexpressible something that destroys communication or marks an exit from one's existence in language. Instead, it makes a claim asking for acknowledgment, which may be given or denied. In either case, it is not a referential statement that is simply pointing to an inner object. [49]

For Das, pain in its articulation may mark a transaction, "the beginning of a relationship, not its end."[50] Events and representations of Abu Ghraib are clearly marked as a denial of this possibility, an attempt to muffle through torture and its images any acknowledgment of this claim. The use of women as well in this staging marks a complex project in which the appropriation of female bodies is given the appearance of a reversal but one which is artifice—women are objectified in their participation across the photos. Such theater successfully removes women as well from their conventional roles as witness and mourner, whose gendered labor has often borne witness to pain and death and marked efforts to articulate the inexpressible. Repositories of pain and remembrance are missing at Abu Ghraib. There is no Antigone—no moment in which a sister mourns her dead brother in defiance of the law. Rather, women are positioned through imperial frames at Abu Ghraib to sexually humiliate and dehumanize, with few of the resources or vocabularies to see their own role in this production. This is apparent in the major tropes which define the event, built upon legal conceptualizations of guilt and responsibility, of individual versus systematic complicity. The militaristic reliance upon chain-of-command and Nuremberg-like defenses by the individual actors in the case speaks to the way in which agency was transformed into passivity, intervention into the spectacle of torture. This world remains a place remembered as without agency, without action by perpetrators— where persons were no longer themselves, no longer there. In such contexts, explanatory discourses and conditions recede and only deeply self-alienated modes of spectatorship persist. In these spaces, we witness the failure of address due to a lack of recognition of punishment's most fundamental property, its infliction of pain upon another. As Judith Butler theorizes, we all come to exist—and make claims for the right to exist— "in the moment of being addressed, and something about our existence proves precarious when that address fails."[51]

As I have argued elsewhere, Abu Ghraib, like Guantánamo and other U.S. military prisons, marks the kind of penal expansion that takes place in the context of wars with no end: wars on drugs, crime, and terror.[52] In the United States, we imprison more than anyone in the world and more than any other society has ever imprisoned for the purposes of crime control, and we do so in a manner that is defined by race. This unprecedented use of imprisonment has largely taken place outside of democratic checks or public interest, in disregard of decades of work by penal scholars and activists who have introduced a vocabulary of warning through terms like "penological crisis," "incarceration binge," "prison-industrial complex," and the "warehousing" of offenders. Such massive expansion has direct effects upon the private lives of prisoners, correctional workers, their families, and their communities. Such unprecedented penal expenditures mark the global emergence of a new discourse of punishment, one whose racial divisions and abusive practices are revised into a technical, legal language of acceptability, one in which Americans are conveniently further distanced from the social realities of punishment through strategies of isolation and exclusion, all conducted in a manner and on a scale which exacerbates the fundamental class, race, and gender contradictions and divisions of democracy. In this respect, the "new war prison" is constituted by both material practices and a discursive language whose expansion and intensification need recognize no limits, no borders, no bounds. The mode of looking which can or will check its power remains an open question.

Emergent modes of penality raise fundamental questions about the nature and possibility of politics, of sociality, and of the place of human suffering and misery in late modern life. They consequently raise profound questions for the social: How do we organize social life in a manner in which impartiality and independent oversight are not enforced but simply expected and understood as essential to democratic life? How do we provide human rights protections and international judicial oversight without creating larger systems of exclusion? How do we ensure that pain, when inflicted, occurs visibly, accountably, and with acknowledgment as opposed to secretly in unknown places? What of due process and the law is left to bring us democratically into these spaces? Contemporary theorists insist that we must know something about social life as an inherent good in itself, worthy of protection. Agamben, for instance, writes:

> One day humanity will play with law just as children play with disused objects, not in order to restore them to their canonical use but free them from it for good. What is found after the law is not a more proper and original use value that precedes the law, but a new use that is born only after it. And use, which has been contaminated by law, must also be freed from its own value. This liberation is the task of study, or of play. And this studious play is the passage that allows us to arrive at that justice that one of Benjamin's posthumous fragments defines as a state of the world in which the world appears as a good that absolutely cannot be appropriated or made juridical (Benjamin 1992, 41). [53]

Something about this possibility demands that we be able to speak through prohibition and discursive foreclosure concerning violence, struggling to put to words and practice a way in which to make violence of the law and the state visible for the sake of the most vulnerable. As this chapter demonstrates, this will mean changing things for distant others but also importantly changing how we live at home. Abu Ghraib is precisely where the spectator at home meets and becomes the perpetrator abroad. In the image wars, it is the field of vision itself that must be interrupted in a manner that shows this continnum as well as the contradictions in state policies where the violence of war and humanitarianism are conflated. We must know how to disrupt the cultural imaginaries that sustain this passivity through regimes based upon surveillance and victimization, spectacle and authority. We should "contemplate how images of suffering are made, how they should be made, how they circulate, the effects they have, and the dilemmas they pose for thoughtful producers and spectators."[54] How might we "picture" in ways that respect the agency and dignity of those shown—against structure? What forms of representation assault or incite the voyeuristic spectator? As Nicholas Mirzoeff asserts, the right to look includes the right to look at what is concealed and hidden in the social and global process, of being able to know the nature of one's own visual self-representation, to be seen as opposed to disappeared. We turn now to a cultural site whose claims depend precisely upon the authority of such a language and vision: the site of science.

6

Prison Science
Of Faith and Futility

Now faith is the substance of things hoped for, the evidence of
things not seen.

—Hebrews, 11:1

The history of the rehabilitative ideal constitutes a kind of thematic
counterpoint of aspirations and doubts.

—Francis Allen, *The Decline of the Rehabilitative Ideal*, 1981

The Peculiarity of Prison Science

The science of punishment, like its object, is peculiar. Its story, as this
chapter seeks to demonstrate, is very much built upon "the substance of
things hoped for," often moving forward precariously upon "the evidence
of things not seen." For an empirical science, one which quite often claims
to be research- or evidence-based, such an assertion may seem strange;
however, it is faith—and its collapse—which marks the most fundamental of shifts in the story of punishment's present. In this chapter, the last
case study of this volume, we turn intentionally to science and its cultural labor in relation to punishment. Efforts to counter penal spectatorship imply the necessity of a hearty and rigorous reflexive critique among
those of us who study punishment. Science plays a profound role in the
history of punishment and its reform efforts. As the spectators with perhaps some of the most important roles to play in the transformation of
punishment, we must be deeply self-aware of the cultural construction
of science even as we are committed to its empirical and theoretical engagement. Consequently, this chapter encourages us to think through the

dimensions of knowledge production surrounding punishment and the role of motifs, images, tropes, and rhetoric in that formation.

In order to demonstrate this, I examine the site of prison science at a specific historical intellectual juncture, one that is routinely identified as the departure point for the crisis of penological modernism—the failure of rehabilitation in the latter part of the twentieth century. I look specifically at the role of science in the admission of that failure as it presents a strategic research site from which to investigate what makes the study of punishment so distinct amidst one of those rare moments where a science must interrogate its foundations and justifications. In such a pursuit, all of the peculiarities of penal knowledge are made manifest: its internal conflictedness, its futility and volatility, its doubts and hopes. And in that process, we are afforded the opportunity to observe the scientist in his suddenly disclosed role as penal spectator and the struggles that ensue, as intellectuals attempt to speak through punishment's contradictions and justify the voice of expertise. As a chapter, it is thus marked by an effort to speak to those who have been long engaged in a critique of penal spectatorship even as they found themselves caught within its tensions. In this respect, this chapter is dedicated to mapping the moments in which social visions emerge—and fail—in relation to punishment.

The performance of science in relation to punishment at the birth of the law and order society is fundamentally melded to something seemingly well beyond the normative constructions of science. In many ways, it is a deeply visible and public moment for the study of punishment. Here, prison science suddenly and forcefully appears in educational settings, media accounts, legislative and policy decisions, courtrooms and justice systems, gossip and conversation. Across this period, criminologists' claims to legitimacy are asserted and hotly debated, key indicators of a deeply cultural moment for the production of prison science. As sociologist of science Thomas F. Gieryn argues:

> What science becomes, the borders and territories it assumes, the landmarks that give it meaning depend upon exigencies of the moment—who is struggling for credibility, what stakes are at risk, in front of which audiences, at what institutional arena? It is exactly this pliability and suppleness of the cultural space "science" that accounts for its long-running success as the legitimate arbiter of reality: science gets stretched and pulled, pinched and tucked, as its epistemic authority is reproduced time and again in a diverse array of settings.[1]

The 1970s forward represent an unusually provocative moment for observing this stretching and pulling, pinching and tucking of science in the study of punishment. It is a moment that permits us to ask questions related to how a very specific group of intellectuals, struggling with an inherently conflicted public institution, lend their work meaning. I follow the lead of sociologists of science and turn to the ways in which scientists depict this process themselves, in their own arguments and publications. For this reason, I rely heavily upon epigraphs, widely used quotations, and exemplary texts. I do this as the ways in which scientists engage their work—the ways in which they research, write and frame their own analyses, the sources they cite, the quotes they repeat—are important indicators of the ways in which proper aims and justifications of penal science are conceptualized in cultural practice. Out of such maneuvers the central images and tropes of science emerge. Such quotation permits me to map a sad, bitter, sometimes savage dialogue directed at the failure of science and the emergent facts of mass incarceration—and in that mapping, examine how scientists, as distinct kinds of observers, with expertise and authority, decide the nature of their engagement with the project of punishment.

I trace the tensions and trajectories that emerge out of these discussions through a close reading of the recent past in penal science, using as a launching point what nearly all criminologists consider to be a key watershed moment, the publication in 1974 of Robert Martinson's "What Works?—Questions and Answers about Prison Reform" in *Public Interest*. If there is a central rhetorical trope for the study of contemporary punishment, it is found in the recurrent motif of "what works." The critical and popular reception of Martinson's study constitutes an emblematic case study, one that asks how science itself is dismantled and then reconstructed by scientists through the coupling of the death of rehabilitation to the life and death of sociologist Robert Martinson, the intellectual largely credited with the idea that "nothing works" in rehabilitative thinking. Here I map moments when Martinson's publication record and personal biography are intentionally positioned to intersect with other claims about what it is to do penal science at precisely the moment prison science confronts the possibility of its own failure. In this invocation, we catch scientists in conflicted, urgent acts of both hope and despair in their own work. At such moments, the interrogation of science—questions concerning its origins, its contributions, its essential properties—are unavoidable. I attempt to conjugate the function and significance of this analytical despair against a resurgent radical hope, all in the context of what it means to pursue the study of punishment. In this process, penal science, because of the centrality of crisis to its contemporary and historical configuration, is specifically invoked, analyzed, and engaged as a site for the enactment ultimately of a new politics of penality and a more reflexive subject position—frames that are inherent to the study of punishment and are placed in high relief when scientific arguments from the late 1960s are juxtaposed with the voices of contemporary criminologists.

On Hope . . . and Despair

> It is confidently predicted that, before the end of this century, prison in [its current] form will become extinct, though the word may live on. (Norval Morris, *The Future of Imprisonment*, 1965)

> We have been gradually escaping from institution responses and one can foresee the period when incarceration will be used still more rarely than it is today. (David Rothman, *The Discovery of the Asylum*, 1971)

In order to understand the dramatic nature of this historical and intellectual shift, one need only look at the scientific texts and research commission publications that precede the turn away from rehabilitation. Penal texts from the 1960s and early 1970s now read like strange storms brewing on the horizon. Clearly, change is imminent, reminding us of Michael Ignatieff's prediction concerning the penal present: "Something fundamental is beginning to happen."[2] There are signs (always) of what is to come but the path has not yet been chosen. In outlining the decisions that must be made, the major intellectual voices of the era point to both the social burdens of the penal past and the possibilities of the future. In one of the most widely read criminal justice publications of the era, *The Challenge of Crime in a Free Society*, the summary report of President Johnson's Commission on Law Enforcement and Administration of Justice, the volume uncannily points toward the strange future that lay ahead.

> The costs of action are substantial. But the costs of inaction are immensely greater. Inaction would mean, in effect, that the Nation would continue to avoid, rather than confront, one of its most critical social problems; that it would accept for the next generation a huge, if now immeasurable,

burden of wasted and destructive lives. Decisive action, on the other hand, could make a difference that would really matter within our time.[3]

Here, action and a passive spectatorship are actively pitted against one another. What the volume does not anticipate is how the very cost of a particular form of penal politics and action, in its choice of ways in which to view the impacts of punishment and informed in part by criminologists and researchers, would lead to the largest criminal justice system and prison population in the world. The manner in which the major commissions and scientific texts of the era missed this possibility is quite staggering; change is anticipated but in far more idealistic and optimistic frames. The American Friends Service Committee captures this directive well in their significant report, *Struggle for Justice*, which points again to the priority of political action and reform in shaping the future of criminal justice in the United States.

> The kinds of action we have described point the way to a criminal justice system that is more humane and more equitable for all the people. More ideas, more actions, more proposals are needed. Work toward such a system of justice will create ripples throughout our whole society, having a salutary effect on all our institutions and policies . . . Thus can continue the long and arduous struggle for justice, a struggle we trust will lead one day to a criminal justice system that will reflect a free and open society.[4]

These politics of desire are characteristic of the spirited rhetoric and emotional fervor of the main scientific statements of the time. Their language invokes a different kind of cultural lens in its understanding of punishment—one which privileges action, work, a collective struggle, a free and open society, and the possibility of change through rippling effects. It is interesting, within such a context, what issues and directives achieved visibility. The President's Commission on Law Enforcement and the Administration of Justice and the American Friends Service Committee insisted that change and reform necessitated a major overhaul of our correctional system. Each pointed insistently at the challenge of crime control in a democracy, including such issues as deep and troubling concerns with class and racial disparity alongside of structural inequalities and the pending crisis of credibility experienced by the American state, given these conditions. Each reflected an increased popular focus on the problematic nature of discretionary justice, the inequities of disparity at every phase of the criminal justice system, and the potentially coercive underpinnings of treatment programs in corrections. In their recommendations, however, each retained the primacy of the individual and the offender as the focal point of justice, maintained a wide breadth of voluntary rehabilitative options, including education, job training, skills development, and treatment interventions. Perhaps most significantly, the burden of change and responsibility for justice was envisioned as shifting from institutions to communities, emphasizing the larger societal role necessary in the administration of justice, including its key objective: the successful reintegration of offenders. These reports, with their optimism and confidence in possibility and their general emphasis upon humaneness and compassion, not only contrast starkly with the shift in political discourse and cultural practice that followed but leave open the question of the role of science in that shift. As political critiques from the left merged with those of the right, creating a dystopian penal outcome that few could possibly have anticipated, many would wonder how scientists did not see the shape of punishment to come and more would commit themselves to reversing the project of mass incarceration with a dedicated rational fervor that would rely upon the rigor and legitimacy of science in new and enhanced ways that continue to lend primary shape to the field today. In short, science would be invoked to save us.

In these pursuits, the work of intellectuals would be fundamentally defined by a tension sustained between two visions—one of deepening despair and the other a cautious hope, often pointing back toward those moments just before the turn occurred. Marc Mauer, director of the highly influential criminal justice watchdog organization, The Sentencing Project, begins his centerpiece in advocacy, *The Race to Incarcerate*, with such a retrospective, directed at Rothman's hopeful optimism:

> In 1971, David Rothman, one of the leading historians of the birth of the penitentiary, closed his highly regarded work, *The Discovery of the Asylum*, with these words ". . . we have been gradually escaping from institution responses and one can foresee the period when incarceration will be used still more rarely than it is today." The value of Rothman's contributions to this field of scholarship should not be diminished by this unfortunate prediction, but rarely has such a gaze into the future proven to be so wide off the mark as this one. [5]

Nils Christie begins the third edition of *Crime Control as Industry* with a note:

> This book is a warning against recent developments in the field of crime control. . . . It is a deeply pessimistic analysis I here present, and as such, in contrast to what I believe is my basic attitude to much in life. . . . But a warning is also an act of some optimism. A warning implies belief in possibilities for change.[6]

These kinds of discourses dominate the contemporary era for those who study punishment and underlie their motives and efforts to communicate science. In Loïc Wacquant's "Deadly Symbiosis: When Ghetto and Prison Meet and Mesh," he insists vehemently and desperately that mass incarceration is not a "destiny" but a democratic decision-making process, "a matter of political choices, and these choices must be made in full knowledge of the facts—and of the consequences!"[7] Convict criminologist John Irwin writes with an exasperated fatigue in his most recent volume, *The Warehouse Prison*, "After I had stood by for 20 years in horror while prison populations exploded, I was compelled to revisit the prison environment to conduct this study."[8] Todd Clear writes of his meditation on pain in punishment, *Harm in American Penology*, that it "grew out of my despair at the changes taking place in the criminal justice system, especially changes in the use of corrections," where, after fifteen years of professional service in the field, he writes, "I was spent. I had lost my heart and my head for the work. . . . this book grew out of my frustration at the field, my disillusionment about reforms, and my personal exhaustion with the day to day effort of trying to make sense of it all."[9] Similarly, at the end of his introduction to *Crime and Punishment in America*, Elliott Currie anticipates

> a society we should not want—one that would have been unrecognizable to the citizens of an earlier, more human and optimistic America: A society in which a permanent state of social disintegration is held in check only by the creation of a swollen apparatus of confinement and control that has no counterpart in our own history or in any other industrial democracy.[10]

Off the mark. Warnings. Choices. Consequences. Horror. Exhaustion. A society we should not want. The main intellectual voices of prison science now are profoundly shaped by a deep sense of experienced cynicism, desperation, and despair. To write of prisons now is to write of a time that breaks from historical precedent in a way that leaves the most objective of scientists speaking in tragic discourses with a futile sense that history is upon us. The scale of imprisonment, its deepening race, class, and gender disparities, its collateral consequences, its implication in cultural, military, and industrial complexes, its exacerbation of the inequities of democracy, its global expansion have all left prison scientists the gloomiest of penal spectators with a distinct and peculiar burden: a scientific counter-effort directed at the overwhelming force of politicized patterns of crime control and incarceration. There is a strange pain to those of us who work in fields that are intractably defined—fields where causality may be privileged but to no avail—where little translates into public discourse of what we actually do—and finally, where what works depends upon a clear understanding of the evidence of the past. The ways in which our recent past has formed us as a field is fundamental—fundamental to who we are as intellectuals, fundamental to the project of punishment, fundamental to how we study punishment and how punishment is understood as a social practice. But of critical importance to this volume, it is also fundamental in its role-modeling, in how authority and expertise engage in multiple tasks: (1) the training of future researchers; (2) the reproduction of knowledge through the frames of research; and (3) a cultural pedagogy through the demonstration of alternative ways of viewing punishment. Ultimately, scientists are penal spectators with a specific burden and complicity, in their centrality to the reproduction and the alteration of the wider cultural penal gaze. In that pursuit, it seems important to do the work of tracing the intellectual origins of such a, for all intents and purposes, miserable trajectory.

The Science of Futility:
Robert Martinson and the Construction of "Nothing Works"

> Hence, I approach with hesitance the task of rational planning for the future of imprisonment. The momentum of futility and brutality in imprisonment is great; the political forces obstructing change are deeply entrenched; and the reformers have no agreed-upon program. They may sometimes concur on what is wrong but they lack the inner compass of shared principles to chart a path to other than ameliorative change. There is a fervor and factionalism, a modishness, in their recommendations that seriously impede correction reform. (Norval Morris, *The Future of Imprisonment*, 1974)

As much as anything, our futile efforts to curb or even understand the dramatic and continuing rise in crime have been frustrated by our optimistic and unrealistic assumptions about human nature . . . I argue for a sober view of man and his institutions that would permit reasonable things to be accomplished, foolish things abandoned, and utopian things forgotten. (James Q. Wilson, *Thinking About Crime*, 1975)

Today, optimism has turned to pessimism, fervent hopes to despair. (LaMar Empey, *Beyond Probation: Juvenile Corrections and the Chronic Delinquent*, 1979)

There are rare moments when a particular study or set of studies achieves a level of public attention and popularity that shapes how science will be done in the future in profound ways. Like popular prisons, films, and scandalous photographs, they attract our attention. This may have little or much to do with the scientific worth of the work, and much may later be attributed to such studies that denies the role of larger cultural, political, and social conditions. Nonetheless, a conjunction occurs and history is made. For sociologists of science, these moments are critical sites for examining the role of science in action and understanding how science, like any cultural artifact, is made. Common history in criminology concedes that the publication of sociologist Robert Martinson's 1974 article, "What Works? Questions and Answers about Prison Reform," in the *Public Interest* signaled the "death knell" of rehabilitation.[11] Few singular works bear the notoriety and celebrity that Martinson's publication carries. For instance, many argue that the work constitutes "the least frequently read but most frequently quoted and cited article in the rehabilitation literature."[12] Its reprints are perpetual, even now. It is one of those rare works of science which, in its time, garnered high levels of both intellectual and public attention, including an appearance by Martinson on CBS's popular news program, *60 Minutes*, and incorporation of his findings in editorials, political speeches, and legislative hearings.[13] It even sparked the establishment in 1977 of a prestigious National Academy of Sciences panel, charged with assessing the effectiveness of rehabilitative efforts. In their conclusions, the panel declared Martinson's study to be reasonable and fair in its assessment of the state of rehabilitation, although subtly implying that Martinson had overemphasized the negative findings of his study.[14] That same year, C. Ray Jeffrey, who would soon be president of

the American Society of Criminology, the largest professional organization of criminologists in the world, would declare, in keeping with the
common consensus of the field at that moment, that "punishment has
failed . . . treatment has failed."[15] The study is, thus, widely and commonly
regarded as having definitively altered the future trajectory of the field by
marking the demise of rehabilitation. In doing so, it introduced one of
the most important frames and lenses through which science is seen and
research is conducted in criminology, what many have labeled a technical
or correctionalist "what works" discourse.[16]

As common as this history may seem, Martinson's work is in many
ways far more opaque. Referred to as the "enfant terrible"[17] of criminology,
Martinson himself is most often remembered as a maverick social scientist
who made very large and general claims about the failure of rehabilitative
treatment, based upon a survey of existing studies, claims now widely considered open to multiple kinds of complex interpretation—both positive
and negative and, more often, somewhere in between. His legacy is largely
a negative one in that his statements were unusually well-received in the
reactive backlash and rise of a post–civil rights law and order movement,
lending Martinson a brief and troubled celebrity status and historically
assigning him some complicity in the rise of mass incarceration. The impact of his work spread quickly and the slogan "nothing works" became
the lynchpin of correctional and crime policy throughout the next few
decades. By the mid-1980s, policy makers, public researchers, and political officials all came to see rehabilitation as substantially discredited and
its pursuit increasingly futile.[18] No political candidate since has successfully run for presidential office on a less than harsh-on-crime, punitive
electoral platform. Martinson and his work sat center stage scientifically
as the policy tide in the United States turned toward a number of radical
penal recommendations, ranging from the abolition of parole to changes
in sentencing structure directed toward harsher, fixed mandatory mini-
mums, the emergence of new definitions of dangerousness and criminality,
new penal directives (such as just deserts and incapacitation), as well as a
spurious claim now and again popularly and a heated exchange internally
among intellectuals, calling for the reaffirmation of rehabilitation—based
upon a dense amalgam of "multiple crime control strategies, including
prevention, deterrence, and rehabilitation."[19] Importantly, many penolo-
gists of the period argue that the critical reaction shared by intellectuals
was further fueled by a public "crisis mentality" which demanded swift
policy and denied analysis by favoring an immediate, reactive dismantling

of rehabilitation, a juncture in which Martinson's claims made a timely, if not perfect, discursive fit.[20] As Don Andrews and his collaborators declare in an important reevaluation of Martinson's work, "'Nothing works' satisfied conservative political reactions to the apparent disorder of the 1960s, liberal sorrow over perceived failures of the Great Society, and the ideological persuasions of those academicians whose truly social visions of deviance asserted that only radical social change could have an impact on crime."[21] Here, we are reminded of Philip Smith's argument as to how transformations in punishment often occur through a kind of semiotic alignment in cultural communication, where authority and the force of punishment are brought into line.[22] Martinson's work assumes center stage then in part because of its cultural fit. This also partially explains why, as legislatures and public opinion steered toward punitiveness, often relying upon Martinson's work to do so, all of Martinson's last publications were directed at qualifying and, in some instances, recanting his previous assertions, but to no avail and little critical reception.[23] The common history ends abruptly with a series of little-known press obituaries, which couple the death of rehabilitation to Martinson's suicide in 1980.

Recent efforts in the study of punishment have attempted to move Martinson out of the central place he inhabits in the history of the turn away from rehabilitation and the rise of law and order politics and a culture of control. Sociologist David Garland argues, "Only the most superficial analysis would therefore seek to explain such an event in the currency of contingent actions without reference to more fundamental historical processes. And yet the standard account of recent penal change attributes this major event to the impact of a series of published criticisms."[24] Garland likens this "standard account" to a progressive, post-Enlightenment fairy tale in its simplistic account of penal change. This kind of explanation is, indeed, substantively weak from a historical or sociological perspective which seeks to account broadly for dramatic penal transformation. The causality attributed to Martinson and other largely conservative and radical penal texts of the period, calling for the dismantling of rehabilitation, appears misplaced when considering a variety of factors. As Garland outlines, Martinson's study was not the first of its kind in the sense that long-standing critiques and negative findings about rehabilitation and the promise of punishment had been present in penology.[25] Similarly, Martinson's findings were open to question and subjected to a rapid and rigorous critical interrogation in which even he himself recanted his early and more negative assertions. Finally, and perhaps most

importantly, penal institutions have a long history of being generally subjected to intense criticism with little change or reform occurring in the
context of bureaucratic inertia—supporters and advocates of the current
institutional paradigms often easily convert criticism into a demand for
more resources, more attention, and a retrenchment of the current ideological framework. As Foucault argued, reform constitutes the core of the
project of the prison and its persistence. Obviously, larger social and cultural forces led to the crisis of penological modernism—with Martinson's
work playing only a small part.

Nonetheless, in textbooks, legislative hearings, popular media accounts
and retrospectives, and most correctional literature, Martinson's "what
works" publication is often explicitly enlisted as the turning point which
marks the demise of rehabilitation and, implicitly, the turn to punitive
politics, a study whose "timing"[26] was history-shaping. The privileging of
such an account within intellectual understandings of the moment reveals
important things about the science of punishment and the manner in
which it is invested with meaning by its practitioners and its public. Why
did criminologists largely come to view their history through the cultural
lens of Martinson's study? As Martinson's research is moved to a more appropriate historical context and we turn to the pressing penal problems of
the moment and the future, it seems critical to revisit how such assertions
and declarations about the role of science did—and might again—assume
center stage and what the role of the scientist as a speaking spectator is
in that process. In that effort, a full analysis of the troubled trajectory of
"what works," especially the ways in which Martinson and his critics attempted to define penal science at an unusually culturally reactive moment, seems critical.

What Works—Once More, With Feeling

> With few and isolated exceptions, the rehabilitative efforts that
> have been reported so far have had no appreciable effect on recidi-
> vism. (Martinson, "What Works?" 1974)

Martinson's concluding sentence above marks most of what is remembered and quoted from the publication of his most important publication, "What Works? Questions and Answers about Prison Reform." It is,
consequently, the central rhetorical maneuver in the body of work which
follows Martinson. A more comprehensive map of the text, however,

outlines a number of key rhetorical conventions and strategies by which the science of the period was defined. Martinson, interestingly, begins the piece by marking the tension between faith and evidence, aspiration and doubt. He explains his reasons for conducting his study in the conclusion of the first paragraph of the essay by insisting, somewhat mundanely, that the "articulate" American public has simply "entered another one of its sporadic fits of attentiveness to the condition of our prisons and to the perennial questions they pose about the nature of crime and the uses of punishment."[27] Far from earth-shattering, Martinson frames his work initially in the routine, chronic problems of reform in punishment where "American prisons, perhaps more than those of any other country, have stood or fallen in public esteem according to their ability to fulfill their promise of rehabilitation."[28] In the second paragraph, however, Martinson anchors the possibility of this long-standing debate about rehabilitation in a manner that would reshape the future of prison studies by arguing such debates persist in the absence of "any systematic empirical knowledge about the success or failure that we have met when we *have* tried to rehabilitate offenders, with various treatments and in various institutional and non-institutional settings."[29] This maneuver quickly and decisively links promise and empiricism, faith and evidence, insisting upon a very distinct vision of science. For Martinson, promise is poised in the form of empirical and positivist science: a comprehensive analytic survey of all existing research on rehabilitation, a method in which scientific rigor will "sketch an answer" to the problem of reform and recidivism which plagues punishment. In this manner, Martinson's argument opens by way of a rhetorical frame which assumes a definition and participates in the construction of science, one in which correctional research is fundamentally wedded in its worth to an instrumentalist notion of crime control. Far from unusual, this remains the frame by which most work in the study of punishment is and has been done—and, I will argue, for reasons that are obvious and not so obvious. As penal spectators, our ways of looking at and understanding punishment are fundamentally transformed in the process.

Martinson's report derived much of its credibility from the manner in which he privileged two criteria: (1) his findings were derived from the vantage point of having examined *all* available rehabilitative literature in the English language from 1945 through 1967, two decades worth of correctional research; (2) via a rigorous scientific standard of empirical criteria. The consensus of his findings culminates in the statement: "With few and isolated exceptions, the rehabilitative efforts that have been reported so far have had no appreciable effect on recidivism."[30] This position is further reinforced in the lengthy volume, *The Effectiveness of Correctional Treatment*, which presents the study-by-study presentation and analyses of Martinson's findings from "What Works?" Martinson's initial platform is expanded with an identical conclusion: "This study uncovered no treatment that holds promise of easily and effectively impacting upon the recidivism of all offenders."[31] Important to Martinson's argument are several factors. His central measurements focus on recidivism rates, which indicate the way in which rehabilitation was being articulated across the field as an end toward crime reduction. A decrease in recidivism was often the sole measure of success, and Martinson's critics would later point out that rehabilitation might be important in correctional settings in its own right without direct correlations to recidivism but in part for its ability to humanize control settings. Rehabilitation was also thought to be a philosophy and professional movement structured deeply enough in penal practice to result in a uniform correctional application that would affect a majority of the offender population. Anything short of this totalizing framework could well be marked a failure—and was. Out of the 231 studies that Martinson examined, the treatment programs and interventions that were analyzed included education/skill training; individual counseling; group counseling; milieu therapy; medicalization; sentencing; decarceration; community punishments; probation/parole/prison; and intensive supervision. In each category, Martinson points to a variety of important limitations in the existing research design and research findings, so much so that "What Works?" is less about the implementation of rehabilitation and more about a methodological critique of contemporary correctional research. In Martinson's climactic conclusion to the article, under the subheading "Does nothing work?" he writes:

> We tried to exclude from our survey those studies which were so poorly done that they simply could not be interpreted. But despite our efforts, a pattern has run through much of this discussion—of studies which "found" effects without making any truly rigorous attempt to exclude competing hypotheses, of extraneous factors permitted to intrude upon the measurements, of recidivism measures which are not all measuring the same thing, of "follow-up" periods which vary enormously and rarely extend beyond the period of legal supervision, of experiments never replicated, of "system effects" not taken into account, of categories drawn up

without any theory to guide the enterprise. It is possible that some of our treatment programs *are* working to some extent, but that our research is so bad that it is incapable of telling.[32]

Here we find implications for the failure of penal science which stands at the heart of penological crisis. Each subsection analyzing a particular treatment concludes with a pragmatic statement which insists that there is "no clear" evidence, only ambiguity, or clear failure (worsening behavior on the part of offenders) of rehabilitative propensities.

From Martinson's evaluation it is clear that the field was operating under a hodgepodge of penal practices under the rubric of rehabilitation. Martinson is among the first to uncover the complex amalgam of penal practices and effects that are symptomatic of modern punishment. His response to this complexity is to argue for the shifting of the penological focus from rehabilitation to a more adequate means of deterrence, epitomized in incapacitation. Martinson's empirical and methodological rigor is perhaps best characterized as an attempt to promote a serious discussion of the point of punishment. But his language ultimately boils down to a much more pragmatic and instrumentalist assessment of "what works." His assertions ultimately initiate a penological engagement which becomes deeply preoccupied with the successes but, even more so, the failures of rehabilitation *as* crime control. In direct opposition to rehabilitation, Martinson argues a theoretical turn, representative of the manner in which concerns from the left and the right would collide, toward the abandonment of treatment programs which he viewed, like many, as built upon a faulty theory of crime as a disease and instead proffered the following perspective:

This opposing theory of "crime as a social phenomenon" directs our attention away from a "rehabilitative"' strategy, away from the notion that we may best insure public safety through a series of "treatments" to be imposed forcibly on convicted offenders. These treatments have on occasion become, and have the potential for becoming, so draconian as to offend the moral order of a democratic society; and the theory of crime as a social phenomenon suggests that such treatments may be not only offensive but ineffective as well. This theory points, instead, to decarceration for low-risk offenders—and, presumably, to keeping high-risk offenders in prisons which are nothing more (and aim to be nothing more) than custodial institutions.[33]

Here, Martinson anticipates and frames the logic for the control and warehouse prison and the rise of incapacitation with its attendant mass incarceration through a liberal framework—a move away from "draconian" practices. This point, Martinson declares, is a place from which we may "begin to learn the facts," including the ability "to judge to what degree the prison has become an anachronism and can be replaced by more effective means of social control."[34]

The politics that follow Martinson's work are fascinating. Near the beginning of the article, under a section titled "The travails of a study," in a moment that uncannily anticipates the impacts of Martinson's own work, he points precisely at the politicization of science, describing New York State's resistance to the release of his study's findings, an investigation they had commissioned in order to qualify for federal monies being released through the 1968 Omnibus Crime Control and Safe Streets Act. As Martinson marks it, the study had come to be seen as a "document whose disturbing conclusions posed a serious threat to the programs which, in the meantime, they had determined to carry forward."[35] The delay in release and publication of the findings is perhaps part of the reason why Martinson opted to publish, some argue, without the input or permission of colleagues Douglas Lipton and Judith Wilks, who had collaborated with Martinson on the study and co-authored its centerpiece, the hefty volume, *The Effectiveness of Correctional Treatment*, published in 1975. Rather, Martinson selected *The Public Interest* as the site from which to launch his critique, a choice that would secure his fame. Founded in 1965 by a group of scholars who were increasingly critical of the roles and strategies of liberals in coordinating social change, the journal sought to build what would ultimately be a neoconservative forum for the discussion of policy, economy, and social science. The journal would be an early home to such voices as Pat Moynihan, Robert Solow, Robert Nisbet, Daniel Bell, James Q. Wilson, Milton Friedman, and Peter Drucker. As retrospectives concerning the journal's recent dissolution have emerged, so have attempts to historicize its proper place. Commentators concede that, in many ways like Martinson, "The founders of the PI believed in something called 'the public interest.' If they were less certain about what that public interest was, they were in agreement that it existed and could be at least partially apprehended and approached by reasonable, decent human beings."[36] For these reasons, Martinson's publication was poised to achieve political attention and media coverage, by making claims to scientific expertise but also by invoking and relying upon a compelling notion of "common sense" in science that would translate popularly into what everyone "already knew" about the failure of rehabilitation and criminology. As Gray Cavender describes in his analysis of Martinson's appearance on CBS's *60 Minutes*, the legitimacy of professionals is invoked, including a Bureau of Prisons Director who states, 'We don't know what causes crime. The behavioral sciences cannot tell us what causes crime. We actually don't know what works or if anything works."[37] Such a discourse facilitates a rhetorical and ideological shift marked by the conclusion of the segment, where anchor Mike Wallace broadly asserts that "sociologists and prisoners agree that punishment should be certain and swift, and that there should be no parole," ending with "A swift, sure painful kick in the backside, Dr. Martinson calls it, will deter a criminal."[38] Amid tones of futility, here science descends into a harsh mode of penal spectatorship, literally invoking the infliction of pain. In the end, Martinson's decision to invest his study with such broad claims, framed by "does nothing work?" would haunt his scientific contribution for posterity.

The Travails of Robert Martinson

> The history of science teaches that all-encompassing solutions are seldom to be found and that neither "breakthroughs" nor "comprehensive approaches" emerge without careful preparation. As corrections comes to accept its place among the experienced empirical sciences, it too will perhaps recognize that it, too, must live with these rather general and sobering facts of life. (Ted Palmer, "Martinson Revisited," 1975)

> There is a mad professor who lives in New York's 20th precinct; his name is Martinson and he has "demonstrated" that "nothing works" in correction. (Robert Martinson, "California Research at the Crossroads," 1976)

Given that Martinson's work was clearly directed at a methodological critique of contemporary correctional research, the publication of "What Works?" in 1974 sparked a seriously reactive and volatile debate that would span the next few decades, with and without Martinson's full participation. In his record of personal correspondence, letters hash out the meaning of the "What Works" publication. Psychiatrists, criminologists, legislators, U.S. Department of Justice researchers, the American Friends

Service Committee, court officers, and law enforcement applaud his work, framing it as "admirable," "fascinating," and "useful," requesting prints for classes and local social service agencies and community literature while others critique his rehabilitation measures and ideological commitments. Sociologist Marvin Wolfgang writes:

> I have just read "What Works?" and wanted to write you at once to say that I found the article impressive in several ways. The analysis is comprehensive and clearly presented. You inform the reader with amazingly succinct summaries, pinpoint the important features, and exercise just caution. The alternative interpretations, in your conclusions, are excellent and stimulating. It is rare these days that my enthusiasm for the scholarly merit in this field is aroused so much as your piece has done.[39]

Others write, "I feel . . . that the whole community of correctional treatment evaluators has been mistreated by the volume. The mistreatment arises more from the organization, emphases, and context of the volume than from the handling of particular reports of research."[40] Across his correspondence, Martinson tirelessly and meticulously reasserts the accuracy and validity of his findings. The initial and most heated of dialogues is captured in an engagement in the *Journal of Research in Crime and Delinquency* in 1975 between Martinson and Ted Palmer, whose own work with the California Youth Authority's Community Treatment Project was directly attacked in Martinson's critique. Here, Palmer challenged the analytical framework of Martinson's work, which, he argued, had "triggered" a "widespread pessimism" in the world of corrections, asking, "Does a careful reading of this challenging and influential article really warrant the pessimistic forecast which has been made, especially by individuals who have drawn upon it to support their suspicions regarding the futility of intervention in general?"[41] Palmer's *Correctional Intervention and Research* (1978), a thick counterargument to Martinson's findings, highlights the notion of perspective in methodological interpretation by reassessing 90 percent of Martinson's original sample of studies, focusing instead upon individual outcomes as opposed to some cumulative effect. He famously found that out of 82 studies, Martinson had himself identified 39 studies (nearly half) as having positive or partially positive results. Here the debate extends into a discussion of whether or not Martinson's survey carried enough evidential weight to merit an abandonment of treatment processes, a tactic that would persist across several key works on rehabilitation in the next few decades.

First, Palmer's main statement contends that 48 percent of Martinson's studies did indeed yield "promising results or positive leads."[42] He argues that the nature of Martinson's evaluation minimized the prevalence of positive treatment findings by employing a categorical or attempted total measurement of effect rather than attending to the rehabilitative impact of individual studies. This, he asserts, is an overly stringent criterion for a determination of rehabilitative success, thereby fundamentally limiting the ability of the survey to endorse any treatment category. Palmer writes, "only an unusually powerful and flexible mode of intervention would have been able to satisfy, even figuratively, Dr. Martinson's criterion of success for methods of treatment as a whole."[43] Palmer contends as well that Martinson inaccurately correlates crime rates and levels of recidivism, which Palmer characterizes as a relationship "logically and statistically, very distant and weak."[44] Palmer's criticisms point to what would become a reasonably popular approach to this debate: the taking of a "some things work" position relative to the level of cost, measurable effectiveness, and analytical interpretation/ideological outlook. In his closing remarks, he reframes the question: "Rather than ask, 'What works—for offenders as a whole?' we must increasingly ask, 'Which methods work best for *which* types of offenders, and under *what* conditions or in what types of setting?"[45] Many would find such nuance less than hopeful, including James Q. Wilson, who wrote that "these hints did not constitute, even generously interpreted, a clear and consistent pattern of success on which a public policy might be based."[46] A growing conservative literature like Wilson's works would provide further shelter for arguments like Martinson's.[47] Others, Francis Cullen, for instance, would argue in retrospect that Palmer's findings had "created a fissure in the 'nothing works doctrine' that could not be fully dismissed and that, under the weight of additional data, would ultimately crack wide open."[48] Ultimately, much of the debate turned into (and to some degree, remains) a discussion as to whether the metaphorical glass is half-empty or half-full, but one framed fundamentally about science's relationship to social change and its possibility. Scholars on both sides characterize the debate as one dominated by style, "treatment destruction techniques,"[49] appeals to common sense, and a reliance upon unnecessary jargon and ritual, and have pointed consistently to the fact that the discussions often centered upon some sense of finality and certainty that the scientific method could never supply in its assessments of the causes of crime and the inner workings of human behavior. Such critiques importantly point to the way in which the cultural constructs of science had been exposed. Largely, however, camps emerged in a manner divided by belief in the possibility or necessity of an overarching treatment framework, one that would and could lend meaning to rehabilitation as a paradigm, a cultural lens, and the scientific basis for its translation into policy and practice. In this regard, the literature that follows Martinson has maintained a strict attention to scientific rigor and an empirical methodicalness, haunted by the question of "what works" and the cultural legitimacy it achieved. As Palmer concludes in his response to Martinson, framed as a warning, Martinson's study in many ways appeared as a type of failed quest or search, a metaphor that would be carried forward across time, "for rapid or glamorous solutions, and for methods that will work with everyone" and, as such, constitute "the search for the impossible, which has ended in so much disillusionment thus far,"[50] what Lab and Whitehead would famously refer to in a later debate concerning ongoing research pursuits framed by Martinson as the "search for the secular grail."[51]

Martinson's response to Palmer is important to map as well in that it speaks to what often underlies much of science and is thus most intriguing in how emotive it is, as opposed to any scientific or analytical quality. Sociologists of culture and cultural criminologists alike have given an important place to the messy mobilization of emotions in our understandings of the cultural contests surrounding meaning-making. Already, by 1975, in his writing, Martinson is angry. And he is deeply concerned with the "hysteria" his work has invoked among "correctional folk," referring to the history of corrections as a "graveyard of abandoned fads." He continues to view science as a site from which to break out of such constraints and enact meaningful change but is struggling to come to terms with the many ways in which research findings can be, in his own words and experience, "misused." In defense of his previous assertions, he makes an explicit rhetorical shift away from intellectual debate, what he refers to as the "interminable intramural bickering about the esoteric mysteries of research design and significance tests and such-like oddities" to a claim to his quest that hinges upon him, and his community who are actively invoked across his reaction, getting "on with the task of searching for methods to reduce the slaughter of the innocents down here in the 20th precinct."[52] In a letter to a colleague who had somewhat provocatively invited Martinson to participate in an "Alternatives to Incarceration" conference, Martinson writes:

Whatever gave you the idea that I consider "Alternative to Incarceration" necessarily a "ridiculous" idea? For some kinds and ages of offenders, it is a very good idea; for others, no. As the criminologist-in-residence to the 20th precinct, NYC, I am opposed to any *idée fixe* in this matter and continue to ask: what will be the overall influence on the crime rates which have my neighbors locked up in their apartments and businesses? What about the victims. . . ? Are they not human also? Do they not bleed as did my son Michael when he was mugged in Central Park?

His appeal to common sense and the personal plight of those caught in crime-ridden contexts powerfully invokes the emergent discourses of the era, those increasingly directed away from sources of criminality and instead directed at targeted incapacitation, deterrence, and the rise of the victim. Also, as was characteristic of his writing, Martinson, without hesitancy, foregrounds his own subject position as a distinct kind of penal spectator, one who has a direct proximity to the experience of crime and victimization. No doubt, such understandings shaped his personal and scientific interpretations of punishment, evidence again of the role of culture in shaping the approaches and worldviews we bring to the construction of science.

His declarations would become far less acerbic by 1977, as major sea changes in the structure of criminal justice became apparent, where in an article in *Federal Probation*, titled "Save Parole Supervision," Martinson decries the movement to abolish parole, insisting that we not "throw out the baby with the bathwater" and that "the overall consequence of abolishment of parole supervision would be to consign larger numbers of offenders to prison."[53] In a letter from *Hofstra Law Review* and their planning of an issue directed at a sentencing symposium, Martinson faces an outright publication rejection unless he can rewrite the article in a manner which "with alteration and substantiation, reflect(s) the shift in attitudes toward sentencing of one individual, and prominent criminologist—yourself."[54] In the winter of 1979, Martinson publishes this piece as part of the symposium, serving as his final word on the subject, in the *Hofstra Law Review* under the title "New Findings, New Views: A Note of Caution Regarding Sentencing Reform," and, in a distinct turn away from his earlier positions, writes:

The purpose of this Article is to suggest that not only must sentencing reform be undertaken with knowledge of such system-wide class disparities, but that *any* reform must be undertaken with great caution. Tinkering with the system runs a major risk of serious, detrimental ramifications. Contrary to common belief, the rate of recidivism . . . in this country is not high, it is quite low. And, contrary to my previous position, some treatment programs *do* have an appreciable effect on recidivism. Some programs are indeed beneficial; of equal or greater significance, some programs are harmful.[55]

His concluding studies point to a powerful transformation that depends upon a quality Martinson always carried in his work—a passionate, reflexive self-awareness—that stands in opposition quite often to the cool, detached objectivity he so adamantly invoked. In the passage above, Martinson offers us a far different vision of crime and punishment than he had depicted previously and also a far different argument concerning the meaning of his work. At that point, as often happens with science, the legacy and interpretation of his work were no longer, if ever, in the hands of the author.

In Memoriam . . . The Discourse of Death in Rehabilitation

> Late one gloomy winter afternoon in 1980, New York sociologist Robert Martinson hurled himself through a ninth-floor window of his Manhattan apartment while his teen-age son looked on. Martinson had become the leading debunker of the idea that society could "rehabilitate" criminals. His melancholy suicide was to be a metaphor for what would follow in American corrections. (Jerome Miller, "The Debate on Rehabilitating Criminals: Is It True that Nothing Works?" 1989)

> He was a liberal trying to end the often barbaric U.S. practice of keeping minor offenders in jail indefinitely unless they proved they had reformed. He was appalled to see his ideas taken up by law and order hardliners. He went back to his data. He had been wrong, he announced in 1979; many rehabilitation schemes had worked. A radio interviewer asked what he thought about his "Nothing Works" theory. "I was talking shit," Martinson replied. A year later, in 1980, he threw himself from the ninth floor window of his Manhattan apartment while his teenage son looked on. (Nick Cohen and Michael Durham, "Out of Control?" 1993)

> Appalled by the way his work had been expropriated, Martinson
> tried to recant, suggesting some schemes had value after all. But
> he had lost his audience. By 1980 his work was even being used to
> justify capital punishment: if prisoners could not be rehabilitated,
> why not kill them? That winter, he jumped to his death from his
> ninth-floor New York apartment. (David Rose, "Evolution of Brit-
> ain's Jail Revolution," 2002)

Martinson revised his assertions and scientific statements a number
of times and in a number of ways through the few remaining years of
his life, but none of these publications received the attention that his
Public Interest piece achieved. In 1980, for reasons that are not clearly
documented, Martinson committed suicide. His death, as demonstrated
above, became a moment in which one of the most intimate, private,
and mysterious acts of Martinson's life was converted, much like his
earlier research, into terms with cultural significance for the study of
punishment. The debate he launched and its primary frames and questions would continue forward into the present through a discourse fundamentally bound up with the "death" of rehabilitation.[56] Out of this has
emerged one of the most profound legacies of Martinson's work: the
creation of a paradigm for saving rehabilitation, in which the study of
punishment is chronically justified through an empirical validity linked
explicitly to crime reduction and the question of what works. In this regard, Martinson opened up—and closed off very quickly—the question
of what constitutes "good" science and serves as one of criminology's
starkest reminders of the problem of its troubled communication to the
public—of the stakes of speaking as penal spectators, with unusual and
peculiar legitimacy and authority.

Reaffirming Science

> This is more than a book about punishment versus rehabilita-
> tion of criminals. It is, to be sure, the first book to defend the
> notion that Americans acted unwisely and too hastily when they
> recently exorcised rehabilitation programs from prisons. But it
> is also an essay on how social movements go awry—on the un-
> anticipated consequences of purposive social action. (Donald
> Cressey, foreword to Cullen and Gilbert's *Reaffirming Rehabilita-
> tion*, 1982)

> The question or questions that have to be asked are: "What types of knowledge are you trying to disqualify when you say that you are a science? What speaking subject, what discursive subject, what subject of experience and knowledge are you trying to minorize when you begin to say: 'I speak this discourse, I am speaking a scientific discourse, and I am a scientist.'" (Michel Foucault, *Society Must be Defended*, 2003)

Threads of Martinson's persistence—or more accurately, the emergent discourses that made up Martinson's time and work and were mobilized by his presence—are apparent across the study of punishment, and in this latter section I will trace some of those connections through three trajectories: the rise of evidence-based criminology, a new emphasis upon theorizing punishment at its foundations, and the emergence of a "new penology" alongside of larger arguments about the crisis of sovereignty and governmentality.

Martinson not only initiated a continuing dialogue over the value of rehabilitation, but his work laid the groundwork for one of the most powerful streams of contemporary criminology, evaluative research predicated upon the evidentiary and effectiveness criteria of "what works." As Francis Cullen argues, Martinson's decision to "frame" his work in the language of "effectiveness" ultimately opened up what he refers to as a "silver lining" in research possibilities by creating room for a narrow but heated debate over "the empirical issue of 'what works.'"[57] "Nothing works" could—and would—then be challenged by its own scientific standards, creating a research trajectory within criminology directed at a very specific understanding of how and why we should study punishment. The debate Martinson initiated followed a distinct formula that can be plotted through the consistent stream of studies dedicated to the problems and polemics of what works, a wave of research literature, generally framed in opposition to Martinson's findings, which has consistently developed across three decades and continues today.[58]

One of the more important methodological developments in this debate includes the rise of a key mode of investigation, the meta-analysis. The rise of meta-analysis as a statistical tool provided a means by which to take disparate studies employing different independent variables measured on different scales and create a dependent variable as a standardized measure of a general effect size. This methodological development permitted a more high-powered analysis and summary of research findings than Martinson's study afforded. Among other things, the validity and reliability of meta-analyses depend upon the kinds of studies which are included in the sample, meaning that they should all be well-designed and methodologically sound according to rigorous scientific standards. For this reason, meta-analyses privilege randomized experiments where control groups are present. Also, variations across the sample can introduce a degree of heterogeneity to the outcome, and the method, because it relies upon published studies, fundamentally skews with a preference toward statistically significant results—what's called publication bias. Given these issues, it is clear that meta-analyses do not reflect all studies published on a particular approach or issue but rather privilege a particular understanding and image of science based on rigorous empirical criteria. This trend is particularly apparent in several of the more famous dialogues on "what works" post-Martinson. Francis Cullen had been central to the development of this discourse and the "saving" of rehabilitation by way of his influential volume with Karen Gilbert in 1983, *Reaffirming Rehabilitation*, followed by a series of published studies where he collaborated with Canadian psychologists Paul Gendreau, Don Andrews, and James Bonta, producing a large set of psychological studies arguing that some positive worth remained to be found in treatment programs.[59] Another heated defense of "nothing works" by criminologist Charles Logan and Gerald Gaes of the Federal Bureau of Prisons in the early 1990s led to the following interesting assertion: "Meta-analysis of research on rehabilitation has not yet established that any particular method of treatment is significantly and reliably effective. We still do not know what 'works' in correctional treatment, *but it wouldn't matter even if we knew, because the fundamental purpose of imprisonment is not the correction but the punishment of criminal behavior*" (emphasis added).[60] Their argument importantly positions empiricism and ideology side by side and, more often than not, blurred in the practice of research and punishment. More significantly, they point beyond the contours of the "what works" debate toward a more foundational justification for corrections as punishment, a crucial turn and articulation that emphasizes much of the underlying stakes that had made what works discussions so heated—a simple cultural privileging of punitiveness over science.

In no volume of the era are these stakes more apparent than Francis Cullen's and Karen Gilbert's work, *Reaffirming Rehabilitation*, published in 1982. In the foreword to the volume, Donald Cressey poignantly points to the value of such a reaffirmation by stating that in fact, the sociology of prison had long argued that institutions which confine are fundamentally ill-adapted to positive effects on human behavior. He agrees, in fact, with Martinson's finding that rehabilitation always existed more as an ideal than a functional pragmatic product of incarceration. However, he insists that rehabilitation "'worked' nonetheless. It worked because 'treatment' came to mean 'We treat them well here.' Humanitarianism was introduced, and defended, in the name of treatment."[61] The underlying justification for the privileging of rehabilitation, regardless of its ability to meet the ends of crime control, is central to, although often muted, in the debates and emergent strategies that follow science post-Martinson. Surprisingly, pragmatically perhaps, Cressey as well mutes this foundation in his conclusion where he argues for the reintroduction of prison labor and a work ethic to correctional environments:

> It doesn't matter, really, that the financial costs of administering justice actually might not decrease as prisoners are put to work. What matters is that humanitarianism could again be made to dominate decision-making in the criminal justice process. Wardens would not be able to say, as they once did, "We treat them well here and as a result they are getting rehabilitated." But they could say—with an equal disregard for factual accuracy—"We treat them well here and as a result their work is reducing our costs." The world runs on healthy hypocrisies.[62]

The peculiarity of the study punishment is deeply bound up with something akin to "hypocrisy" —not that correctional science has been intentionally hypocritical but that it has always felt compelled to explain its existence and its relationship to the state and governance through its ability/ success to regulate crime against the ironies of the world's most conflicted, dysfunctional institution, when it would appear that most criminologists would prefer to argue for treatment, for rights, and for rehabilitation on humanitarian grounds as safeguards of American prison conditions. This is the work of punishment that underlies the call of "what works" and it is this theme that persists across Cullen and Gilbert's volume both overtly and, other times, beneath the surface of other kinds of arguments and justifications. As they state it:

> [O]ur purpose for undertaking this volume is not to provide further enlightenment either about the inadequacies of state enforced therapy or about the viability of determinate sentencing. Instead, it is quite the

opposite: to warn of the dangers of embracing a punishment philosophy and to propose that we should not reject rehabilitation but rather reaffirm a rehabilitation that is properly tempered by considerations limiting the coercive potential of the state. . . . that the goal of our criminal justice system should be to improve rather than to damage an offender, and that for society's own welfare, criminal punishment should reflect not our basest instincts (vengeance) but our most noble values. . . . Only the ideology of rehabilitation contains at its core a benevolence consistent with the tradition of liberal reformism.[63]

In an era in which the causes of crime had been framed as so deeply structural that little could be accomplished within the frames of criminology and criminal justice practice, the question increasingly emergent was less one of what works and more one of what is to be done?[64] In the absence of grand structural transformations, in the solidification of a punitive turn, in the turn from causes to pragmatics, how would science commit to the problem of punishment? For Cullen and Gilbert, reclaiming rehabilitation was a key strategy in penal politics that could only be overlooked "at a cost of considerable human misery."[65] This is the most persistent theme in the volume, one which insists that "rehabilitation is not simply an evil but a source of actual and potential good that can be abandoned only at considerable risk,"[66] the only remaining "justification of criminal sanctioning that obligates the state to care for an offender's needs or welfare,"[67] a mechanism of accountability for correctional officials, states, and democracy. Cullen and Gilbert conclude largely with a set of deeply interrelated questions bound up with how to negotiate a new mode of scientific and penal engagement. At the ends of liberal reform, how will a humanizing ideology be given voice?

Will the medium be a justice model that is rooted in despair and not optimism, that embraces punishment and not betterment, that disdains inmate needs and disadvantages in favor of a concern for sterile and limited legal rights, and whose guiding principle of reform is to have the state do less for its captives rather than more? Or will, as we fear, this vacuum remain unfilled and the liberal camp be left without an ideology that possesses the vitality—as has rehabilitation over the past 150 years—to serve as a rallying cry for or motive force behind reforms that will engender lasting humanizing changes?

If unfilled, the authors foresee a set of conservative values directed at crime control but engaged through practices and frameworks designed to encourage choosing broadly and as a society "inhumanity over humanity, injustice over justice, cruelty over kindness, vengeance over mercy, insensitivity over caring, despair over hope," leaving those most directly impacted by crime—victims—with little recourse to anything less than vengeance. In the end, they not only leave us with difficult, ethical choices about science as penal spectators, but even more significantly, demonstrate an important obligation and cultural labor in that role as scientists.

Whether Americans were through with rehabilitation or not, prisons were on the verge of massive, exponential population increases. It is important to consider how this debate in many ways hinged—and continues to center itself upon—a decision about the cultural parameters of social justice. Post-Martinson some of the most significant studies, Supreme Court decisions, and policy shifts have revolved around the common acknowledgment that the criminal justice system cannot tackle social structure, that "root" causes are out of reach, and that crime and punishment are phenomena which spiral through long, interconnected chains of social problems and complex, dysfunctional institutions. Such tactics are evident in Morris and Tonry's theory on the interchangeability of intermediate punishments, where they argue "the criminal law cannot rectify social inequalities; those inequalities will inexorably infect rational punishment policies," a situation, they add, which "leaves an uneasy sense of moral imbalance and forces us to the consideration of how deserved punishments can operate fairly in a world of social inequality."[68] Cullen and Gilbert argue as well near the end of their volume that "true criminal justice ultimately awaits true social justice. . . . This might strike some as a pessimistic thought, but it is also an appropriately sobering one."[69] The dilemma such a shift poses for the criminologist is where to anchor one's central questions, of how to conduct research in a meaningful way, and of how one is to approach pessimism, or more appropriately, the fundamental social tragedies and pains which undergird punishment. In short, the question is one of how culturally we will construct science and be attentive to those constructions as such, thereby lending them alterability. In the midst of such confusion, Cullen and Gilbert point to what future work and a more complex theorizing of punishment would insist upon, that the lines which distinguish rehabilitation and retribution were elusive and not easily harnessed.

By 2004, in the Presidential Address to the American Society of Criminology, then President Francis Cullen titled his speech, "The Twelve People Who Saved Rehabilitation: How the Science of Criminology Made a Difference," and argued that what was needed was "a vibrant movement to reaffirm rehabilitation and to implement programs based on the principles of effective intervention."[70] As Cullen prefaces the talk in his published abstract:

> I contend that the saving of rehabilitation was a contingent reality that emerged due to the efforts of a small group of loosely coupled research criminologists. These scholars rejected the "nothing works" professional ideology and instead used rigorous science to show that popular punitive interventions were ineffective, that offenders were not beyond redemption, and that treatment programs rooted in criminological knowledge were capable of meaningfully reducing recidivism. Their story is a reminder that, under certain conditions, the science of criminology is capable of making an important difference in the correctional enterprise, if not far beyond.[71]

This turn by science toward humanization is a critical and cultural one, reflective once again of that peculiarity that defines the study of punishment. As Cullen goes on to argue, there was something to the kind of science that was being done which led to historical contingencies in their favor: "They were skilled scientists, both theoretically and empirically. Using different techniques, they were able to marshal substantial data—rooted in sound criminological understandings of crime—that showed the limits of punishment and the poverty of the view that 'nothing works' to change offenders."[72] In short, what they produced was "good" science. For Cullen, ultimately that involves an effort to be "criminologically relevant,"[73] empirically rigorous, accessible in order to "increase the chances that criminology will make a difference."[74]

Such a discourse reflects the substantive way in which debates about the value of rehabilitation and the notion of what works marked a turn toward applied, evaluative research; the possibility of humanizing increasingly isolated prison systems with unprecedented exclusionary technologies; and the mapping of collateral consequences of mass incarceration. Such a convergence in science intersects importantly with notions of a new penology and the complex workings of a shift toward governing at

a distance. Here, criminology reflects the tensions of its foundational—
and perhaps inevitable—collusions with the state in any effort to garner
research funding or impact public policy and bridge knowledge, a tension
that is increasingly built into the socialization processes of criminal justice professionals and academics. Such critiques also mark the contours
of a continuing dialogue over what it means culturally to make a genuine
effort at institutional change and social transformation.

Evidence-based Research

> In criminology, cognitive passion used to be directed towards
> causation. To be sure, the quest was utilitarian (the correctional
> attitude was to find out the causes of crime in order to do some-
> thing about it). But appreciation was also possible: it once seemed
> intellectually interesting to know why people committed crime.
> Now the Holy Grail of causation has been displaced by the Holy
> Grail of evaluation. Disillusioned with basic research and the quest
> for root causes, prepared to settle for limited intellectual horizons
> and constrained by the demands of funding agencies, criminolo-
> gists started a decade ago asking the question, What works? As we
> saw when considering "new behaviourism," the trend was to leave
> behind conventional causal questions and move in an even more
> explicitly technicist and correctional direction. (Stanley Cohen,
> *Visions of Social Control,* 1985)

> Virtually every article on correctional rehabilitation begins by
> reviewing the demise of the "nothing works" philosophy purport-
> edly ushered in by Martinson (1974). The latent message to other
> researches is unmistakable: Question the value of offender reha-
> bilitation and risk similar vilification for apostasy. Being branded
> with the "Scarlet M" (for Martinson) can have serious repercus-
> sions for one's professional reputation and ability to obtain grant
> funding or gainful employment. (Douglas B. Marlowe, "When
> 'What Works' Never Did: Dodging the 'Scarlet M' in Correctional
> Rehabilitation," 2006)

The debate about what works in the study of punishment has led to important trends broadly in criminology, including the rise of evidence-based
research. This vision of science rises specifically out of a commitment to

a more rigorous and empirical investigation directed at a concerted effort to move knowledge into practice. In this manner, it is very much a legacy of Martinson's watershed publication. It reflects a public turn in the commission of criminology, specifically one in which the social scientist enters into a direct dialogue with professionals, politicians, and policy makers—in a sense, a public criminology. In criminology, this movement has most often occurred in a manner where the scientist as expert takes on the responsibilities of validating policy and monitoring government decision-making in a direct and overt effort to make policy makers more responsible for political choices about crime policy. As such, it is an effort in many ways to speak truth to power while rebuilding a legitimate role for penal science and criminology more broadly, again a moment in which a semiotic alignment of cultural values is pursued. It is importantly grounded in a fundamental optimism about the power of research to lay out a clear vision for practice and the possibility of social change. Such a cultural vision of science is one that is fundamentally framed through a promise of utility and certainty (where crime control, largely as crime prevention, remains a viable end for criminology).

Evidence-based research practices, borrowing from trends in other fields, particularly medicine, are built upon ethical and institutional motives to move the scientific method and research findings into the culture of professional settings through evaluation; the creation of guidelines; distribution to media, policy, and legislative sources; the construction of crime information databases; and a newfound ability to capture and record the daily discretionary acts of justice in a systematic way. Lawrence Sherman has referred to the role of the criminologist in such a paradigm shift as the "evidence cop," whose commitments are directed toward scientific evidence in a manner that moves practice beyond "local custom, opinions, theories, and subjective impressions" and away from "the mythic power of subjective and unstructured wisdom."[75] Proactive, preventative, with unprecedented information processing possibilities in problem-solving and community contexts, evidence-based research holds out the promise of monitoring outputs and outcomes at all levels of justice organization. As Sherman puts it:

> For every claim that X causes Y, evidence-based thinking asks only "what is the evidence?" and not "who says so?" The answer can then be graded from weak to strong based on standard rules of scientific interference. A before-after comparison is stronger than a simultaneous correlation,

and a randomized controlled test is stronger than a longitudinal cohort analysis. Strong evidence trumps weak, irrespective of how articulate or charismatic the person presenting the evidence may be. In this respect, evidence-based practice is no different from the basic epistemology of science.[76]

For these reasons, Sherman argues, evidence-based research can accommodate any management structure or paradigm as policing as science is solely present to evaluate "what works, and how we know what works," to "[support], rather than [replace], other paradigms for doing police work."[77] Significantly, Sherman marks part of the justification for this turn in the obstacles such research must anticipate: "Applying it to policing predictably creates cultural wars over important values: autonomy, accountability, wisdom, and the philosophy of knowledge. To the extent that the values of the larger culture show decreasing respect for rules, expertise and authority derived from printed words . . . , evidence-based policing will face many obstacles to implementation within policing."[78]

Sherman's most influential what works study, the voluminous meta-analysis *Preventing Crime: What Works, What Doesn't, What's Promising*, conducted at the request of U.S. Congress and released in 1997, analyzes hundreds of crime prevention programs, gang violence prevention, community-based mentoring programs, after-school programs, family- and school-based programs, community policing initiatives like neighborhood watches, drug treatment interventions, and a variety of popular, "get tough" programs like boot camps, home confinement, electronic monitoring. Importantly, the study found little impact and evidence to support popular programs like boot camps and midnight basketball. More significantly, Sherman claimed, once again, that there was simply not enough rigorous science taking place in criminology to evaluate what works in crime prevention.

In corrections, where prison populations and state budgets have expanded exponentially, evidence-based work is bound up not simply with the impact of programs upon criminal behavior but the effectiveness of funds spent and larger sets of cost-benefit analyses. Housed under a what works discourse, evidence-based corrections is largely broken into two types of research: (1) basic research which "examines what works best when implemented properly under controlled conditions" and (2) outcome research which "examines the results each individual program, agency, or facility is achieving."[79] This kind of research has focused on juvenile correctional facilities, boot camps, prisoner reentry, broader criminological interventions, supermax, etc., and has often been directed oppositionally, arguing against the implementation of particular kinds of popular programs, including boot camps and supermax confinement. What works now is directed at methodologies used to identify effectiveness and in degrees and gradations: what doesn't work, what is promising, what works, and what is unknown, all in an effort to guide policy and practice strategically. This movement as well has led to fundamental reorientations in how universities, professional organizations, and international collaborations prioritize criminological questions and train future researchers.[80]

In this regard, science is not simply about understanding the world around us but is integral in its governance. Out of such an arrangement, complex schemes of negotiation emerge in the now dependent relationships which structure scientific expertise, political intent, and public will. Contemporary critiques of what works and evidence-based discourses have pointed to the manner in which science becomes susceptible to policy pressures and political values.[81] As Tim Hope writes, such research relies upon an "Enlightenment view of science: specifically that the method of scientific reasoning itself is *infallible* as a method for testing the validity of truth-claims; that there is a unitary methodology of science, which has a *monopoly* on all truth-claims that wish to invoke scientific authority, and that scientifically validated knowledge is *superior* to other sources as a guide to progress."[82] What is produced in this exchange is most likely less of a science and more like institutional negotiations over the meanings of science in the midst of complex and often conflicting interests. Borrowing from Ulrich Beck's notion of an emergent scientized consciousness with a high level of reflexivity, Hope argues: "Contrary to the aspiration of the primary scientific ideal, reflexive scientization emerges not to make the world simpler and easier to understand but as a tool to help govern a complex society, whose complexity is continuously expanding as a result of the application of science itself to social problems. The emergence of evidence-based policy making and new forms of policy-oriented science (like the mode of 'crime science' described here), is not a coincidence— each supports the other symbiotically in the construction of political programmes . . . and is likely to be on the look out for ideas, evidence, even legitimacy, to substantiate its promise."[83] These kinds of contexts are to some degree simply a part of how public science is done. In high-crime societies like the United States, where crime and punishment are so rigidly politicized, these meanings are potentially more volatile and the contribution of a depoliticized science that is solely "evidence-based" potentially problematic—especially if effective science or "scientific merit" is less important in shaping public discourse than science which achieves political endorsement, national funding, and media coverage, outside of theoretical contribution and solely on the basis of types of questions asked. In this realm of "scientized consciousness," the work of punishment becomes even more complex and culturally contingent. As Ulrich Beck argues in his theorizations of risk society, and as the legacy of Robert Martinson reminds us, the more deeply science comes to predominate, the more fallible and responsible for its own claims—and disasters—it becomes.

Evidence-based what works discourse has a complex double-edged quality to it. As science in action, its social, cultural, and political uses aren't controlled or predictable with any degree of certainty. The new penology marks the more problematic aspects of such directions. Centered in correctional managerialism, actuarial justice, and the privileging of custody, the discourses, objectives, and techniques of the new penology share key elements with what works models. Grounded similarly in the crisis of the state, a heightened perception of high crime against the futility of punishment, and a hardening of popular attitudes toward criminals, both discourses speak to the limits of science. However, the new penology is marked by an expansion and elaboration of exclusionary tactics through the convergence of scientific and bureaucratic mechanisms as managerial strategies, practiced and implemented through new technological possibilities in the realm of empirical classification and social control. More significantly, the new penology, through such public and private convergences, extends outward into the production of identities and subjectivities well beyond crime across the social fabric—governance at a distance and through crime.[84] Such a perspective relates specifically to the despair and futility of nothing works in that, as an actuarial objective, it "does not offer an answer to this perceived hopelessness. Instead, it takes for granted that no answer exists, and offers the placating alternative of at least managing this hopelessness in a less burdensome and more efficient fashion . . . a chance to succeed, although only through a redefinition of goals."[85] The linkages between what works discourses and the new penology are complex, but importantly, many of the aims, methods, and techniques of evidence-based research are potentially and aptly directed at new penology objectives with their privileging of "techniques for identifying, classifying and managing groups assorted by levels of dangerousness."

In such worlds, science can collide again with familiar terms in a way that "takes crime for granted . . . accepts deviance as normal . . . is skeptical that liberal interventionist crime control strategies do or can make a difference. Thus its aim is not to intervene in individuals' lives for the purpose of ascertaining responsibility, making the guilty 'pay for their crime' or changing them. Rather it seeks to regulate groups as part of a strategy of managing danger."[86]

In keeping with new penology claims, much of the contemporary study of punishment has concerned itself with the absence of social vision and meta-narratives that might anchor the practice of punishment in democratic, humane discussions. As Adrian Cherney argues, "Any form of social policy hinges on more than a rational analysis of 'what works.' Instituting change in how society responds to social problems depends also on the ability to articulate a vision—a public ideal around which reform can be mobilized."[87] The pragmatics of what works discourse is perfectly understandable, even admirable, but to pursue such a vision of science without reflexively factoring in the symbolic, political, in short, cultural aspects of its production is to operate in a nonexistent vacuum. Or, as Ian Loader positions it, a scientific consciousness emerges in "the reconstitution of a technocratic, expert-driven rationalization aimed at stripping crime of its dramatic emotionality so as to render it susceptible to scientific intervention and control."[88] In the turn to a deeper theorization of punishment, it has become evident precisely how vast and fundamental a role politics, symbolism, emotion, and culture play in laying out the most fundamental aspects of punishment's practice. As the foundations of punishment, its functions, and its effects continue to be elaborated—as we explore the ways in which its practice and policies carry a fundamental sociopolitical volatility and contradiction—the question of "what works" perhaps remains premature. Perhaps there is a role for scientists as well in communicating to professionals, politicians, and the public the complexity of punishment and the peculiarity of a science that takes punishment as its object. For Hannah Arendt, the trouble with the rise of experts is "not that they are cold-blooded enough to 'think the unthinkable,' but that they do not *think*," or at least think about how they think, and the "purely speculative character of the whole enterprise is forgotten."[89]

In the end, it is difficult to underestimate the impact of "what works" not simply upon the study and practice of punishment but upon the culture and practice of criminology broadly, including the creation of policy, the training of future experts, the formation of expert advisory boards across the globe, and the reworking of state-criminology relations and alliances. The studies that derive out of this debate identify themselves as directed toward policy and political affirmations—cues to the appropriate manner in which penality should be organized, implemented, and to what ends. If the rehabilitative/punishment debate provides any sort of consensus, it is found in the continued intellectual and professional perseverance within corrections toward "what works."

> On close inspection neither alliance nor enmity is quite as simple as it seems, and individuals can almost always tell more than one story, sometimes contradictory, about themselves. Failures of imagination, then, may be failures to see how many imaginations are at play and how they might, in fact, "struggle it out," for if we cannot escape our history, we might at least make better use of it. I am not willing to give up the hope suggested by these efforts. They represent the possibility that we might be able to imagine and work for something else, to interrupt the terms we have been given. Surely that imagining—which both uses and pushes against the frameworks we already have—is the only way that these places and those consigned to live and work in them can be thought otherwise.[90]

Robert Martinson's work and place in the politics surrounding rehabilitation are crucial to any understanding not only of the intellectual debates and scholarship surrounding punishment during that period and forward but of the role of culture and spectatorship more broadly in science. Criminologists since that moment routinely employ his name as a watershed mark that maps how both alliances and fragmentations emerged in the 1970s "post-Martinson." His name remains central to intellectual assumptions of the cultural life of the time, a turning point in the rise of conservative law and order politics, a media figure/celebrity, and a dreaded harbinger of punishment to come. Finally, certainly Martinson remains pivotal in understanding that as late as the 1970s, those who study punishment were struggling with their identity as scientists, out of which emerges a legacy of discourse built around the practical but also instrumentalist and technical question of "what works," an assertion of the usability of science in policy and consequently a stake for credibility and legitimacy by penal scholars. These kinds of rhetorical slogans and the way they embody particular ideologies are crucial not simply in understanding the metaphors by which we govern and do science but in understanding also how we break out of them—a possibility that is distinctly linked to why we might want to insist upon a routine reflexive self-examination of scientists as cultural actors and penal spectators.

For example, let us assume, as impossible as it is and should be in the production of any science, that criminology achieves a for-once-and-for-all-readily-agreed-upon consensus that, scientifically, rehabilitation *does not* work. And by this, I mean that there are no programs or interventions in prisons and correctional settings that clearly promise to reduce recidivism or positively change human behavior—and to render our situation more dystopic, let us assume there never will be—that nothing will ever work. Imagine, as did Donald Clemmer, Gresham Sykes, Erving Goffman, and Michel Foucault, that the sociology of punishment has proven the prison is structurally predisposed to creating tensions and hierarchies that will always fundamentally distort efforts to create healthy patterns of decision making and will always divest, rather than invest, individuals with social skills and capital. Let us assume, somewhat differently, that Martinson was right and that "there is a more radical flaw in our present strategies—that education at its best, or that psychotherapy at its best, cannot overcome, or even appreciably reduce, the powerful tendency for offenders to continue in criminal behavior."[91] Let us assume that out of this discovery comes a massive rise in imprisonment with technologies capable of a kind of human exclusion that has no precedent. Let us assume the worst: that our science fails us. Then what? Social scientists of punishment would once again be forced to ask themselves who they are, what it is that they do, and, most importantly, why. I believe that even in the imagined absence of scientific evidence, caught between spectatorship or engagement, passively observing or witnessing, criminologists would—and must—hold forth that there are better ways to respond to criminals, to imagine alternative foundations for social action and change, including the denial of prisons and death houses, through strategies built upon all the complexities of human rights, democracy, and the constant assertion that the science of punishment is always more than a well-intended, utilitarian dream of crime control and social order. This is where the work of punishment for scientists begins—and, perhaps someday, ends. Until then, the cultural lenses and rhetorical tropes through which we conduct our craft will continue to have powerfully predictable—and, Martinson might tell us, unpredictable—shaping power.

7

Prison Otherwise
Cultural Meanings beyond Punishment

> Many years ago Durkheim claimed that society could not only understand but also reconstitute itself through its collective representations. If he is correct, as I have been arguing, then coming to terms with the symbolic logics of culture should be the first and not the last step in any analysis and reform of criminal justice.
>
> —Philip Smith, *Punishment and Culture*, 2008

> In the late modern world, then, the fundamental subject matter of criminology—crime and its causes, crime control, fear of crime, policing, punishment—is recast. Now, fear of crime may well emerge from mediated representation, punitive attitudes from social and personal precariousness. . . . A new sort of criminology will be needed.
>
> —Jeff Ferrell, Keith Hayward, and Jock Young,
> *Cultural Criminology: An Invitation*, 2008

I began this volume with a discussion of my own introduction to incarceration in the United States. It was during those first trips to prison in graduate school as an instructor and a tourist when a tension in my own relationship to punishment materialized. Caught between passivity and engagement, lacking the cultural vocabularies and political will to interrogate that tension, penal spectators often miss the ways in which their struggles with how to look and act meaningfully in proximity to pain are submerged. Punishment, I have argued, is a crucial testing ground and resource for understanding our relationship to that pain. Across this volume, I point to some of the ways in which that test and the tensions of cultural response materialize. They are, more often than not, moments that we rarely think through as settings where our own relationships to the practice of punishment emerge. And yet, they are sites in which the meanings of punishment proliferate and run up against one another, inflecting the tone and nature of our relationships to exclusion, pain, and suffering. As penal spectators, we watch across vast mediascapes where penality flourishes explicitly and implicitly in narratives and commentaries structured through penal correlates of prison, surveillance, judgment, and accusation. We visit death camps, assassination sites, crime scenes, battle grounds, war zones, third world poverty, and defunct prisons. We look to prisons in distant locations in the context of wars against terror and vicariously explore the meanings and limits of acts rendered both visible and invisible within them. We hear about and produce criminological and sociolegal studies which attempt to intervene and speak back to torture, war prisons, and mass incarceration but rarely speak self-reflexively of our own places in that dialogue and in proximity to pain. In this way, we live our everyday lives amid complex, but often fleeting, anecdotal appearances of the penal, even as punishment emerges as a structuring force in globalizing frameworks. In these contexts, we could benefit profoundly from a structure of critique, a framework from which to challenge our distanced selves in relation to our own place in punishment.

In this concluding chapter, I explore this possibility while revisiting the key cases, concerns, and emergent themes in this volume. This effort begins with an assessment of the conditions under which the cultural work of punishment so often fails. Second, in an effort to carve out space for alternative discourse and practices, I discuss some preliminary starting points where a new kind of work and subject position in relationship to punishment might begin. In this pursuit, I identify what I consider to be some key exemplars and forces for change. In all of this, I argue that cultural analysis has a special role in the transformation of the passivity of penal spectatorship to an informed and engaged mode of citizenship, which requires a critical engagement with the work of punishment. The chronology of chapters in this volume has reflected something of the shape and aims of this final chapter. Beginning with cultural meanings and images of punishment we are most likely to share, those that circulate and are visualized daily in mass media, we then moved into settings that are more selective and challenging in their relationship to spectatorship. Prison tours represent important ways in which to bring citizens into contact with their penal history and the challenges of punishment in late modernity. However, cultural imaginaries run rampant in the newly opened spaces of the prison, where visitors play a powerful consumer role, shaping tours around the thrills and spectacle of punishment as opposed to its empirical realities. The international scandals of U.S. war prisons further problematize the notion of penal spectatorship, leaving us in unstable territory on multiple levels amid a new and complex legal architecture where ordinary American actors engage in the most egregious act of spectatorship—torture. The chapter on prison science reflects a transitional point, marking the destructiveness of spectatorship in expertise but also its possibility as a powerful arbiter in reshaping the work of punishment and our penal future. This final chapter is, in that spirit, very much directed at encouraging the pursuit and cultivation of a new and more radical set of theoretical questions, empirical methods, and cultural imaginaries for that future. Such work begins precisely where our cultural efforts in the project of punishment have failed.

How the Work of Punishment Fails

The failure of punishment as a cultural practice and the triumphant rise of punitiveness above other kinds of cultural meanings are implied in the very scale of punishment in the United States, marked by a passive national commitment to mass incarceration and the death penalty over alternative modes of accountability. The preservation of humaneness in the project of punishment depends upon a self-conscious social awareness of its limits and the idea that, rationally, its invocation and practice are among the most tragic of social processes, always last resorts. Contemporary penal patterns in the United States explicitly deny this post-Enlightenment framework, leaving penal spectatorship a fleeting marker of a weakened civic relationship and proximity to punishment. There are, in this sense, specific sets of cultural conditions which facilitate this failure and, across this volume, each of the cases examined share a set of characteristic features. These include such dimensions as: a distinct social distance from punishment by a privileged and politically powerful group of citizens; a convergence of punishment with an emotive response to the insecurity and uncertainty of late modernity, defined by a passive fear, anger, and blame; the normalization of penal excess and the failure of penal restraint; a majoritarian sense of legitimacy and authority derived from cultural play with penal judgment; and finally, a dangerous potentiality of punishment, foreshadowed in each of these cases.

The most important prerequisite for the failure of the work of punishment is social distance. Penal iconography is given an incredibly privileged and salient role in the formation of cultural understandings about punishment, particularly for citizens who remain fundamentally distanced from the day-to-day practice of punishment. Films, television, games, and the Internet often serve as our first access points and cultural resources from which to make sense of punishment and its proper place in the social order. Punishment remains a site of discursive fascination and proliferation across media genres and platforms precisely because of its distance and invisibility. The prison tour, even as it brings visitors into contact with the original architecture and machinery of the penitentiary, acts carefully to distance us as outsiders in its privileging of cultural associations and stereotypical images of criminals over a more thoughtful structure which links history with the unprecedented contemporary dimensions and sociology of imprisonment. Similarly, the scandalous photos of Abu Ghraib were shocking in part due to the privilege of distance, as these were acts and practices that occurred across American war prisons, had institutional roots at home in domestic efforts at isolation like supermax, and were juridical outcomes of the pursuit of a new legal architecture in the war on terror which openly privileged exception and executive power.

In each of these cases, distance affords spectators a space in which they need not do many things, including engage the complexities, contradictions, and tragic qualities of punishment nor reflect upon their own role in its formation. This is particularly critical because, at such a distance, direct deliberation and interrogation of punishment rarely materialize in the everyday life of the spectator. Rather, punishment circulates as a cultural distraction or social oddity. Efforts to counter such distance and the mythologies which derive from it are examined closely in the volume's final case study in relation to the prison scientist. Here, it is the criminologist who speaks most directly back to those myths but must necessarily engage in a careful form of auto-critique in order not to replicate or exacerbate the very penal conditions she seeks to map and change. Importantly, this aggravation and intensification of punishment by experts depends as well upon a false sense of distance from the pain of punishment, most often in the form of a detached objectivity that allows professionals, politicians, and citizens alike to deny the painful foundations of punishment. Methodological and theoretical distance from the violence of punishment thus plays a profound role in diluting efforts to limit and redirect punitive tendencies, instead framing "what works" around instrumentalist concerns that deny the vastly symbolic and volatile role punishment plays across culture.

This distance, of course, is an energetic structuring force which lends the prison a mystical quality, further feeding the reproduction and growth of cultural fantasy. This voyeuristic fascination with the spectacle of imprisonment brings many visitors to the gates of defunct prisons, now open for tours. Similarly, prison films and documentaries merge generic conventions and fantasies of imprisonment, privileging in fictional and nonfictional contexts cultural stereotypes centered upon brutality, sex, and the thrill of escape. As Philip Smith carefully demonstrates, efforts at bureaucratic closure and restrictions in accessing punishment have in fact made the prison's symbolism via fantasy more vigorously attractive.[1] A powerful way in which to alter these imaginaries is through direct engagements with punishment and the punished via critically constructed encounters which rigorously emphasize commonality as opposed to difference and the tragic mundaneness of punishment over its spectacle. Beyond direct encounters with punishment, building the problem of pain and its infliction more transparently and reflexively into the very institutions that have concealed its presence—law, criminal justice, academe, the state—represents a fundamental way in which to restructure penality in everyday life, all measures which will be discussed in greater depth in the second half of this chapter.

This reconstruction must occur against an intensely difficult and complex set of late modern conditions, many of which invoke the very emotions, reactions, and subjectivities which lend punishment its distinct volatility. Late modernity is defined by rapid and radical global changes in technology, economy, and the shifting political boundaries and sovereignty of nation-states, all of which occurs against the backdrop of burgeoning factions of collective violence deriving from deeply riven and increasingly emergent structural inequalities. In such contexts, increasing feelings of uncertainty and anxiety make recourse to punishment and exclusion highly seductive possibilities. It is this reactive emotionality against the uncertainty of late modernity which marks the second of conditions shared across our case studies and which, particularly in its disguise as a "righteous anger," captivating fear, or essentializing judgment, we must seek to moderate more deliberately amid all the insecurities of late modern life. This convergence of fear and anger is particularly treacherous in its creation of pathways toward an exclusionary vindictiveness which in turn reflects the very precariousness of what it means to count or be included in late modernity.[2] In short, as Ferrell, Hayward, and Young insist below, it is the very fragility of inclusion itself—for everyone—that deepens the attraction to exclusion.

> The profoundly precarious position of most of those "included" in late modern society in turn spawns anger, vindictiveness, and a taste for exclusion. From this precarious social perch, it can all too easily seem that the underclass unfairly live on our taxes and commit predatory crime against *us*. It can seem that *we* are afflicted by our own hard work and decency, while *they* are free to hang about and pursue pleasure. It can seem that they are all we are not, are not restrained by the same late modern inequities as we are.[3]

Distortions of the structural forces that constrain us all lend themselves to the frameworks of blame and accusation which have always attended punitiveness. In late modernity, this constellation of interactions and social forces reflects a new and fundamental set of social facts we will not soon evade. Amid such conditions, we must choose how to live, and one of the most convenient emotive passages through such a context is a distanced but impulsive and irrational anger, built upon fear or sheer passivity, which asserts identity and rights claims through an exclusion of others. Here, certain subjectivities loom more readily than others, as Ian Loader and Neil Walker elaborate:

> Individuals who live, objectively or subjectively, in a state of anxiety do not make good democratic citizens. . . . Fearful citizens tend to be inattentive to, unconcerned about, even enthusiasts for, the erosion of basic freedoms. They often lack openness or sympathy towards others, especially those they apprehend as posing a danger to them. They privilege the known over the unknown, us over them, here over there. They often retreat from public life, seeking refuge in private security "solutions" while at the same time screaming anxiously and angrily from the sidelines for the firm hand of authority—for tough "security" measures against crime, or disorder, or terror. Prolonged episodes of violence, in particular, can erode or destroy people's will and capacity to exercise political judgement and act in solidarity with others . . . Fear, in all these ways, is the breeding ground, as well as the stock-in-trade, of authoritarian, uncivil government.[4]

Throughout this volume, fear and passive anger coupled with blame have been fast friends to punitiveness, flourishing through distance. Such forces materialize in the propensity to pounce on wounded or vulnerable individuals (epitomized in the photographs at Abu Ghraib) and the leap to inflict pain without allegation, oversight, investigation, or evidence of actual misconduct (embodied in the very legal structure of new war prisons and the war on terror). Such formations take shape as well in the accusational frameworks of crime news commentary, the overworked imaginings of violence and predatoriness in representations and tours of prisons, and the irritation and sense of futility, however comprehensible, of crime experts with "failed" efforts to get at the roots of crime or rehabilitation, hallmarks of the birth of "law and order" societies. In such frameworks, exacerbated by distance, there is little room for thoughtful and judicious deliberation, reasoned debate, or compassion. It will require a new kind of concerted, deliberate civic and intellectual work to bring such voices back.

This merging of insecurity and anger is the subject of much commentary in late modernity, positioned, as discussed in this volume's chapter on theory, importantly across a continuum of social violence. Arjun Appadurai refers to it as a "surplus of rage":

> The large-scale violence of the 1990s appears to be typically accompanied by a surplus of rage, an excess of hatred that produces untold forms of degradation and violation, both to the body and the being of the victim: maimed and tortured bodies, burned and raped persons, disemboweled women, hacked and amputated children, sexualized humiliation of every type. What are we to do with this surplus, which has frequently been enacted in public actions, among friends and neighbors, and is no longer conducted in the covert ways in which the degradation of group warfare used to occur in the past?[5]

In his larger work, Appadurai attributes many critical qualities to this kind of violence, but perhaps most interesting in relationship to our case is that such violence no longer requires concealment but is comfortable in its forthrightness, echoing Garland's findings on the deep, visible cultural support for public torture lynchings in the United States. As we saw at Abu Ghraib, American soldiers were not simply caught engaging in torture but carelessly, jokingly, and deliberately recording and distributing those images with a clear lack of reservation or reluctance in the infliction of pain or their role in its production. The Bush administration has been forthright, if not celebratory, in its unabashed efforts to expand executive power and open up new penal spaces beyond constitutional and international law. The overt ways in which crass consumption underpins prison tourism and the overtly voyeuristic uses of images of prison life in efforts to attain high levels of ratings and media viewership indicate something profoundly disconcerting about contemporary limits to punishment. In fact, any efforts at cultural justifications of punishment or penal restraint are conspicuously absent, replaced by normalized narratives and images of excess. The normalization of this violence is demonstrated in the sheer extensionality of penality across social life in a manner that is hardly remarked upon.

What is peculiarly striking in our map of penal spectatorship is the manner in which a particular way of looking at and understanding punishment is taken for granted. In its most dangerous manifestations, spectatorship normalizes what should be abhorred. Even within intellectual and scientific enterprise, the pain of punishment is often muted and its gravity diluted. At the heart of punishment is always the deliberate infliction of pain on another—a violation that, ironically, may be but is not always at the core of crime itself. Few scholars of punishment have given this foundational point its due, a social fact that reveals punishment is fundamentally a moral problem, aggravated always in its intent. In the face of such ironies, democracy at best can engage in this project thoughtfully, reluctantly, and with a leniency that reflects an understanding of the complex origins of violence. Instead, contemporary punishment is a practice marked by excess, indicative of the ironies of modernity, including the exaggeration of the prevalence of civilized sensibilities in modern life. In increasingly global contexts, where new interdependencies and the reduction of social distance are one set of outcomes, another set includes the devolution of social relationships. Penal scholar John Pratt argues that alongside of the rationalization of punishment we have also witnessed the resurgence of "emotive and ostentatious punishment," where "decivilizing effects" occur.[6] Against the weakening of the sovereign state, as risk and danger become mass mediated hallmarks of everyday life, insecurities and intolerance take on new potential, with myth and fantasy sometimes privileged above reason and objectivity—a tension we have seen played out repeatedly across our cases. Penal excesses then rise up not as anomalies but as carefully conditioned sets of historical outcomes.

Because punishment tends to be majoritarian, it brings with it a surplus of authority. As discussed in the introduction of this volume, a large and important group of Americans are dramatically impacted by the experience of punishment. These are communities defined by race and class, marginalized and minoritized within the larger social order. As a majoritarian way of looking, penal spectatorship is necessarily directed at minorities and thereby grounded dangerously in democratic principles. As Appadurai argues, such identities may be described as majoritarian not simply because they are larger in number but because they are efforts to close disturbing gaps, to control, assert sovereignty and superiority, and thus represent an "anxiety of incompleteness."[7] This subject position is inevitably about complex intersections between distant events and proximate fears, sparked by uncertainty and mediated images and experiences. Amid such insecurities, observers pursue meaning, superiority, distinction, and certainty through the segregation and exclusion of others. Consequently, each of the sites this volume examines carries with it evidence of an experience of authority and legitimacy which derives from and depends upon majoritarian spectatorship and judgment. Angry news commentators who speak for the crime victim, the citizen who considers herself democratically informed by simply being a regular viewer of prison documentaries, the tour guide who reconstructs the spectacle of violence to titillate consumer-citizens all belie contests over identity and a vicarious pleasure in the judgment of others who can be conveniently distinguished from ourselves. Because legitimacy has historically depended upon penal restraint and a deliberate rationalizing of state violence through the rule of law, such a shift toward a new and unfettered penal judgment, grounded in cultural imaginaries, is particularly insidious.

Finally, each of these cases is linked together by way of a deep and extensive potentiality centered upon how each foreshadows not simply particular trajectories in the practice of punishment but also the ways in which those trajectories are bound up with larger responses to pain and human suffering. Each maps how extensive, dangerous, and yet unremarked upon are our relationships to punishment and the infliction of pain upon each other. Acting as harbingers and portents, they reflect dangerous convergences that we must work to maintain within the line of vision, even as they recede or are normalized. Such work will require the reconstruction of the fundamental values of democracy, its checks and balances, its fundamental commitments to the protection of minorities (as opposed to majorities), to offset such normalized excesses and invisible convergences in penality. Each of these sites provides a valuable window into the nature of penal potentiality. Each, as a space in process, reflects cultural efforts to make passive spaces provocative, to invoke penality for complex reasons, ranging from consumption to preservation to critique to war. Each is culturally seductive in its imagining, carrying with it a volatile way of looking that is not clearly anchored in the painful foundations of punishment. More significantly, in a contemporary framework, much of this cultural participation occurs against the absence of the punished and, more insidiously, the absence of any perception of a need or necessity to ground punishment in relation to those who experience it. Here, frameworks of judgment, accusation, and blame assume an aloof legitimacy and authority that prohibits deliberation or discussion and instead encourages discursive foreclosure. Even prison science, whose spectatorship is grounded in an effort to speak back to these complex dimensions, is a story at best of a struggle (and often a failed one) to speak truth to power and with authority in a manner that alters contemporary penal trajectories. In this way, ultimately, each of these sites expresses an emergent cultural propensity, one in which the most punitive aspects of punishment are privileged in the cultural imaginary and where political power, in the rise of the executive, the victim, and new categories of war, detention, and terror, finds fuel in the abstract imagining of a distant other.

Such conditions necessitate a deeper interrogation of the terms that drive us when our deepest, harshest invocations of passion and rage at another surface and why that response is so often designed through frameworks of punitiveness and retribution. In a culture that mass incarcerates, such outrage and accusation deserves a rich sociological context. Mass incarceration, as coined and described by David Garland, implies two things fundamentally: a rate of imprisonment that contrasts sharply with historical and comparative norms for similar societies, and a demographic concentration of imprisonment which results in the systematic imprisonment of entire groups of the broader population. Punishment on such a scale and with such effects strictly defies the cultural imaginary which invokes individualized, anecdotal cases of violence as a foundation for punitiveness. Within such a context, we must better justify and explain why, even in the most extreme cases, we ought to struggle to retain the humanity of individuals, others as well as ourselves, against such punitive proclivities. This framework must develop against punishment because penality will never assist us in the development of such a reflexivity. Because of its distinct relationship to the infliction of pain, punishment is, in fact, foundationally about denying this very structure in its invocation. In this way, it acts always as a site for easy justification—through naturalized assumptions of deterrence, desert, incapacitation, or revenge. To invoke Ignatieff, for penal spectators, punishment is not about the strangers at our door but about the strangers who have broken through our neighbor's door, whom we imagine at our own door, violating our most intimate, sacred spaces through our own fictive potentiality as victims. In a penal system where half the prisoners are nonviolent, where the disproportional majority are African American, where the mentally ill are now concentrated in a manner without precedent, outrage at imagined violence and offenders is distinctly inappropriate and misleading. Consequently, the structures through which we maintain such forms of cultural participation deserve careful and critical exposure.

Beyond this, the identity which such fictional violence and subjectivity affords puts victims and perpetrators at risk. It also puts culture at risk, as well as the very idea and possibility of thoughtful, critical penal reflection and restraint. Against the contemporary scale of U.S. imprisonment, the question of how punishment and its spectators are historically and culturally situated then assumes a complex urgency. How might a different kind of subjectivity other than that of the playful, anxious, or volatile passivity of the penal spectator materialize? How might such knowledge become the grounds for a cultural work other than a distant yet severe punitiveness? Such a reorientation will involve more than a transformation within prisons or the communities that surround and populate them. It will involve a transformation in the understanding of human need as well as the possibility and necessity of cultural transformation. It will also involve an understanding that ignorance itself is socially constructed and will require a concerted effort to understand the conditions under which we seek to know and not know. How do we, in fact, bring to bear—and prohibit—certain kinds of knowledge in public, popular, and social contexts? What cultural work do such practices require? Such a transformation will necessarily be grounded in a reflexive cultural critique and rigorous attention to the structure of address—out of which may arise a deeper personal and social investment in the work and worth of human interaction.

Where Work Begins

Amid such deep discontinuities, there are, surprisingly, numerous starting points for altering the path we are on. First, we must get at the cultural imagination as directly as we can by strategizing ways in which to demystify punishment and its voyeuristic appeal. This depends of course upon making punishment more visible and developing more structured ways for meaningful encounters with its complexity. Only by diminishing both the mystery and fantasies of punishment may we begin to elaborate the shared bond between the punisher and the punished and the complicity and responsibility of "distant" community members in the infliction of pain. Such efforts, caught up in the complexities of culture, are no doubt tricky and without predictability. I am reminded of Austin Sarat's controversial call to televise executions in an effort to bring us closer to our own roles in the practice of capital punishment. In supporting such a possibility, Sarat insists that "the presence of the camera would signify the flood of thousands, or millions, of uncontrollable looks into the execution chamber," bringing with them many things, "resistances, demands, assertions of power, some calling for more vengeful pain, some for the end of death imposed in the name of popular sovereignty."[8] In any case, we would be that much closer to a debate about capital punishment which might actually get at the core of its practice, as opposed to its corollary issues—the conviction of the innocent, the problems of lethal injection, disparity and inequality in death's application. I am not suggesting that this specific strategy is a particularly powerful way in which to break down the distance of the penal spectator. In fact, it might only further sensationalize punishment for many. However, such a tactic foregrounds the powerful presence of the penal spectator that is already present in the administration of death:

> Ghoulish or not, the public is always present at an execution. It is present as a juridical fiction, but as more than a fiction, as an authorizing audience unseeing and unseen, but present nonetheless. This is the haunting reality of state killing in a constitutional democracy. So long as there is capital punishment in the United States, the only question is the terms of our presence.[9]

The only hope we truly have in such encounters is the possibility of cultural disruption in all of its unpredictability.

There are many examples of such intersections on the ground, most of which originate at the concrete point in which the practice of punishment meets society. First, in such efforts, we must not leave behind the millions who have been impacted by incarceration most directly. In the deepest, harshest corners of the American penal system—including supermax and death row—there are necessary efforts at humanization and the disruption of penal spectatorship which must be pursued, even with the awareness, as Lorna Rhodes reminds us, that we will never achieve our full humanity in such settings. Rhodes points toward the power of the most fundamental of social interactions, for example, simple tier walks by administrative staff, where those in power listen directly, albeit briefly, to prisoners in isolation voicing their most basic needs.[10] Such bare bones pursuits magnify the critical work required to maintain the most minimal structure of address. Megan Comfort's meticulous ethnography of the experiences of women with incarcerated partners demonstrates how deeply the penitentiary penetrates the lives of those who sustain relationships with the imprisoned, women who in complex and contradictory ways take on the characteristics of penal life themselves.[11] Similarly, recent work on capital punishment has demonstrated how dramatically the life ways and trajectories of the families of the condemned are damaged in the pursuit of death.[12] Such work has profound implications for the vast and deep array of social networks and communities caught up in penal configurations, illuminating how carceral borders and the experience of imprisonment increasingly blur distinctions between inside and out. We are only beginning to map the ways in which the prison-industrial complex has negatively reshaped entire towns and communities, and continued research on these dynamics, including the collateral consequences of mass incarceration, with a deep and critical eye toward cultural meanings, is imperative. In the end, however, the question of how to alter penal configurations depends deeply upon those who are more often than not removed from the tangibility of punishment and the communities most impacted by it. Here, making evident ways for spectators and citizens to see their interdependencies to the project of punishment and their agency in altering the nature of those commitments is vital. That work begins by linking voices, agencies, and services together which historically have been institutionally and structurally isolated from one another, with a unified commitment toward moving away from punishment as a public good of the first order. Such efforts will require much work on the part of distanced spectators, including a rethinking of the parameters of community, who counts and who does not, in short, rethinking what it means to be social. In this sense, this kind of work is the inverse of punishment which, as we have seen, seeks to sever the social in all of its humanizing commitments.

Restorative justice frameworks have played a profound role in efforts to reconstruct social relationships in such a manner.[13] Such contexts depend upon a voluntary and public airing of experiences of harm by victims and offenders. But this is only part of the restorative justice model. A far more critical component insists that communities take on a mediating role in the framing of this harm, preparing safe spaces for both the victim and the offender to work through their experiences, advising and providing parameters for the requirements of accountability. Here, we see the way in which community members serve as built-in limits for proclivities toward punitiveness. Restorative justice frameworks insist upon a movement away from the infliction of pain and the experience of harm and redirect personal and social efforts toward reparation and healing. It is easy to see how such a framework models the revitalization of civic life and democratic society necessary to respond to a citizenry whose public commitments have been dramatically weakened in punitive pursuits. Here is a way also to train citizens, students, practitioners, and academics to foreground their relationships and obligations to pain and its remedy.

Most of these efforts point importantly to the artificiality and illusion of distance on the part of penal spectators. For instance, take the formation of citizens' circles, voluntary groups established to better facilitate a variety of reentry processes. In the formation of the circle, community members, drawn broadly from a variety of professional and life experiences, join together to assist the newly released prisoners in their transition back into the community. Participants include an array of social service agents—social workers, mental health and substance abuse professionals, children's services representatives as well as correctional administrators, officers, case workers, students, and citizens. Here, the community establishes itself in a collaborative effort to brainstorm solutions to housing, employment, and other special needs of the individual reentering society. In these environments, I have observed citizens check their jargon and humanize their labels for prisoners, openly discussing the difficulties and work involved in such shifts. I have seen community members build empathy and understanding for the complex conditions to which prisoners return after imprisonment. For restorative justice proponents, this shift in ways of looking reflects an essential transformation, one which acknowledges how the community is fundamentally implicated in all of the complexity of these relationships. Consequently, it is easier to visualize the critical role community actors have in moderating and limiting punishment, developing more direct and meaningful efforts to attend to the needs of the victim and the offender, and finally insuring that reparation is about healing, accountability, and transformation, not an isolating vindictiveness or punitiveness. Such efforts redirect us toward the equally important commonalities and distinctions in experiences for those imprisoned and those distanced from them, experiences that are critical in building a culture of support as opposed to harm. Restorative justice then is a useful model on the ground in which the shared experiences of prisoners and those removed from punishment may build humanizing strategies.

Bringing citizens into a direct and meaningful encounter with the conditions of the imprisoned is only part of the answer, however. Certainly, the majority of citizens are not going to pursue these kinds of voluntary or public service commitments. More importantly, such starting points are limited in that the origin of punishment is not in the prison but in the vicarious judgment that is given such powerful license in late modern society and circulates broadly and amorphously across culture. As we have seen throughout this volume, the meanings of punishment are bound up with larger frameworks of individual rationalization and decision making that do not occur with direct reference to official practices of punishment but rather revolve around myriad settings where the worth of the self is pitted against the relationship to another. This contest is worth thinking through carefully. We have perhaps an infinite number of ways in which to respond to the violence, vulnerability, and suffering of this other, but most reactions will follow one of two paths. One is a choice to care—a force that is in and of itself humanizing, cognizant of structures of interdependence and the ways in which human suffering is mapped through chains of pain that are networked and layered throughout human relations: a role which echoes that of the witness. The other is a choice to dominate—to take the need, weakness, and vulnerability of another and place it on display in a manner that translates into power, authority, and a claim to legitimacy: the role of the spectator. In such moments, as we choose our ways of being, we ultimately decide how we will relate to one another. The former insists upon an effort to locate and display the compassion possible of the other, the self, and the social relationship.

The deep complexities of such an engagement may not be apparent at first glance. But one need only imagine the righteous anger toward those who might violate us, our loved ones, or the most vulnerable. Who does not experience some affinity to the anger, the need for retribution and vindication, that characterizes the crime victim? More significantly, who does not experience something much less, the passing sensation of curiosity and voyeuristic inquisitiveness into the worlds of pain others are caught up in? But to give in to those experiences or, more specifically, to make that kind of experience a primary path in social interaction, a dominant cultural logic, is to put all—including ourselves, and especially those who have experienced victimization and pain—at great risk. It is precisely in these instances that the community is called upon to intervene, that the spectator is asked to move in closer and identify him- or herself as a social being, a mediator in the context of pain and harm with careful attention and concern for the fragility of human relationships.

It is in this moment that the penal spectator's very distance takes on meaningful potentiality. As Luc Boltanski writes, it is this very detachment and impartiality which takes on authority and legitimacy, as "It is because the spectator is without ties and prior commitments that his report, his testimony, can be put forward as credible."[14] Beyond such authority, however, to take up the cry of the victim and no one else at a distance (which would be inauthentic at any rate) is also to leave the victim alone, powerless, and caught within isolating, alienating structures of retribution and vengeance. It is in fact plausible that many victims may not find their way to forgiveness or to spaces apart from the pain and grief of loss and violence. Such a possibility is precisely what demands the action of the engaged but somewhat distanced actor who attempts to procure safe spaces for this pain, watching out and acting gently against processes that might lead victims through endless cycles of hatred and rage. There may be no more powerful way in which to speak back to the violence and pain that defines crime and punishment. Thus, it is critical that we attempt to imagine ways for these kinds of relationships to take shape.

From within our case studies, there is evidence of practical ways in which to begin to fashion alternative approaches such as those above. For example, prison tourism clearly emerges as a cultural practice caught problematically in fundamental tensions of consumption and spectacle. Nonetheless, there are ways to hold the imagination of the tourist accountable, if only temporarily. Tour administrators can self-reflexively point to these tensions, building in moments along the way for visitors to confront their own place in the project of punishment, linking history to contemporary patterns in mass incarceration, and reflexively pointing toward the problems of spectatorship—how the very positions from which we look shape our understandings of punishment. Eastern State Penitentiary marks a key case where many tensions in punitive and recreational discourses collide, but a marked effort to inform the tourist of these tensions is evident in many of its tour designs and exhibits. One of the most successful models for such an engagement, referenced as well in chapter 4 on prison tourism, is the Inside-Out Prison Exchange Program, a national initiative directed at transforming ways of thinking about crime and justice. This program was established in 1997 to bring college students and incarcerated individuals together in a classroom setting in the hopes of developing an innovative partnership between institutions of higher learning and prison systems locally and nationally. The program, in all of its objectives, challenges the comfortable frames of penal spectatorship. It aims to counter predominant stereotypes and myths about prisons and prisoners through *personal* engagement. It attempts to locate and display the ways and positions from which we see, encouraging participants to view crime and justice issues from new perspectives. Inside-Out insists as well that this way of seeing be linked to empowerment and agency and the project of assisting students (free and incarcerated) in seeing themselves as actors in relation to issues of crime and justice. It is consequently a program where participants are designated as potential agents of social change, where all are implicated in commitments to public service and more meaningful citizenship. Finally, Inside-Out has successfully initiated a problem-solving, grassroots community which, through education on the ground, hopes to transform public thought and opinion on mass incarceration through cross-dialogues between free and incarcerated citizens. Not coincidentally, Inside-Out has become an important way to bring professors and college courses back into prisons, without funding, under the strategic umbrella of strengthening liberal arts education.

Each of these efforts is underpinned by a commitment to pushing participants to the place where acknowledgment of the distinctiveness of contemporary penal patterns and predicaments becomes undeniable—realities which run counter to the assumed aims of punishment, foreground the role of other, more insidious motives, and force a restructuring in social orientation and ways of looking at punishment. Each attempts to circumvent a harsh penal judgment only loosely related or informed by empirical realities of punishment. More broadly and away from the centers of punishment, there are emergent strategies for how to interrupt these subjectivities where they are perhaps most prolific—amid cultural representations of punishment. A truly cultural criminology will devise a rich and complex set of methods and theoretical frames for these pursuits. We might begin by mapping how punishment and state control both dominate and evade representation. As we have seen, the ironies and contradictions of punishment emerge in any effort at its representation.

Strategizing ways in which to locate the vulnerability of punishment and the state to images opens up the possibility of an intervention that self-reflexively takes shape via representation. Such efforts will include a commitment and attention to photography, documentary, filmmaking, culture jamming, new media, convergence culture, and deep image ethnographies of everyday life—where contests of inclusion and exclusion are played out across cultural discourse.[15] Within such emergent media environments, a variety of alternative and disruptive structures are possible, including the exploration and application of new media, such as YouTube, weblogs, and online social networks (such as Facebook), for democratizing and educational purposes. In this respect, the radical technological environments of late modernity can serve as vehicles for collective problem-solving, public deliberation, grassroots creativity, and new communities. In his groundbreaking work on convergence culture, Henry Jenkins powerfully maps how such engagements can generate skills and expertise in collaboration, negotiation, and the building of community across a field of new and old media, through cultural interplay and its tensions.[16]

At a far deeper level, we can benefit profoundly from substantive efforts directed at alternative conceptualizations of the self and its relationship to others. In particular, a deeper interrogation of the ambiguities and complexities of late modern identities and subjectivities promises to open up commonalities and points of identification which might lead us away from punitiveness. For instance, as discussed earlier in this volume, Jonathan Simon argues that most Americans now conceptualize themselves through the lens of crime and as its potential victim, a subject position which plays a powerful role in the shaping of punitive discourse and penal spectatorship. Yet such standpoints might also be complicated in ways that build empathy and humanize the distanced citizen to the plight of the mass incarcerated. For instance, the homogeneity of the victim subject is perhaps at least interrupted by the experience of its counterpoint, the surveilled—which at various points includes all of us, who through the expansion of penality across the fabric of social life, are routinely state targets as students, parents, educators, workers, consumers (in debt), citizens, etc. There is, consequently, a plurality of perspectives from which to encourage individuals to think through the extensiveness of the carceral in their own lives and how intensified such experiences must be for the mass incarcerated. In this way, we might remap predominant subjectivities or at least disrupt them by pushing against their reductiveness and pointing to the complexity and ambiguities of late modern identity.

Another way to alter the trajectory of subjectivity is through a disruption of the collective. The moral superiority and authoritative judgment of the group depend upon a supportive audience of spectators whose anger and vindictiveness have achieved consensus as the overarching emotional framework for action. In such contexts, we must work to check the collective and its susceptibility to punitive proclivities. Compellingly, often a single voice of dissent in deliberative frameworks is enough to partially reframe and alter collective decision making, another reason why democratic frameworks that are richly diverse and inclusive of oppositional voices are far better consensus-builders. Even if that consensus remains punitive, the group must now justify its decision making in terms accountable to the claims of the minority and its opposition. Here are contexts then where pointing out the irrationality of punitiveness will help garner penal restraint, if only through forcing the semblance of appearing rational as opposed to vindictive, shaming audiences into disguising baser motives.

At this point, I would like to turn briefly to some of the more recent accounts of penal restraint and explore the nature of their justifications. Many have mapped frameworks for how a decreased reliance upon imprisonment and a cessation of mass incarceration might develop. For instance, most penal commentators point to the limits of state and federal budgets in a dramatic time of economic downturn, where crises in other social institutions—economy, health care, education—have assumed center stage over crime and punishment.[17] Fiscal cost is already beginning to limit the construction and use of prisons—as I write these lines, my home state of Ohio is planning to close six prisons in response to statewide budget cuts in the face of economic recession. However, such restrictions on the use of punishment, as welcome as they may be, are not grounded in emergent shifts in cultural discourses on punishment, nor are they carefully thought out solutions to the problem of punishment. In fact, restrictions on punishment, in this case, are corollaries and unanticipated consequences of mass incarceration and the economic stressors it has helped create. Funding cuts may even heighten punitiveness, as they often translate into fewer prison programs and opportunities for treatment as well as more volatile conditions due to the transfer of prison populations from closed facilities to other, already overcrowded institutions. Unless economic arguments against punishment are pitched within a new and rational narrative of punishment, old discourses lie in wait.

Similarly, others point to styles of governance and the role of political contest in the historical transformation of punishment. Attention to the political dimensions of culture has demonstrated that openings in public decision making emerge under specific conditions of governance.[18] For instance, it appears as if, finally, we may be entering a post–Bush administration era which offers some checks on executive power, closes war prisons, and at least attempts to return constitutional rights to the center of democratic deliberations. However, pragmatic, administrative, and proceduralist reforms will never necessarily challenge or force an interrogation of cultural values and the dangerous convergences of democracy and punishment. A healthy and critical self-doubt in the project of punishment is, in this case, a valuable cultural resource, although difficult to sustain. In short, we must continue to struggle to understand the cultural conditions under which political fatigue and fervor in relation to punitiveness arise. A critical self-awareness of the role of law and institutions in the production of pain amid democratic contexts is crucial in such a pursuit. This turn would seek not only to bring back and render more transparent legislative deliberation, judicial review, adversarial frameworks, and the inherent tension in balancing liberty and security, but also would strive to build a deepening sensitivity and thorough understanding of why checks and balances are critical in the production and prohibition of pain.

In this respect, democratic commitments always depend upon something more, as Ignatieff argues, including the idea that individuals matter intrinsically—that human dignity matters. Rights as foundational commitments to individual dignity ought to limit government action and the force of punishment in times of safety and danger alike if democracies are to prevail without betraying what they stand for. With the recognition and understanding of why such commitments exist, there are deliberate ways in which penal restraint might be democratically modeled in the institutional structure, logics, and missions of our professional lives. So much of this shift depends upon a self-conscious auto-critique—one, for example, where researchers seriously consider ways in which to translate a recognition of shared humanity into our work and into the practice of values on the ground, all of which might then percolate into a larger political will and cultural shift in attitudes toward punishment. As Loader and Walker argue, democracy by recognition necessarily seeks out the widest range of individuals and organizations impacted by the state's decision making, those who have by way of diversity of experience and expertise committed themselves to democratic dialogue and contest. They write:

> Recognition registers the vital importance of a state that governs security by fostering routine democratic deliberation among all those affected by its decisions about security problems—about how and whether demands for order can be met, how the state should allocate its limited resources, or how it is to wield its regulatory capacities. The task here is to devise and sustain mechanisms of public conversation and contestation in respect of security problems and how to apprehend them, mechanisms whose guiding orientation is that of inclusion.[19]

Importantly, underpinning the foundations of democracy is a deeper commitment to an inclusiveness that understands care depends upon a prior recognition of other people as human beings.

There are, finally, alternative ways to think both more broadly and more thoroughly about our social commitments and cultural investments in punishment and what these commitments reveal about our understandings of social obligation in relationship to the predominant role of pain and exclusion in our world. Importantly, exclusion always passes through institutions. It is generated through the family, economy, health care, educational, and political systems. We work hard in the United States to make those exclusions appear self-generated, products of individual action, deserving of punishment. Such strategies and logics produce new and darker regimes of exclusion that extend well beyond the punished, to those who are assigned little or no worth across a broad network of social institutions and settings. In this way, punishment and the punished are always our closest witnesses of the ways in which the social destinies of our most vulnerable are ordered. Jonathan Simon provides us with a way to think through this measure when he concludes his volume *Governing Through Crime* with a powerful discussion of how a war against cancer might imply a different mode of governance and another kind of emergent political subjectivity. In this context, still troubled by war metaphors, prevention is key, but in a manner where victims are empowered and institutions committed through knowledge, science, research, and treatment, where professional training is extensive, where networks and information are crucial and proliferating, built, most importantly, around individuals who have the disease and the families and friends who support them—all of which has radically shifted the cancer patient, Simon argues, into a rights-bearing subject over the last four decades. This subject, however, implies a vastly different sociality, where stigma is surpassed and the public good built not just upon the health, vitality, and protection of its subjects but on how we as a society choose to deal with some of our largest social problems and the needs of our most vulnerable citizens: the elderly, the sick, and the dying. Such a turn would mark a profound site from which to re-envision otherness as among us, part of us and the ones we love. Models and sites for a different social order do exist, but remain secondary to other modes of subjectivity built around crime. A better work of punishment insists that the pursuit and elaboration of these models become primary.

"Culture Will Make Trouble"

In his volume *Culture and Punishment*, Philip Smith points to how shared collective and civil discourse can limit power and the trajectory of punishment. He carefully maps how reforms in punishment, like the resurgence of the chain gang, failed precisely because of semiotic links to slavery in popular consciousness that could not be controlled or eliminated. Similarly, the guillotine and electric chair eventually failed as cultural understandings of the body and the integrity of the individual shifted. And now, resistance to panoptic surveillance and the rationalization of power undercut some of the most contemporary understandings and policies on governance and social control. Smith makes a profound observation about these possibilities and the role of culture in limiting punishment in his conclusion.

> Potential counter-discourses will spring forth weed-like from the fertile, symbol-rich soils of punishment. This is not a field where authority can easily plough under unwanted meanings. Culture will make trouble whether or not we take the time to plant the seeds of deliberately chosen counter-myth. Should we feel ethically compelled, our findings have indicated some effective pathways for such critical activity. We might invoke and mobilize sacred awe to counter the dominance of reason, or show the existence of disorders and degradations and call for a cleanup, or raise doubt and ambivalence where certainty seemed to reign, or flag category violations that abuse the primitive classifications of our civilization. Through all these means a braking influence can be exerted on that runaway train of disciplinary society.[20]

This volume has been decidedly deterministic and ethically compelled in its efforts to counter cultural myth and raise doubt against the certainty of punitiveness. It has been a deliberate effort to hold those most distanced from punishment and least impacted by its effects accountable. Consequently, my assessment of punishment and culture has been one that points incessantly and unremittingly at how cultural meanings fail. Importantly, this was never to deny that alternative meanings exist and deep contests are not under way, but rather to point to the fact that when punitiveness takes hold, when discourse hardens into dominant ideology, its grasp, especially in the case of punishment, is difficult to loosen and pain prevails. Simultaneously, however, I take heart in culture—where penal meanings will always be plural and tricky to harness, where dominance will always be susceptible to semiotic subterfuge. It is this kind of criminology, one that is premised in culture, that best promises to bring us back to our own role in the project of human exclusion. Here, amid a heightened sense of vulnerability with seemingly no precedent, individuals and societies make decisions about the way forward. Crime and punishment have always been the testing grounds for such extremities, marking the limits of the social bond, betraying the fundamental flaws and insecurities that define what it means to be human. Consequently, they demand similarly and incessantly a call for concepts—ideas and practices that might lead us beyond penality by way of a creative, ethical commitment, a work of punishment worth pursuing.

Notes

CHAPTER 1

1. Donald Clemmer, *The Prison Community* (Boston: Christopher Publishing House, 1940); Gresham M. Sykes, *The Society of Captives: A Study of a Maximum Security Prison* (Princeton, NJ: Princeton University Press, 1958); and Erving Goffman, *Asylums: Essays on the Social Situation of Mental Patients and Other Inmates* (Garden City, NY: Anchor Books, 1961).

2. President's Commission on Law Enforcement and the Administration of Justice, *The Challenge of Crime in a Free Society: A Report* (Washington, DC: U.S. GPO, 1967); American Friends Service Committee, *Struggle for Justice: A Report on Crime and Punishment in America* (New York: Hill & Wang, 1971); David Rothman, *Conscience and Convenience: The Asylum and Its Alternatives in Progressive America* (Boston: Little, Brown, 1980); Nicole Hahn Rafter, *Partial Justice: Women in State Prisons, 1800–1935* (Boston: Northeastern University Press, 1985).

3. William J. Bennett, John J. DiIulio, Jr., and John P. Walters, *Body Count: Moral Poverty--And How to Win America's War against Crime and Drugs* (New York: Simon & Schuster, 1996); Norval Morris and Michael Tonry, *Between Prison and Probation: Intermediate Punishments in a Rational Sentencing System* (New York: Oxford University Press, 1991); Nils Christie, *Crime Control as Industry: Towards Gulags, Western Style* (New York: Routledge, 2000).

4. Marc Mauer and Tracy Huling, "Young Black Americans and the Criminal Justice System," Washington, DC: *The Sentencing Project*, 1995.

5. Michelle Brown, "Back Against the Wall: Correctional Workers and the Collateral Consequences of Mass Imprisonment." Unpublished manuscript, 2009.

6. Marie Gottschalk, "Two Separate Societies: One in Prison, One Not," *Washington Post*, April 14, 2008. http://www.washingtonpost.com/wp-dyn/content/article/2008/04/14/AR2008041402451.html (accessed December 5, 2008).

7. Robert Cover, "Violence and the Word," *Yale Law Journal* 95 (1986): 1601–1629.

8. Austin Sarat and Thomas R. Kearns, "A Journey Through Forgetting: Toward a Jurisprudence of Violence," in *The Fate of Law*, ed. Austin Sarat and Thomas R. Kearns (Ann Arbor: University of Michigan Press, 1991), 222.

9. Ibid., 239.

10. Ibid., 247.

11. Lucia Zedner, "Dangers of Dystopias in Penal Theory," *Oxford Journal of Legal Studies* 22 (2002): 341–366.

12. David Garland, *Punishment and Modern Society: A Study in Social Theory* (Chicago: University of Chicago Press, 1990), 274.

13. Austin Sarat, *When the State Kills: Capital Punishment and the American Condition* (Princeton, NJ: Princeton University Press, 2001), 245.

14. Judith Butler, *Precarious Life: The Powers of Mourning and Violence* (New York: Verso, 2004), 151.

15. bell hooks, *Teaching to Transgress: Education as the Practice of Freedom* (New York: Routledge, 1994), 59.

16. Patricia J. Williams, *The Alchemy of Race and Rights* (Cambridge, MA: Harvard University Press, 1991).

17. Stanley Cohen, *Visions of Social Control: Crime, Punishment, and Classification* (New York: Blackwell, 1985), 237.

18. C. Wright Mills, *The Sociological Imagination* (New York: Oxford University Press, 1959).

19. American Friends Service Committee, Struggle for Justice, 154.

20. Patricia O'Brien, *Making It in the "Free World": Women in Transition from Prison* (Albany: State University of New York Press, 2001). 53.

CHAPTER 2

1. Giorgio Agamben, *Remnants of Auschwitz: The Witness and the Archive* (New York: Zone Books, 2002), 17.

2. Ibid., 20.

3. Susan Sontag, *Regarding the Pain of Others* (New York: Farrar, Strauss, and Giroux, 2003), 7.

4. Marc Mauer, *The Race to Incarcerate* (New York: New Press, 2006), 129.

5. Jonathan Simon, *Governing Through Crime: How the War on Crime Transformed American Democracy and Created a Culture of Fear* (New York: Oxford University Press, 2007).

6. Ibid., 106.

7. Ibid.

8. Ibid., 100.

9. Ibid., 140.

10. João Biehl, Byron Good, and Arthur Kleinman, "Introduction: Rethinking Subjectivity," in *Subjectivity: Ethnographic Investigations*, ed. João Biehl, Byron Good, and Arthur Kleinman (Berkeley: University of California Press, 2007), 5.

11. Ibid., 14.

12. Leslie McAra and Sarah Armstrong, *Perspectives on Punishment* (Oxford, UK: Oxford University Press, 2006), 23.

13. Philip Smith, *Punishment and Culture* (Chicago: University of Chicago Press, 2008), 56.

14. See David Garland, *Punishment and Welfare: A History of Penal Strategies* (Aldershot: Gower, 1985); *Punishment and Modern Society: A Study in Social Theory* (Chicago: University of Chicago Press, 1990).

15. Michel Foucault, *Discipline and Punish: The Birth of the Prison* (New York: Pantheon Books, 1977), 104.

16. Garland, *Punishment and Modern Society*, 17.

17. Garland and Young, *The Power to Punish*, 22.

18. Ibid., 23.

19. Jeff Ferrell, Keith Hayward, and Jock Young, *Cultural Criminology: An Invitation* (Los Angeles: Sage, 2008).

20. David Garland, "Concepts of Culture in the Sociology of Punishment." *Theoretical Criminology* 10, 4 (2006): 419–447.

21. Ulrich Beck, "Beyond Class and Nation: Reframing Social Inequalities in a Globalizing World," *British Journal of Sociology* 58 (2007): 679–705.

22. Zygmunt Bauman, "Social Issues of Law and Order," *British Journal of Criminology* 40 (2000): 206.

23. João Biehl, *Vita: Life in a Zone of Social Abandonment* (Los Angeles: University of California Press, 2005). Biehl provides a powerful visual vector from which to map social exclusion through his inclusion of a series of provocative photographs by Torben Eskerod.

24. Nancy Scheper-Hughes, "Coming to Our Senses: Anthropology and Genocide," in *Annihilating Difference: The Anthropology of Genocide*, ed. Alexander Hinton (Berkeley: University of California Press, 2002), 370.

25. Ibid.

26. Ibid., 373–374.

27. The nature of this form of inquiry is carefully analyzed in chapter 6 on prison science, the last case study of the volume.

28. Jonathan Simon, "The Ideological Effects of Actuarial Practices," *Law & Society Review* 22, 4 (1988): 771.

29. Ibid., 792.

30. See Loïc Wacquant, *Urban Outcasts: A Comparative Sociology of Advanced Marginality* (Cambridge: Polity Press, 2007); *Punishing the Poor: The New Government of Social Insecurity* (Durham, NC: Duke University Press, 2009); *Deadly Symbiosis: Race and the Rise of Neoliberal Penality* (Cambridge: Polity Press, 2008).

31. This relationship is more thoroughly elaborated in chapter 5 on new war prisons.

32. Giorgio Agamben, *Homo Sacer: Sovereign Power and Bare Life* (Stanford: Stanford University Press, 1998), 11.

33. McRobbie, "Vulnerability, Violence, and (Cosmopolitan) Ethics," 84.

34. Michael Ignatieff, *The Needs of Strangers* (New York: Viking Penguin, 1986), 14.

35. Ibid., 17.

36. Ibid.

37. Ibid., 50–51.

38. Ibid., 34.

39. Hannah Arendt, *The Human Condition* (Chicago: University of Chicago Press, 1958), 120.

40. Jacques Derrida, "By Force of Mourning," in *The Work of Mourning,* ed. Pascale-Anne Brault and Michael Naas (Chicago: University of Chicago Press, 2001).

41. Elaine Scarry, *The Body in Pain: The Making and Unmaking of the World* (New York: Oxford University Press, 1985), 169.

42. Ibid.

43. Ibid., 171.

44. Ibid.

45. Lorna A. Rhodes, *Total Confinement: Madness and Reason in the Maximum Security Prison* (Berkeley: University of California Press, 2004), 68.

46. Bauman, "Social Issues of Law and Order," 207.

47. Garland, *Punishment and Modern Society.*

48. Zygmunt Bauman, *Liquid Modernity* (Cambridge: Polity, 2000), 139.

49. Ibid., 139.

50. Ibid., 139–140.

51. Ibid., 218.

52. Butler, *Precarious Life,* 140.

53. Ibid., 150.

54. Arthur Kleinman and Joan Kleinman, "The Appeal of Experience; The Dismay of Images: Cultural Appropriations of Suffering in our Times," in *Social Suffering,* ed. Arthur Kleinman, Veena Das, and Margaret Lock (Berkeley: University of California Press, 1997), 19.

55. Ibid., 19.

56. Butler, *Precarious Life,* 147.

CHAPTER 3

1. Ray Surette, *Media, Crime, and Criminal Justice: Images and Realities* (Pacific Grove, CA: Brooks/Cole Publishing, 1992), 1.

2. Angela McRobbie and Sarah L. Thornton, "Rethinking 'Moral Panic' for Multi-mediated Social Worlds," *British Journal of Sociology* 46, 4 (1995): 571.

3. Austin Sarat, "State Killing in Popular Culture," in *When the State Kills: Capital Punishment and the American Condition* (Princeton, NJ: Princeton University Press, 2001); Ray Surette, *Media, Crime, and Criminal Justice: Images*

and Realities (Pacific Grove, CA: Brooks/Cole Publishing, 1992); Alison Young, *Imagining Crime: Textual Outlaws and Criminal Conversations* (Thousand Oaks, CA: Sage, 1996); Nicole Rafter, *Shots in the Mirror: Crime Films and Society* (New York: Oxford University Press, 2006).

4. Austin Sarat, "Imagining the Law of the Father: Loss, Dread, and Mourning in *The Sweet Hereafter*," *Law & Society Review* 34 (2000): 3.

5. Jeff Ferrell and Clinton Sanders, eds., *Cultural Criminology* (Boston: Northeastern University Press, 1995), 308.

6. David Garland, "On the Concept of Moral Panic," *Crime Media Culture* 4, 1 (2008): 9–30.

7. Judith Butler, *Precarious Life: The Powers of Mourning and Violence* (New York: Verso, 2004), 146.

8. Ibid., 2.

9. Ibid., 145.

10. David Garland, *Punishment and Modern Society: A Study in Social Theory* (Chicago: University of Chicago Press, 1990), 255.

11. Ibid., 17.

12. Ibid., 276.

13. Rafter, *Shots in the Mirror*, 6.

14. Ibid., 7.

15. Claire Valier, *Crime and Punishment in Contemporary Culture* (New York: Routledge, 2004).

16. Rafter, *Shots in the Mirror*.

17. Erving Goffman, *Asylums: Essays on the Social Situation of Mental Patients and Other Inmates* (Garden City, NY: Anchor Books, 1961), 12.

18. Gresham Sykes, *The Society of Captives: A Study of a Maximum Security Prison* (Princeton, NJ: Princeton University Press, 1958), 79.

19. Rafter, *Shots in the Mirror*.

20. Mark Kermode, *The Shawshank Redemption* (London: British Film Institute, 2003), 84.

21. Ibid., 87.

22. Ibid., 86.

23. Michel Foucault, *Discipline and Punish: The Birth of the Prison* (New York: Pantheon Books 1977), 307.

24. Garland, *Punishment and Modern Society*, 9.

25. For an exploration of alternative and racialized functions of spectacle and panoptic surveillance in cinema, see Giovanni Tiso ("The Spectacle of Surveillance: Images of the Panopticon in Science-Fiction Cinema" (2000) at http://homepages.paradise.net.nz/gtiso/filmessay, accessed 11/13/2006).

26. William J. Mitchell, *City of Bits: Space, Place, and Infobahn* (Cambridge, MA: MIT Press, 1995), 5.

27. Tiso, "The Spectacle of Surveillance."

28. Foucault, *Discipline and Punish*, 143.

29. Ibid.

30. Ibid., 228.

31. Andrew Ross, *No-Collar: The Humane Workplace and Its Hidden Costs* (New York: Basic Books, 2003), 59.

32. Steven A. Kohm, "The People's Law versus Judge Judy Justice: Two Models of Law in American Reality-Based Courtroom TV" *Law & Society Review* 40, 3 (2006): 693–728.

33. Foucault, *Discipline and Punish*, 227.

34. http://www.csmonitor.com/2007/0212/p99s01–duts.html.

35. Jane Mayer, "Whatever It Takes: The Politics of the Man behind '24,'" *The New Yorker*, February 19, 2007 at http://www.newyorker.com/reporting/2007/02/19/070219fa_fact_mayer.

36. See advertisements: Evi Girling, "'Looking Death in the Face': The Benetton Death Penalty Campaign," *Punishment & Society* (2004); Mona Lynch, "Selling Securityware: Transformations in Prison Commodities Advertising, 1949–99," *Punishment & Society* (2002); novels: John Bender, *Imagining the Penitentiary: Fiction and the Architecture of Mind in Eighteenth-Century England* (Chicago: University of Chicago Press, 1987); television: Richard Sparks, *Television and the Drama of Crime: Moral Tales and the Place of Crime in Public Life* (Philadelphia: Open University Press, 1992); webcam images: Mona Lynch, "Punishing Images: Jail Cam and the Changing Penal Enterprise," *Punishment & Society* (2004); photographs: Susan Sontag, *Regarding the Pain of Others* (New York: Farrar, Straus, and Giroux, 2003); postcards: David Garland, "Capital Punishment and American Culture," *Punishment & Society* (2005); art: Anne Brydon and Pauline Greenhill, "Representations of Crime: On Showing Paintings by a Serial Killer," in *Crime's Power: Anthropologists and the Ethnography of Crime*, ed. Philip C. Parnell and Stephanie C. Kane (New York: Palgrave, 2003); political slogans: Hall et al., *Policing the Crisis: Mugging, the State and Law and Order* (London: Macmillan, 1978); Stuart Scheingold, *Politics of Law and Order: Street Crime and Public Policy* (New York: Longman, 1984); Katherine Beckett, *Making Crime Pay: Law and Order in Contemporary American Politics* (New York: Oxford University Press, 1997); institutional architecture: Bender, *Imagining the Penitentiary*; Norman Johnston, *Forms of Contraint: A History of Prison Architecture* (Urbana: University of Illinois Press, 2000); professional and trade journals: Lorna Rhodes, *Total Confinement: Madness and Reason in the Maximum Security Prison* (Berkeley: University of California Press, 2004); conversational chat and gossip: Evi Girling, Ian Loader, and Richard Sparks, *Crime and Social Change in Middle England: Questions of Order in an English Town* (New York: Routledge, 2000); Theodore Sasson, *Crime Talk: How Citizens Construct a Social Problem* (New York: Aldine de Gruyter, 1995).

37. Bender, *Imagining the Penitentiary*, 15.

38. Ibid., 5.

39. Ibid., 21, 84.

40. Ibid., 228.

41. David Wilson and Sean O'Sullivan, "Re-theorizing Penal Reform Functions in Prison Film," *Theoretical Criminology* 9, 4 (2005): 471–491.

42. Sarat, "Imagining the Law of the Father," 40.

43. Philip Smith, *Punishment and Culture* (Chicago: University of Chicago Press, 2008), 25.

44. Ibid., 37.

45. Ibid., 43.

46. Sontag, *Regarding the Pain of Others*, 7.

47. Valier, *Crime and Punishment in Contemporary Culture*, 253.

48. Sontag, *Regarding the Pain of Others*, 117.

49. Ibid., 110.

50. Ibid., 195.

51. Stanley Cohen, *States of Denial: Knowing About Atrocities and Suffering* (Malden, MA: Blackwell, 2001), 195.

52. Angela McRobbie, "Vulnerability, Violence and (Cosmopolitan) Ethics: Butler's *Precarious Life*," *British Journal of Sociology* 57, 1 (2006): 84.

53. Young, *Imagining Crime*, 212.

54. Butler, *Precarious Life*, 144.

55. Ibid., 150.

56. Ibid., 213.

57. Ibid., 151.

58. Sarat, "Imagining the Law of the Father," 9.

59. Ibid.

60. Rafter, *Shots in the Mirror*, 230–231.

61. Arjun Appadurai, *Modernity at Large: Cultural Dimensions of Globalization*, Public Worlds, vol. 1 (Minneapolis: Minnesota University Press, 1996), 587.

CHAPTER 4

1. Kenneth Foote, *Shadowed Ground: America's Landscapes of Violence and Tragedy* (Austin: University of Texas Press, 2003), 294.

2. Ibid., 6.

3. "Closed Ohio Prison Extends Visiting Hours," *USA Today*, August 9, 2002, Section: Life, p. 02d.

4. See John Lennon and Malcolm Foley, *Dark Tourism: The Attraction of Death and Disaster* (London: Continuum, 2000).

5. Carolyn Strange and Michael Kempa, "Shades of Dark Tourism: Alcatraz and Robben Island," *Annals of Tourism Research*, 30, 2 (2003): 387.

6. Chris Rojek, *Ways of Escape: Modern Transformations of Leisure and Travel* (London: Macmillan, 1993).

7. A.V. Seaton, "War and Thanatourism: Waterloo 1815–1914," *Annals of Tourism Research*, 26, 1: 130–158.

8. Strange and Kempa, "Shades of Dark Tourism," 386–405.

9. See Jacob A. Riis, *How the Other Half Lives: Studies Among the Tenements in New York* (New York: Penguin Books, 1997); Luc Sante, *Evidence* (New York: Farrar, Straus and Giroux, 1992); Susan Sontag, *Regarding the Pain of Others* (New York: Farrar, Straus and Giroux, 2003); Alan Trachtenberg, *Reading American Photographs: Images as History: Mathew Brady to Walker Evans* (New York: Hill & Wang, 1989).

10. See http://realitytoursandtravel.com/.

11. See http://www.favelatour.com.br/indexing.html.

12. David Rothman, *The Discovery of the Asylum: Social Order and Disorder in the New Republic* (Boston: Little, Brown, 1971).

13. Charles Dickens, *American Notes*—chap. 7 at http://www.online-literature.com/dickens/americannotes/.

14. Ibid.

15. Gustave de Beaumont and Alexis de Tocqueville, and Francis Lieber, translator, *On the Penitentiary System in the United States and Its Application in France* (Philadelphia: Carey, Lea, and Blanchard, 1833), 38.

16. Ibid.

17. Norman Johnston, *Eastern State Penitentiary: Crucible of Good Intentions* (Philadelphia: Philadelphia Museum of Art, 2000), 35.

18. Ibid., 50.

19. Michel Foucault, *Discipline and Punish: The Birth of the Prison* (New York: Pantheon Books, 1977), 202.

20. John Urry, *The Tourist Gaze: Leisure and Travel in Contemporary Societies* (London: Sage, 1990).

21. Ibid., 3.

22. Ibid.

23. Interview at Eastern State Penitentiary.

24. Philip Smith, *Punishment and Culture* (Chicago: University of Chicago Press, 2008), 92.

25. Ibid.

26. West Virginia Penitentiary publicity flyer, Moundsville Economic Development Council.

27. Jennifer Gonnerman, "The Riot Academy," *Village Voice* (May 24–30, 2000).

28. See website: http://www.wvpentours.com/main.php. Accessed May 19, 2008.

29. See websites: www.wvpentours.com; http://www.mrps.org/; http://www.easternstate.org/

30. "Restoring Our Local Landmark!" The Mansfield Reformatory Preservation Society. See website: http://www.mrps.org/home.htm. Accessed May 19, 2008.

31. Ibid.

32. See historic site mission: http://www.easternstate.org/contact/. Accessed March 21, 2008.

33. West Virginia Penitentiary publicity flyer, Moundsville Economic Development Council.

34. Based on Eastern States 2006 promotional brochure: "Terror Behind the Walls: Halloween at Eastern State Penitentiary."

35. Based on Eastern States 2006 promotional brochure: "Terror Behind the Walls: Halloween at Eastern State Penitentiary." Admission costs: $20–30.

36. Interview at Eastern State Penitentiary.

37. West Virginia Penitentiary publicity flyer, Moundsville Economic Development Council.

38. Avery Gordon, *Ghostly Matters: Haunting and the Sociological Imagination* (Minneapolis: University of Minnesota Press, 1997), 194.

39. Ibid., 134–135.

40. Ibid., 202.

41. Ibid.

42. The Inside-Out Prison Exchange Program is a national program, founded by Lori Pompa, that originated in conjunction with Temple University and a maximum security prison outside Philadelphia in 1997. In 10 years, the program has expanded to include over 1,000 inside and 1,000 outside students, as well as instructors from 81 colleges and universities in 31 states with courses implemented in federal, state, and local prisons and jails. The mission of the program is to deepen the conversation about issues of crime and justice by bringing college students—particularly those pursuing careers in criminal justice—together w/incarcerated men and women to study as peers in seminars behind prison walls. See http://www.temple.edu/inside-out/.

43. David Garland, "Penal Excess and Surplus Meaning," *Law & Society Review*, 39, 4 (2005): 793–834.

44. Urry, *The Tourist Gaze*, 102.

45. Gillian Rose, *Visual Methods* (Thousand Oaks, CA: Sage, 2007): 183.

CHAPTER 5

1. Michael Ignatieff, *The Needs of Strangers* (New York: Viking Penguin, 1984), 52.

2. See the Emmy Award–winning *Ghosts of Abu Ghraib*, the Academy Award–winning *Taxi to the Dark Side*, and Erroll Morris's *Standard Operating Procedure.*

3. *Taxi to the Dark Side* exposes practices at Bagram through a homicide case.

4. See Anthony R. Jones and George R. Fay, *Investigation of Activities at Abu Ghraib* (2004); Reed Brody, *The Road to Abu Ghraib* (Human Rights Watch, June 2004), http://www.hrw.org/reports/2004/usa0604/.

5. Via private meetings, torture memos, and vetoes of bills designed to limit interrogation techniques.

6. Robert Cover, "Violence and the Word," *Yale Law Journal* 95 (1986): 1601.

7. Elaine Scarry, *The Body in Pain: The Making and Unmaking of the World* (New York: Oxford University Press, 1985), 27.

8. Brody, *The Road to Abu Ghraib.*

9. See *Ghosts of Abu Ghraib.*

10. *Article 15-6 Investigation of the 800ᵗʰ Military Police Brigade*, Conducted by Major General Antonio M. Taguba, issued May 2004 at http://news.findlaw. com/hdocs/docs/iraq/tagubarpt.html.

11. Ibid., 5. See also Michelle Brown, "'Setting the Conditions' for Abu Ghraib: The Prison Nation Abroad," *American Quarterly* 57, 3 (2005): 973–997.

12. See interviews in *Ghosts of Abu Ghraib.*

13. Ibid.

14. See Philip Gourevitch and Errol Morris, "Annals of War: Exposure: The Woman Behind the Camera at Abu Ghraib," *The New Yorker*, at: http://www. newyorker.com/reporting/2008/03/24/080324fa_fact_gourevitch.

15. See Philip Zimbardo, *The Lucifer Effect* (New York: Random House, 2007).

16. Gourevitch and Morris, "Annals of War: Exposure."

17. Jean Baudrillard, "War Porn," *Journal of Visual Culture* (2006): 5 (1).

18. Susan Sontag, "What Have We Done?" *The Guardian* (2003): 2.

19. "Iraq Prisoner Abuse 'Un-American,' Says Rumsfeld," *Washington Times*, May 7, 2004; online at http://www.washingtontimes.com/news/2004/ may/07/20040507-115901-67361/.

20. David Garland, "Penal Excess and Surplus Meaning," *Law and Society Review* (2005); Max Gordon, "Abu Ghraib: Postcards from the Edge" at: http:// www.opendemocracy.net/ 2004; Michael L. Niman, "Strange Fruit in Abu Ghraib: The Privatization of Torture," *The Humanist* (2004); Hazel Carby, "A Strange and Bitter Crop: The Spectacle of Torture" (2004) at: http://www.opende-mocracy.net/.

21. Garland, "Penal Excess and Surplus Meaning," 795.

22. Ibid., 829.

23. Zimbardo, *The Lucifer Effect*; Daniel Goldhagen, *Hitler's Willing Execu-tioners: Ordinary Germans and the Holocaust* (New York: Alfred A. Knopf, 1996).

24. Lesley Gill, *The School of the Americas: Military Training and Political Violence in the Americas* (Durham, NC: Duke University Press, 2004), 13.

25. Stephen Eisenman, *The Abu Ghraib Effect* (London: Reaktion Books, 2007), 111.

26. Ibid., 17.

27. Chris Greer and Yvonne Jewkes, "Extremes of Otherness: Media Images of Social Exclusion," *Social Justice* (2005): (32)1: 29.

28. Stanley Cohen, *States of Denial: Knowing about Atrocities and Suffering* (Malden, MA: Blackwell, 2001), 194.

29. João Biehl, Byron Good, and Arthur Kleinman, "Introduction: Rethinking Subjectivity," in *Subjectivity: Ethnographic Investigations*, ed. João Biehl, Byron Good, and Arthur Kleinman. Berkeley: University of California Press, 2007, 4–5.

30. Karen J. Greenberg and Joshua L. Dratel, eds., *The Torture Debate in America* (New York: Cambridge University Press, 2006), 2.

31. Eisenman, *The Abu Ghraib Effect*, 111.

32. Mark Hamm, "'High Crimes and Misdemeanors': George W. Bush and the Sins of Abu Ghraib," *Crime, Media, Culture* 3(3) (2007): 259–284.

33. Elaine Scarry, *The Body in Pain: The Making and Unmaking of the World* (New York: Oxford University Press, 1985).

34. Giorgio Agamben, *State of Exception* (Chicago: University of Chicago Press, 2005), 121.

35. Judith Butler, *Precarious Life: The Powers of Mourning and Violence* (New York: Verso, 2004), 53.

36. Amy Kaplan, "Violent Belongings and the Question of Empire Today—Presidential Address to the American Studies Association, October 17, 2003," *American Quarterly* 56, 1 (March 2004): 14.

37. Agamben, *State of Exception*, 4.

38. Ibid.

39. Nicholas Mirzoeff, "Invisible Empire," *Radical History Review* 95 (2006): 22.

40. David Luban, "Liberalism, Torture, and the Ticking Bomb," in *The Torture Debate in America*, ed. Karen J. Greenberg (Cambridge: Cambridge University Press, 2006), 35–83.

41. Baudrillard, "War Porn," 86.

42. Ibid.

43. Ibid., 830.

44. Mark Benjamin, "Sympathy for Charles Graner," at http://www.salon.com/news/feature/2008/12/01/graner/print.html, accessed December 7, 2008.

45. Cohen, *States of Denial*.

46. See Michael Hallett, "Militarism and Colonialism in the Global Punishment Economy," in *Visions for Change: Crime and Justice in the 21st Century*, 5th edition, ed. Roslyn Muraskin and Albert R. Roberts (New York: Prentice Hall, 2008).

47. Mary Bosworth, "Race and Punishment," *Punishment and Society* 2, 1 (2000).

48. Veena Das, "Language and Body: Transactions in the Construction of Pain," in *Social Suffering*, eds. Arthur Kleinman, Veena Das, and Margaret Locke (Berkeley: University of California Press, 1997), 68.

49. Ibid., 70.

50. Ibid., 78.

51. Butler, *Precarious Life*.

52. See Brown, "'Setting the Conditions' for Abu Ghraib: The Prison Nation Abroad," 973–997; Michelle Brown. "The New Penology in a Critical Context," in *Advancing Critical Criminology: Theory and Application*, ed. Walter DeKeseredy and Barbara Perry (Lanham, MD: Lexington Books, 2006).

53. Agamben, *State of Exception*, 64.

54. Mark Reinhardt and Holly Edwards, "Traffic in Pain," in *Beautiful Suffering: Photography and the Traffic in Pain*, ed. Mark Reinhardt, Holly Edwards, and Erina Duganne (Chicago: University of Chicago Press, 2007) 12.

CHAPTER 6

1. Thomas F. Gieryn, *Cultural Boundaries of Science: Credibility on the Line* (Chicago: University of Chicago Press, 1999), x–xi.

2. Michael Ignatieff, *A Just Measure of Pain: The Penitentiary in the Industrial Revolution, 1750–1850* (New York: Pantheon, 1978), 216.

3. President's Commission on Law Enforcement and the Administration of Justice, *The Challenge of Crime in a Free Society* (Washington, DC: U.S. GPO, 1967).

4. American Friends Service Committee, *Struggle for Justice* (New York: Hill & Wang, 1971).

5. Marc Mauer, *Race Incarcerate* (New York: New Press, 2006), 16.

6. Nils Christie, *Crime Control as Industry: Towards Gulags, Western Style* (New York: Routledge, 2000): 13, 16.

7. Loïc Wacquant, "Deadly Symbiosis: When Ghetto and Prison Meet and Mesh," *Punishment and Society* 3 (2001):95–134.

8. John Irwin, *The Warehouse Prison: Disposal of the New Dangerous Class* (Los Angeles: Roxbury, 2005).

9. Todd Clear, *Harm in American Penology: Offenders, Victims, and Their Communities,* (Albany: State University of New York Press, 1994), xiii.

10. Elliott Currie, *Crime and Punishment in America* (New York: Metropolitan Books, 1998), 11.

11. Ted Palmer, "Martinson Revisited," *Journal of Research in Crime and Delinquency Davis California* 12 (1975): 133.

12. Rick Sarre, "Beyond 'What Works?'" A 25-Year Jubilee Retrospective of Robert Martinson's Famous Article," *Australian and New Zealand Journal of Criminology* (2001): 38; F. D. Cousineau and D. B. Plecas, "Justifying Criminal

Justice Policy with Methodologically Inadequate Research," *Canadian Journal of Criminology* 24 (1982); Paul Gendreau and R. R. Ross, "Revivifications of Rehabilitation: Evidence from the 1980s," *Justice Quarterly* 4, 3 (1987): 349–407.

13. Gray Cavender, "Media and Crime Policy: A Reconsideration of David Garland's The Culture of Control," *Punishment and Society* 6, 3 (2004).

14. Lee Sechrest, Susan O. White, and Elizabeth D. Brown, eds., *The Rehabilitation of Criminal Offenders: Problem and Prospects* (Washington, DC: National Academy of Sciences Press, 1979).

15. Francis Cullen and Karen Gilbert, *Reaffirming Rehabilitation* (Cincinnati: Anderson Publishing, 1982), 1.

16. A simple key word search in criminal justice abstracts successfully demonstrates the importance of Martinson's introduction of "what works/nothing works" discourse, yielding over 250 hits from his publication to the present.

17. Edgardo Rotman, *Beyond Punishment: A New View on the Rehabilitation of Criminal Offenders* (New York: Greenwood Press, 1990).

18. Francis T. Cullen and P. Gendreau, "The Effectiveness of Correctional Rehabilitation: Reconsidering the 'Nothing Works' Debate," in *The American Prison: Issues in Research Policy*, ed. L. Goodstein and D. L. MacKenzie (New York: Plenum, 1989): 25.

19. Christy Visher, "Incapacitation and Crime Control: Does a 'Lock 'em Up' Strategy Reduce Crime?" *Justice Quarterly* 4 (1987): 519.

20. Michael Sherman and Gordon Hawkins, *Imprisonment in America: Choosing the Future* (Chicago: University of Chicago Press, 1981), 3.

21. Don A. Andrews, Ivan Zinger et al., "A Human Science Approach or More Punishment and Pessimism: A Rejoinder to Lab and Whitehead," *Criminology* 28 (1990): 370–371.

22. Philip Smith, *Punishment and Culture* (Chicago: University of Chicago Press, 2008).

23. Robert Martinson, "New Findings, New Views: A Note of Caution Regarding Sentencing Reform," *Hofstra Law Review* 7 (1979): 242–258; Martinson, "California Research at the Crossroads," *Crime & Delinquency* (1976); Martinson, "Restraint and Incapacitation: An Analytical introduction," in *Crime and Deterrence and Offender Career* (New York: City College of the City University of New York, 1975); Martinson, "What Works? Questions and Answers about Prison Reform," *Public Interest* 35 (1974): 22–54; Robert Martinson and Judith Wilks, "Save Parole Supervision," *Federal Probation* 41 (1977): 23–27; Martinson, "Is the Treatment of Criminal Offenders Necessary?" *Federal Probation* 40 (1976); Martinson and Wilks, *Knowledge in Criminal Justice Planning: A Preliminary Report* (New York: The Center for Knowledge in Criminal Justice Planning, 1976).

24. David Garland, *The Culture of Control* (Chicago: University of Chicago Press, 2001), 63.

25. The "failure" of rehabilitation had been iterated earlier by previous studies, one example being a less widely received article by Walter Bailey ("100 Reports of Empirical Evaluations of Correctional Treatment: 1940–1960" [1966]) which provided a limited content analysis of a series of reports, each of which had empirically examined the effects of rehabilitation through assessments of studies of "correctional treatment." Bailey's report, like Martinson's, was designed to examine representative samples of scientific assessments of rehabilitation across penology. Both are directed at presenting themselves as barometers of the state of rehabilitation based on scientific expertise. Bailey concludes that the validity of treatment is more ambiguous than previously thought, due to slight levels of success and inconsistent application, lending these studies and rehabilitation in practice an overall characterization of unreliability—not unlike Martinson's study. See Walter C. Bailey, "Correctional Outcome: An Evaluation of 100 Reports," *Journal of Criminal Law, Criminology and Police Science* 57, 2 (1966): 153–160. Other studies include: William C. Berleman and Thomas W. Steinburn, "The Value and Validity of Delinquency Prevention Experiments," *Crime & Delinquency* (1966); Donald R. Cressey, "The Nature and Effectiveness of Correctional Techniques," *Law and Contemporary Problems* 23 (1958): 754–771; Martin Gold, "A Time for Skepticism." *Crime & Delinquency* 20 (1974): 20–24; Bernard C. Kirby, "Measuring Effects of Treatment of Criminals and Delinquents," *Sociology and Social Research* 38 (1954): 368–374; James Robison and Gerald Smith, "The Effectiveness of Correctional Programs," *Crime and Delinquency* 17 (1971): 67–80; Barbara Wootton, *Social Science and Social Pathology* (London: Allen & Unwin, 1959); David F. Greenberg, "The Correctional Effects of Corrections: A Survey of Evaluations," in *Corrections and Punishment*, ed. D. F. Greenberg (Newbury Park, CA: Sage, 1977).

26. Francis T. Cullen, "The Twelve People Who Saved Rehabilitation: How the Science of Criminology Made a Difference," *Criminology* 43 (2005): 1.

27. Martinson, "What Works?" 22.

28. Ibid.

29. Ibid.

30. Ibid., 25.

31. Douglas Lipton, Robert Martinson, and Judith Wilks, *The Effectiveness of Correctional Treatment: A Survey of Treatment Evaluation Studies* (New York: Praeger, 1975).

32. Ibid., 48–49.

33. Ibid., 49–50.

34. Ibid., 50.

35. Ibid., 23.

36. Adam Wolfson, "About the Public Interest," *Public Interest* (Spring 2005). Accessed 8–25–07 at http://findarticles.com/p/articles/mi_m0377/is_159/ai_n13779489/print.

37. Gray Cavendar, "Media and Crime Policy: A Reconsideration of David Garland's *The Culture of Control*," *Punishment and Society* (2004): 341.

38. Ibid.

39. Center for Knowledge in Criminal Justice Planning—Letter: Marvin Wolfgang.

40. Center for Knowledge in Criminal Justice Planning— File 72 Letter: Stuart Adams.

41. Palmer, "Martinson Revisited."

42. Ted Palmer, *Correctional Intervention and Research: Current Issues and Future Prospects* (Lexington, MA: Lexington Books, 1978), 20.

43. Palmer, "Martinson Revisited," 141.

44. Palmer, *Correctional Intervention and Research,* 56.

45. Palmer, "Martinson Revisited," 150.

46. James Q. Wilson, "'What Works?' Revisited: New Findings on Criminal Rehabilitation," *Public Interest* (Fall 1980): 3.

47. Marvin Frankel, *Criminal Sentences: Law Without Order* (New York: Hill & Wang, 1973); Andrew von Hirsch, *Doing Justice: The Choice of Punishments— The Report of the Committee for the Study of Incarceration* (New York: Hill & Wang, 1976); David Fogel, *We Are the Living Proof . . . the Justice Model of Corrections* (Cincinnati: Anderson, 1975); Ernest Van Den Haag, *Punishing Criminals* (New York: Basic Books, 1975).

48. Cullen, "The Twelve People Who Saved Rehabilitation," 10.

49. Michael Gottfredson, "Treatment Destruction Techniques," *Journal of Research in Crime and Delinquency* (January 1979): 39–54.

50. Palmer, "Martinson Revisited," 151.

51. Steven P. Lab and John T. Whitehead, "From 'Nothing Works' to 'the Appropriate Works': The Latest Stop on the Search for the Secular Grail," *Criminology* 28 (1990): 405.

52. Martinson, "California Research at the Crossroads," 191.

53. Martinson and Wilks, "Save Parole Supervision," 23.

54. Center for Knowledge in Criminal Justice Planning, file 20: *Hofstra Law Review.*

55. Martinson, "New Findings, New Views," 244.

56. David Greenberg, "The Incapacitative Effect of Imprisonment: Some Estimates," *Law & Society Review* 9, 41 (1975): 541–580; Palmer, "Martinson Revisited"; Wilson, "'What Works?' Revisited," 3–17; Sherman and Hawkins, *Imprisonment in America,* 3; Cullen and Gilbert, *Reaffirming Rehabilitation*; Paul Gendreau and R. R. Ross, "Revivifications of Rehabilitation; Visher, "Incapacitation and Crime Control"; Cullen and Gendreau, "The Effectiveness of Correctional Rehabilitation"; Norval Morris and Michael Tonry, *Between Prison and Probation: Intermediate Punishments in a Rational Sentencing System* (New York: Oxford University Press, 1991).

57. Cullen, "The Twelve People Who Saved Rehabilitation," 10.

58. See Gendreau and Ross, "Revivification of Rehabilitation"; Steven P. Lab and John T. Whitehead, "An Analysis of Juvenile Correctional Treatment," *Crime*

& *Delinquency* 34 (1988): 60–83; D. A. Andrews, Ivan Zinger et al., "Does Correctional Treatment Work? A Clinically Relevant and Psychologically Informed Meta-Analysis," *Criminology* 28 (1990): 369–404; Lab and Whitehead, "From 'Nothing Works' to 'The Appropriate Works'; Charles H. Logan and Gerald G. Gaes, "Meta-Analysis and the Rehabilitation of Punishment," *Justice Quarterly* 10 (1993): 245–263; Daniel Glaser, "What Works, and Why It Is Important: A Response to Logan and Gaes," *Justice Quarterly* 11 (1994): 711–723.

   59. Andrews, Zinger et al., "A Human Science Approach or More Punishment and Pessimism"; Francis T. Cullen, Kristie R. Blevins, Jennifer S. Trager, and Paul Gendreau, "Rise and Fall of Boot Camps: A Case Study in Common-Sense Corrections," *Journal of Offender Rehabilitation* 40 (2005): 53–70; Cullen and Gendreau, "From Nothing Works to What Works"; Cullen and Gendreau, "The Effectiveness of Correctional Rehabilitation"; Francis T. Cullen, John Paul Wright, Paul Gendreau, and D. A. Andrews, "What Correctional Treatment Can Tell Us About Criminological Theory: Implications for Social Learning Theory," in *Learning Theory and the Explanation of Crime: A Guide for the New Century*, ed. Ronald L. Akers and Gary F. Jensen (New Brunswick, NJ: Transaction Publishers, 2003), 339–362; Paul Gendreau, Francis T. Cullen, and James Bonta, "Intensive Rehabilitation Supervision: The Next Generation in Community Corrections," *Federal Probation* 58 (1994): 72–78; Paul Gendreau, Claire Goggin, Francis T. Cullen, and Mario Paparozzi, "The Common-Sense Revolution and Correctional Policy," in *Offender Rehabilitation and Treatment: Effective Programs and Policies to Reduce Re-Offending*, ed. James Maguire (Chichester, UK: John Wiley and Sons, 2002).

   60. Logan and Gaes, "Meta-Analysis and the Rehabilitation of Punishment."

   61. Cullen and Gilbert, *Reaffirming Rehabilitation*, xix.

   62. Ibid., xxiii.

   63. Ibid., 19–20.

   64. Stanley Cohen, *Visions of Social Control: Crime, Punishment, and Classification* (New York: Polity Press/Blackwell, 1985).

   65. Cullen and Gilbert, *Reaffirming Rehabilitation*, 21.

   66. Ibid., 246.

   67. Ibid., 247.

   68. Morris and Tonry, *Between Prison and Probation*, 103.

   69. Cullen and Gilbert, *Reaffirming Rehabilitation*, 185.

   70. Cullen, "The Twelve People Who Saved Rehabilitation."

   71. Ibid., 1.

   72. Ibid., 5.

   73. Cullen, "The Twelve People Who Saved Rehabilitation."

   74. Ibid., 27.

   75. Lawrence W. Sherman, *Evidence-based Policing* (Washington, DC: Police Foundation, 1998); Lawrence W. Sherman, Denise Gottfredson, Doris MacKenzie, John Eck, Peter Reuter, and Shawn Bushway *Preventing Crime: What*

Works, What Doesn't, What's Promising (Washington, DC: U.S. Office of Justice Programs, 1997); "Evidence-based Policing" (Washington, DC: Police Foundation, Ideas in American Policing Series, 1998), 4; 2002 (www.policefoundation. org). "Evidence-Based Policing: Social Organization of Information for Social Control," in Elin Waring and David Weisburd, eds., *Crime and Social Organization*, Vol. 10, Advances in Criminological Theory (New Brunswick and London: Transaction Publishers, 2001), 217–248.

76. Sherman, "Evidence-Based Policing: Social Organization of Information for Social Control," 222.

77. Ibid., 231.

78. Ibid., 245.

79. Doris Layton MacKenzie, "Corrections and Sentencing in the 21st Century: Evidence-Based Corrections and Sentencing," *The Prison Journal* 81, 3 (2001): 299–312.

80. See the Campbell Collaboration.

81. Tim Hope, "Pretend It Works: Evidence and Governance in the Evaluation of the Reducing Burglary Initiative," *Criminal Justice: The International Journal of Policy and Practice* 4, 3 (2004): 287–308.

82. Ibid., 290.

83. Ibid., 302.

84. Jonathan Simon, *Governing Through Crime* (New York: Oxford University Press, 2007).

85. Kimberly Kempf-Leonard and Elicka S. L. Peterson, "Expanding Realms of the New Penology," *Punishment & Society* 2, 1 (2000): 68.

86. Malcolm Feeley and Jonathan Simon, "Actuarial Justice: The Emerging New Criminal Law," in *Crime and the Risk Society*, ed. Pat O'Malley (Brookfield, VT: Ashgate, 1998), 375.

87. Adrian Cherney, "Beyond Technicism: Broadening the 'What Works' Paradigm in Crime Prevention," *Crime Prevention and Community Safety: An International Journal* (2002): 49–59.

88. Ian Loader, "Fall of the 'Platonic Guardians': Liberalism, Criminology and Political Responses to Crime in England and Wales," *British Journal of Criminology* 46 (2006): 561–586.

89. Hannah Arendt, *On Violence* (New York: Harcourt, Brace & World, 1970), 6–7.

90. Lorna Rhodes, *Total Confinement: Madness and Reason in the Maximum Security Prison* (Berkeley: University of California Press, 2004).

91. Martinson, "What Works?" 49.

CHAPTER 7

1. Philip Smith, *Punishment and Culture* (Chicago: University of Chicago Press, 2008).

2. Jock Young, *The Vertigo of Late Modernity* (Los Angeles: Sage, 2007).

3. Jeff Ferrell, Keith Hayward, and Jock Young, *Cultural Criminology* (Los Angeles: Sage, 2008), 62.

4. Ian Loader and Neil Walker, *Civilizing Security* (Cambridge: Cambridge University Press, 2007), 8.

5. Arjun Appadurai, *Fear of Small Numbers: An Essay on the Geography of Anger* (Durham, NC: Duke University Press, 2006), 10.

6. See John Pratt, "Emotive and Ostentatious Punishment: Its Decline and Resurgence in Modern Society," *Punishment & Society* 2, 4 (2000): 417–439.

7. Ibid., 53.

8. Austin Sarat, *When the State Kills: Capital Punishment and the American Condition* (Princeton, NJ: Princeton University Press), 194.

9. Ibid., 205.

10. Lorna Rhodes, *Total Confinement: Madness and Reason in the Maximum Security Prison* (Berkeley: University of California Press, 2004).

11. Megan Comfort, *Doing Time Together: Love and Family in the Shadow of the Prison* (Chicago: University of Chicago Press, 2008).

12. Elizabeth Beck, Sarah Britto, and Arlene Andrews, *In the Shadow of Death: Restorative Justice and Death Row Families* (New York: Oxford University Press, 2007).

13. See Howard Zehr, *Changing Lenses: A New Focus for Crime and Justice* (Scottdale, PA: Herald Press, 1990); Dennis Sullivan and Larry Tifft, eds., *Handbook of Restorative Justice: A Global Perspective* (New York: Routledge, 2006).

14. Luc Boltanski, *Distant Suffering: Morality, Media and Politics* (Cambridge: Cambridge University Press, 1999).

15. See Ferrell, Hayward, and Young, *Cultural Criminology*; Bruce Hoffman and Michelle Brown, "Staging an Execution: The Media at McVeigh," in *Framing Crime: Cultural Criminology and the Image*, ed. Keith Hayward and Michael Presdee (London: Routledge, 2009). Hayward and Presdee's volume, *Framing Crime*, is generally directed at such concerns as well.

16. Henry Jenkins, *Convergence Culture: Where Old and New Media Collide* (New York: New York University Press, 2006).

17. Marie Gottschalk, *The Prison and the Gallows: The Politics of Mass Incarceration in America* (New York: Cambridge University Press, 2006).

18. James Q. Whitman, *Harsh Justice: Criminal Punishment and the Widening Divide Between America and Europe* (New York: Oxford University Press, 2003); Vanessa Barker, "The Politics of Punishing: Building a State Governance Theory of American Imprisonment Variation," *Punishment & Society* 8, 1 (2006): 5–32.

19. Ian Loader and Neil Walker, *Civilizing Security* (Cambridge: Cambridge University Press, 2007), 220.

20. Smith, *Punishment and Culture*, 183.

References

Agamben, Giorgio. *Homo Sacer: Sovereign Power and Bare Life.* Stanford: Stanford University Press, 1998.
———. *Remnants of Auschwitz: The Witness and the Archive.* New York: Zone Books, 2002.
———. *State of Exception.* Chicago: University of Chicago Press, 2005.
Allen, Francis A. *The Decline of the Rehabilitative Ideal: Penal Policy and Social Purpose.* New Haven, CT: Yale University Press, 1981.
American Friends Service Committee Working Party. *Struggle for Justice: A Report on Crime and Punishment in America.* New York: Hill & Wang, 1971.
Andrews, D. A., Ivan Zinger, Robert D. Hoge, James Bonta, Paul Gendreau, and Francis T. Cullen. "Does Correctional Treatment Work? A Clinically Relevant and Psychologically Informed Meta-Analysis." *Criminology* 28 (1990): 369–404.
———. "A Human Science Approach or More Punishment and Pessimism: A Rejoinder to Lab and Whitehead." *Criminology* 28 (1990): 419–429.
Appadurai, Arjun. *Modernity at Large: Cultural Dimensions of Globalization.* Minneapolis: University of Minnesota Press, 1996.
———. *Fear of Small Numbers: An Essay on the Geography of Anger.* Durham, NC: Duke University Press, 2006.
Arendt, Hannah. *The Human Condition.* Chicago: University of Chicago Press, 1958.
———. *On Violence.* New York: Harcourt, Brace & World, 1970.
Armstrong, Sarah, and Lesley McAra, eds. *Perspectives on Punishment: The Contours of Control.* New York: Oxford University Press, 2006.
Bailey, Walter C. "Correctional Outcome: An Evaluation of 100 Reports." *The Journal of Criminal Law, Criminology, and Police Science* 57 (1966): 153–160.
Barker, Vanessa. "The Politics of Punishing: Building a State Governance Theory of American Imprisonment Variation." *Punishment & Society* 8 (2006): 5–32.
Baudrillard, Jean. "War Porn." *Journal of Visual Culture* 5 (2006): 86–88.
Bauman, Zygmunt. *Modernity and the Holocaust.* Ithaca, NY: Cornell University Press, 1989.
———. *Liquid Modernity.* Cambridge: Polity Press, 2000.

————. "Social Issues of Law and Order." *British Journal of Criminology* 40 (2000): 205–221.

Beaumont, Gustave de, and Alexis de Tocqueville. *On the Penitentiary System in the United States, and Its Application in France.* Philadelphia: Carey, Lea & Blanchard, 1833.

Beck, Elizabeth, Sarah Britto, and Arlene Andrews. *In the Shadow of Death: Restorative Justice and Death Row Families.* New York: Oxford University Press, 2007.

Beck, Ulrich. "Beyond Class and Nation: Reframing Social Inequalities in a Globalizing World." *British Journal of Sociology* 58 (2007): 679–705.

Beckett, Katherine. *Making Crime Pay: Law and Order in Contemporary American Politics.* New York: Oxford University Press, 1997.

Bender, John. *Imagining the Penitentiary: Fiction and the Architecture of Mind in Eighteenth-Century England.* Chicago: University of Chicago Press, 1987.

Benjamin, Mark. "Sympathy for Charles Graner." *Salon*, December 1, 2008. http://www.salon.com/news/feature/2008/12/01/graner/print.html (accessed December 7, 2008).

Bennett, William J., John J. DiIulio, Jr., and John P. Walters. *Body Count: Moral Poverty—And How to Win America's War against Crime and Drugs.* New York: Simon & Schuster, 1996.

Berleman, William C., and Thomas W. Steinburn. "The Value and Validity of Delinquency Prevention Experiments." *Crime & Delinquency* 15 (1966): 471–478.

Biehl, João. *Vita: Life in a Zone of Social Abandonment.* Berkeley: University of California Press, 2005.

Biehl, João, Byron Good, and Arthur Kleinman. "Introduction: Rethinking Subjectivity." In *Subjectivity: Ethnographic Investigations*, ed. João Biehl, Byron Good, and Arthur Kleinman. Berkeley: University of California Press, 2007.

Blanchot, Maurice. *The Infinite Conversation.* Minneapolis: University of Minnesota Press, 1992.

Boltanski, Luc. *Distant Suffering: Morality, Media, and Politics.* Cambridge: Cambridge University Press, 1999.

Bosworth, Mary. "Race and Punishment." *Punishment & Society* 2 (2000): 114–118.

Brody, Reed. *The Road to Abu Ghraib.* New York: Human Rights Watch, 2004. Available at http://www.hrw.org/reports/2004/usa0604/.

Brown, Michelle. "'Setting the Conditions' for Abu Ghraib: The Prison Nation Abroad." *American Quarterly* 57 (2005): 973–997.

————. "The New Penology in a Critical Context." In *Advancing Critical Criminology: Theory and* Application, ed. Walter DeKeseredy and Barbara Perry. Lanham, MD: Lexington Books, 2006.

————. "Back Against the Wall: Correctional Workers and the Collateral Consequences of Mass Imprisonment." Unpublished manuscript, 2009.

Brydon, Anne, and Pauline Greenhill. "Representations of Crime: On Showing Paintings by a Serial Killer." In *Crime's Power: Anthropologists and the Ethnography of Crime*, ed. Philip C. Parnell and Stephanie C. Kane. New York: Palgrave Macmillan, 2003.

Butler, Judith. *Precarious Life: The Powers of Mourning and Violence*. New York: Verso, 2004.

Carby, Hazel. "A Strange and Bitter Crop: The Spectacle of Torture." openDemocracy News Analysis, created October 10, 2004. http://www.opendemocracy.net/media-abu_ghraib/article_2149.jsp (accessed October 15, 2006).

Cavell, Stanley. "Comments on Veena Das's Essay 'Language and Body: Transactions in the Construction of Pain.'" In *Social Suffering*, ed. Arthur Kleinman, Veena Das, and Margaret Lock. Berkeley: University of California Press, 1997.

Cavender, Gray. "Media and Crime Policy: A Reconsideration of David Garland's *The Culture of Control*." *Punishment & Society* 6 (2004): 335–348.

Cherney, Adrian. "Beyond Technicism: Broadening the 'What Works' Paradigm in Crime Prevention." *Crime Prevention and Community Safety: An International Journal* 4 (2002): 49–59.

Christie, Nils. *Crime Control as Industry: Towards Gulags, Western Style*. New York: Routledge, 2000.

Clear, Todd R. *Harm in American Penology: Offenders, Victims, and their Communities*. Albany: State University of New York Press, 1994.

Clemmer, Donald. *The Prison Community*. Boston: Christopher Publishing House, 1940.

Cohen, Nick, and Michael Durham. "Out of Control?" *The Independent*, February 14, 1993, 17.

Cohen, Stanley. *Folk Devils and Moral Panics*. London: MacGibbon & Kee, 1982.

———. *Visions of Social Control: Crime, Punishment, and Classification*. New York: Blackwell, 1985.

———. *States of Denial: Knowing About Atrocities and Suffering*. Malden, MA: Blackwell, 2001.

Comfort, Megan. *Doing Time Together: Love and Family in the Shadow of the Prison*. Chicago: University of Chicago Press, 2008.

Cousineau, F. Douglas, and Darryl B. Plecas. "Justifying Criminal Justice Policy with Methodologically Inadequate Research." *Canadian Journal of Criminology* 24 (1982): 307–321.

Cover, Robert. "Violence and the Word." *Yale Law Journal* 95 (1986): 1601–1629.

Cressey, Donald R. "The Nature and Effectiveness of Correctional Techniques." *Law and Contemporary Problems* 23 (Autumn 1958): 754–771.

Cullen, Francis T. "The Twelve People Who Saved Rehabilitation: How the Science of Criminology Made a Difference." *Criminology* 43 (2005): 1–42.

Cullen, Francis T., Kristie R. Blevins, Jennifer S. Trager, and Paul Gendreau. "Rise and Fall of Boot Camps: A Case Study in Common-Sense Corrections." *Journal of Offender Rehabilitation* 40 (2005): 53–70.

Cullen, Francis T., and Paul Gendreau. "The Effectiveness of Correctional Rehabilitation: Reconsidering the 'Nothing Works' Debate." In *The American Prison: Issues in Research and Policy*, ed. Lynne Goodstein and Doris Layton MacKenzie. New York: Plenum Press, 1989.

———. "From Nothing Works to What Works: Changing Professional Ideology in the 21st Century." *Prison Journal* 81 (2001): 313–338.

Cullen, Francis T., and Karen E. Gilbert. *Reaffirming Rehabilitation*. Cincinnati, OH: Anderson, 1982.

Cullen, Francis T., John P. Wright, Paul Gendreau, and D. A. Andrews. "What Correctional Treatment Can Tell Us about Criminological Theory: Implications for Social Learning Theory." In *Social Learning Theory and the Explanation of Crime: A Guide for the New Century*, ed. Ronald L. Akers and Gary F. Jensen. New Brunswick, NJ: Transaction Publishers, 2003.

Currie, Elliott. *Crime and Punishment in America*. New York: Metropolitan Books, 1998.

Das, Veena. "Language and Body: Transactions in the Construction of Pain." In *Social Suffering*, ed. Arthur Kleinman, Veena Das, and Margaret Lock. Berkeley: University of California Press, 1997.

Derrida, Jacques. "By Force of Mourning." In *The Work of Mourning*, ed. Pascale-Anne Brault and Michael Naas. Chicago: University of Chicago Press, 2001.

Dickens, Charles. *American Notes*. New York: St. Martin's Press, 1985.

Dratel, Joshua. "The Curious Debate." In *The Torture Debate in America*, ed. Karen J. Greenberg. Cambridge: Cambridge University Press, 2006.

Eisenman, Stephen. *The Abu Ghraib Effect*. London: Reaktion Books, 2007.

Empey, LaMar T. "Foreword," in Charles A. Murray and Louis A. Cox, Jr., *Beyond Probation: Juvenile Corrections and the Chronic Delinquent*. Beverly Hills, CA: Sage, 1979.

Feeley, Malcolm M., and Jonathan Simon. "The New Penology: Notes on the Emerging Strategy of Corrections and Its Implications." *Criminology* 30 (1992): 449–474.

Feeley, Malcolm, and Jonathan Simon. "Actuarial Justice: The Emerging New Criminal Law." In *Crime and the Risk Society*, ed. Pat O'Malley. Brookfield, VT: Ashgate, 1998.

Ferrell, Jeff, Keith Hayward, and Jock Young. *Cultural Criminology: An Invitation*. Los Angeles: Sage, 2008.

Ferrell, Jeff, and Clinton R. Sanders, eds. *Cultural Criminology*. Boston: Northeastern University Press, 1995.

Fishman, Mark. "Crime Waves as Ideology." *Social Problems* 25 (1978): 531–543.

Fogel, David. *We Are the Living Proof: The Justice Model for Corrections*. Cincinnati, OH: Anderson, 1975.

Foote, Kenneth E. *Shadowed Ground: America's Landscapes of Violence and Tragedy*. Austin: University of Texas Press, 2003.

Foucault, Michel. *Discipline and Punish: The Birth of the Prison.* New York: Pantheon Books, 1977.

———. *The History of Sexuality.* New York: Vintage Books, 1990.

———. "To Punish Is the Most Difficult Thing There Is." In *Power: Essential Works of Michel Foucault 1954–1984,* volume 3, ed. James D. Faubion. New York: New Press, 2000.

———. *Society Must Be Defended: Lectures at the Collège de France, 1975–76.* New York: Picador, 2003.

Frankel, Marvin E. *Criminal Sentences: Law Without Order.* New York: Hill & Wang, 1973.

Franklin, Adrian. "The Tourist Syndrome: An Interview with Zygmunt Bauman." *Tourist Studies* 3 (2003): 205–217.

Garland, David. *Punishment and Welfare: A History of Penal Strategies.* Aldershot: Gower, 1985.

———. *Punishment and Modern Society: A Study in Social Theory.* Chicago: University of Chicago Press, 1990.

———. *The Culture of Control: Crime and Social Order in Contemporary Society.* Chicago: University of Chicago Press, 2001.

———, ed. *Mass Imprisonment: Social Causes and Consequences.* Thousand Oaks, CA: Sage Publications, 2001.

———. "Capital Punishment and American Culture." *Punishment & Society* 7 (2005): 347–376.

———. "Penal Excess and Surplus Meaning: Public Torture Lynchings in Twentieth-Century America." *Law & Society Review* 39 (2005): 793–834.

———. "Concepts of Culture in the Sociology of Punishment." *Theoretical Criminology* 10 (2006): 419–447.

———. "On the Concept of Moral Panic." *Crime Media Culture* 4 (2008): 9–30.

Garland, David, and Peter Young. *The Power to Punish: Contemporary Penality and Social Analyses.* Brookfield, VT: Ashgate, 1983.

Gendreau, Paul, Francis T. Cullen, and James Bonta. "Intensive Rehabilitation Supervision: The Next Generation in Community Corrections?" *Federal Probation* 58 (1994): 72–78.

Gendreau, Paul, Claire Goggin, Francis T. Cullen, and Mario Paparozzi. "The Common-Sense Revolution and Correctional Policy." In *Offender Rehabilitation and Treatment: Effective Programmes and Policies to Reduce Re-Offending,* ed. James McGuire. New York: Wiley, 2002.

Gendreau, Paul, and Robert R. Ross. "Revivification of Rehabilitation: Evidence from the 1980s." *Justice Quarterly* 4 (1987): 349–407.

Gieryn, Thomas F. *Cultural Boundaries of Science: Credibility on the Line.* Chicago: University of Chicago Press, 1999.

Gill, Lesley. *The School of the Americas: Military Training and Political Violence in the Americas.* Durham, NC: Duke University Press, 2004.

Girling, Evi. "'Looking Death in the Face': The Benetton Death Penalty Campaign." *Punishment & Society* 6 (2004): 271–287.

Girling, Evi, Ian Loader, and Richard Sparks. *Crime and Social Change in Middle England: Questions of Order in an English Town*. New York: Routledge, 2000.

Glaser, Daniel. "What Works, and Why It Is Important: A Response to Logan and Gaes." *Justice Quarterly* 11 (1994): 711–723.

Goffman, Erving. *Asylums: Essays on the Social Situation of Mental Patients and Other Inmates*. Garden City, NY: Anchor Books, 1961.

Gold, Martin. "A Time for Skepticism." *Crime & Delinquency* 20 (1974): 20–24.

Goldhagen, Daniel Jonah. *Hitler's Willing Executioners: Ordinary Germans and the Holocaust*. New York: Knopf, 1996.

Gonnerman, Jennifer. "The Riot Academy." *Village Voice*, May 30, 2000, 62–66.

Gordon, Avery F. *Ghostly Matters: Haunting and the Sociological Imagination*. Minneapolis: University of Minnesota Press, 1997.

Gordon, Max. "Abu Ghraib: Postcards from the Edge." openDemocracy News Analysis, created October 14, 2004. http://www.opendemocracy.net/media-abu_ghraib/article_2146.jsp (accessed October 15, 2006).

Gottfredson, Michael R. "Treatment Destruction Techniques." *Journal of Research in Crime and Delinquency* 16 (1979): 39–54.

Gottschalk, Marie. *The Prison and the Gallows: The Politics of Mass Incarceration in America*. New York: Cambridge University Press, 2006.

———. "Two Separate Societies: One in Prison, One Not." *Washington Post*, April 14, 2008. http://www.washingtonpost.com/wp-dyn/content/article/2008/04/14/AR2008041402451.html (accessed December 5, 2008).

Gourevitch, Philip, and Errol Morris. *Standard Operating Procedure*. New York: Penguin Press, 2008.

Greenberg, David F. "The Incapacitative Effect of Imprisonment: Some Estimates." *Law & Society Review* 9 (1975): 541–580.

———. "The Correctional Effects of Corrections: A Survey of Evaluations." In *Corrections and Punishment*, ed. David F. Greenberg. Beverly Hills, CA: Sage, 1977.

Greenberg, Karen J., and Joshua L. Dratel, eds. *The Torture Papers: The Road to Abu Ghraib*. New York: Cambridge University Press, 2005.

———. *The Torture Debate in America*. New York: Cambridge University Press, 2006.

Greenhouse, Carol. "Solidarity and Objectivity: Re-reading Durkheim." In *Crime's Power: Anthropologists and the Ethnography of Crime*, ed. Philip C. Parnell and Stephanie C. Kane. New York: Palgrave Macmillan, 2003.

Greer, Chris, and Yvonne Jewkes. "Extremes of Otherness: Media Images of Social Exclusion." *Social Justice* 32 (2005): 20–31.

Hall, Stuart, Charles Critcher, Tony Jefferson, John Clarke, and Brian Robert. *Policing the Crisis: Mugging, the State and Law and Order*. London: Macmillan, 1978.

Hallett, Michael. "Militarism and Colonialism in the Global Punishment Economy." In *Visions for Change: Crime and Justice in the 21st Century*, 5th edition, ed. Roslyn Muraskin and Albert R. Roberts. New York: Prentice Hall, 2008.

Hamm, Mark. "'High Crimes and Misdemeanors': George W. Bush and the Sins of Abu Ghraib." *Crime Media Culture* 3 (2007): 259–284.

Hoffman, Bruce, and Michelle Brown. "Staging an Execution: The Media at McVeigh." In *Framing Crime: Cultural Criminology and the Image*, ed. Keith Hayward and Mike Presdee. London: Routledge, 2009.

hooks, bell. *Teaching to Transgress: Education as the Practice of Freedom*. New York: Routledge, 1994.

Hope, Tim. "Pretend It Works: Evidence and Governance in the Evaluation of the Reducing Burglary Initiative." *Criminal Justice: The International Journal of Policy and Practice* 4 (2004): 287–308.

Ignatieff, Michael. *A Just Measure of Pain: The Penitentiary in the Industrial Revolution, 1750–1850*. New York: Pantheon Books, 1978.

———. *The Needs of Strangers*. New York: Penguin Books, 1984.

Irwin, John. *The Warehouse Prison: Disposal of the New Dangerous Class*. Los Angeles: Roxbury, 2005.

Jenkins, Henry. *Convergence Culture: Where Old and New Media Collide*. New York: New York University Press, 2006.

Jenkins, Philip. *Using Murder: The Social Construction of Homicide*. New Brunswick, NJ: Aldine Transaction, 1994.

Johnston, Norman. *Eastern State Penitentiary: Crucible of Good Intentions*. Philadelphia: Philadelphia Museum of Art, 2000.

———. *Forms of Constraint: A History of Prison Architecture*. Urbana: University of Illinois Press, 2000.

Jones, Anthony R., and George R. Fay. *Investigation of Activities at Abu Ghraib*. 2004. Available at http://news.findlaw.com/hdocs/docs/dod/fay82504rpt.pdf.

Kaplan, Amy. "Violent Belongings and the Question of Empire Today: Presidential Address to the American Studies Association, October 17, 2003." *American Quarterly* 56 (2004): 1–18.

Kempf-Leonard, Kimberly, and Elicka S. L. Peterson. "Expanding Realms of the New Penology: The Advent of Actuarial Justice for Juveniles." *Punishment & Society* 2 (2000): 66–97.

Kermode, Mark. *The Shawshank Redemption*. London: British Film Institute, 2003.

Kirby, Bernard C. "Measuring Effects of Treatment of Criminals and Delinquents." *Sociology and Social Research* 38 (1954): 368–374.

Kleinman, Arthur, and Joan Kleinman. "The Appeal of Experience; The Dismay of Images: Cultural Appropriations of Suffering in Our Times." In *Social Suffering*, ed. Arthur Kleinman, Veena Das, and Margaret Lock. Berkeley: University of California Press, 1997.

Kohm, Steven A. "The People's Law versus Judge Judy Justice: Two Models of Law in American Reality-Based Courtroom TV." *Law & Society Review* 40 (2006): 693–728.

Lab, Steven P., and John T. Whitehead. "An Analysis of Juvenile Correctional Treatment." *Crime & Delinquency* 34 (1988): 60–83.

———. "From 'Nothing Works' to 'the Appropriate Works': The Latest Stop on the Search for the Secular Grail." *Criminology* 28 (1990): 405–417.

Lennon, John, and Malcolm Foley. *Dark Tourism: The Attraction of Death and Disaster.* London: Continuum, 2000.

Lipton, Douglas, Robert Martinson, and Judith Wilks. *The Effectiveness of Correctional Treatment: A Survey of Treatment Evaluation Studies.* New York: Praeger, 1975.

Loader, Ian. "Fall of the 'Platonic Guardians': Liberalism, Criminology and Political Responses to Crime in England and Wales." *British Journal of Criminology* 46 (2006): 561–586.

Loader, Ian, and Neil Walker. *Civilizing Security.* Cambridge: Cambridge University Press, 2007.

Logan, Charles H., and Gerald G. Gaes. "Meta-Analysis and the Rehabilitation of Punishment." *Justice Quarterly* 10 (1993): 245–263.

Luban, David. "Liberalism, Torture, and the Ticking Bomb." In *The Torture Debate in America,* ed. Karen J. Greenberg. Cambridge: Cambridge University Press, 2006.

Lynch, Mona. "Selling 'Securityware': Transformations in Prison Commodities Advertising, 1949–99." *Punishment & Society* 4 (2002): 305–319.

———. "Punishing Images: Jail Cam and the Changing Penal Enterprise." *Punishment & Society* 6 (2004): 255–270.

MacKenzie, Doris Layton. "Evidence-Based Corrections: Identifying What Works." *Crime & Delinquency* 46 (2000): 457–471.

———. "Corrections and Sentencing in the 21st Century: Evidence-Based Corrections and Sentencing." *The Prison Journal* 81 (2001): 299–312.

Marlowe, Douglas B. "When 'What Works' Never Did: Dodging the 'Scarlet M' in Correctional Rehabilitation." *Criminology & Public Policy* 5 (2006): 339–346.

Martinson, Robert. "What Works? Questions and Answers About Prison Reform." *Public Interest* 35 (Spring 1974): 22–54.

———. "Restraint and Incapacitation: An Analytical Introduction." In *Crime and Deterrence and Offender Career.* New York: City College of the City University of New York, 1975.

———. "California Research at the Crossroads." *Crime & Delinquency* 22 (1976): 180–191.

———. "Is the Treatment of Criminal Offenders Necessary?" *Federal Probation* 40 (1976): 3–9.

———. "New Findings, New Views: A Note of Caution Regarding Sentencing Reform." *Hofstra Law Review* 7 (1979): 243–258.

Martinson, Robert, and Judith Wilks. Knowledge in Criminal Justice Planning: A Preliminary Report. New York: The Center for Knowledge in Criminal Justice Planning, 1976.

———. "Save Parole Supervision." *Federal Probation* 41 (1977): 23–27.

Mauer, Marc. *Race to Incarcerate*. New York: New Press, 2006.

Mauer, Marc, and Tracy Huling. "Young Black Americans and the Criminal Justice System: Five Years Later." Washington, DC: *The Sentencing Project*, 1995.

Mayer, Jane. "Whatever It Takes: The Politics of the Man Behind '24.'" *New Yorker*, February 19, 2007–February 26, 2007, 66, 68, 70, 72, 77–78, 80, 82.

McAra, Leslie, and Sarah Armstrong. *Perspectives on Punishment*. Oxford, UK: Oxford University Press, 2006.

McRobbie, Angela. "Vulnerability, Violence and (Cosmopolitan) Ethics: Butler's Precarious Life." *British Journal of Sociology* 57 (2006): 69–86.

McRobbie, Angela, and Sarah L. Thornton. "Rethinking 'Moral Panic' for Multimediated Social Worlds." *British Journal of Sociology* 46 (1995): 559–574.

Miller, Jerome G. "The Debate on Rehabilitating Criminals: Is It True that Nothing Works?" *Washington Post*, March 1989. http://www.prisonpolicy.org/scans/rehab.html (accessed January 7, 2009).

Miller, Toby. "Historical Citizenship and the Fremantle Prison Follies: Frederick Wiseman Comes to Western Australia." *Continuum: The Australian Journal of Media and Culture* 7 (1994).

Mills, C. Wright. *The Sociological Imagination*. New York: Oxford University Press, 1959.

Mirzoeff, Nicholas. "Invisible Empire: Visual Culture, Embodied Spectacle, and Abu Ghraib." *Radical History Review* 95 (Spring 2006): 21–44.

Mitchell, William J. *City of Bits: Space, Place, and the Infobahn*. Cambridge, MA: MIT Press, 1995.

Morris, Norval. *The Future of Imprisonment*. Chicago: University of Chicago Press, 1965, 1974.

Morris, Norval, and Michael Tonry. *Between Prison and Probation: Intermediate Punishments in a Rational Sentencing System*. New York: Oxford University Press, 1991.

Niman, Michael I. "Strange Fruit in Abu Ghraib: The Privatization of Torture." *The Humanist* 65 (July/August 2004): 18–23.

O'Brien, Patricia. *Making It in the "Free World": Women in Transition from Prison*. Albany: State University of New York Press, 2001.

Palmer, Ted. "Martinson Revisited." *Journal of Research in Crime and Delinquency* 12 (1975): 133–152.

———. *Correctional Intervention and Research: Current Issues and Future Prospects*. Lexington, MA: Lexington Books, 1978.

Pratt, John. "Emotive and Ostentatious Punishment: Its Decline and Resurgence in Modern Society." *Punishment & Society* 2 (2000): 417–439.

President's Commission on Law Enforcement and the Administration of Justice. *The Challenge of Crime in a Free Society: A Report.* Washington, DC: U.S. Government Printing Office, 1967.

Rafter, Nicole Hahn. *Partial Justice: Women in State Prisons, 1800–1935.* Boston: Northeastern University Press, 1985.

Rafter, Nicole. *Shots in the Mirror: Crime Films and Society.* Second Edition. New York: Oxford University Press, 2006.

Reinhardt, Mark. "Picturing Violence: Aesthetics and the Anxiety of Critique." In *Beautiful Suffering: Photography and the Traffic in Pain,* ed. Mark Reinhardt, Holly Edwards, and Erina Duganne. Chicago: University of Chicago Press, 2007.

Reinhardt, Mark, and Holly Edwards. "Traffic in Pain." In *Beautiful Suffering: Photography and the Traffic in Pain,* ed. Mark Reinhardt, Holly Edwards, and Erina Duganne. Chicago: University of Chicago Press, 2007.

Rhodes, Lorna A. *Total Confinement: Madness and Reason in the Maximum Security Prison.* Berkeley: University of California Press, 2004.

Riis, Jacob A. *How the Other Half Lives: Studies Among the Tenements of New York.* New York: Penguin Books, 1997.

Robison, James, and Gerald Smith. "The Effectiveness of Correctional Programs." *Crime & Delinquency* 17 (1971): 67–80.

Rojek, Chris. *Ways of Escape: Modern Transformations in Leisure and Travel.* London: Palgrave Macmillan, 1993.

Rose, David. "Focus: Crime and Punishment: Evolution of Britain's Jail Revolution: The Orthodoxy that 'Nothing Works' Has Been Overturned." *The Observer,* May 5, 2002, 20.

Rose, Gillian. *Visual Methods.* Thousand Oaks, CA: Sage, 2007.

Ross, Andrew. *No-Collar: The Humane Workplace and Its Hidden Costs.* New York: Basic Books, 2003.

Rothman, David. *The Discovery of the Asylum: Social Order and Disorder in the New Republic.* Boston: Little, Brown, 1971.

———. *Conscience and Convenience: The Asylum and Its Alternatives in Progressive America.* Boston: Little, Brown, 1980.

Rotman, Edgardo. *Beyond Punishment: A New View on the Rehabilitation of Criminal Offenders.* New York: Greenwood Press, 1990.

Sante, Luc. *Evidence.* New York: Farrar, Straus and Giroux, 1992.

Sarat, Austin. "Imagining the Law of the Father: Loss, Dread, and Mourning in *The Sweet Hereafter.*" *Law & Society Review* 34 (2000): 3–46.

———. *When the State Kills: Capital Punishment and the American Condition.* Princeton, NJ: Princeton University Press, 2001.

Sarat, Austin, and Nasser Hussain. "Toward New Theoretical Perspectives on Forgiveness, Mercy, and Clemency: An Introduction." In *Forgiveness, Mercy, and Clemency*, ed. Austin Sarat and Nasser Hussain. Stanford: Stanford University Press, 2007.

Sarat, Austin, and Thomas R. Kearns. "A Journey Through Forgetting: Toward a Jurisprudence of Violence." In *The Fate of Law*, ed. Austin Sarat and Thomas R. Kearns. Ann Arbor: University of Michigan Press, 1991.

Sarre, Rick. "Beyond 'What Works?' A 25-Year Jubilee Retrospective of Robert Martinson's Famous Article." *Australian and New Zealand Journal of Criminology* 34 (2001): 38–46.

Sasson, Theodore. *Crime Talk: How Citizens Construct a Social Problem.* Hawthorne, NY: Aldine de Gruyter, 1995.

Scarry, Elaine. *The Body in Pain: The Making and Unmaking of the World.* New York: Oxford University Press, 1985.

Scheingold, Stuart. *The Politics of Law and Order: Street Crime and Public Policy.* New York: Longman, 1984.

Scheper-Hughes, Nancy. "Coming to Our Senses: Anthropology and Genocide." In *Annihilating Difference: The Anthropology of Genocide*, ed. Alexander Laban Hinton. Berkeley: University of California Press, 2002.

Seaton, A. V. "War and Thanatourism: Waterloo 1815–1914." *Annals of Tourism Research* 26 (1999): 130–158.

Sechrest, Lee, Susan O. White, and Elizabeth D. Brown, eds. *The Rehabilitation of Criminal Offenders: Problems and Prospects.* Washington, DC: National Academy of Sciences, 1979.

Sherman, Lawrence W. *Evidence-Based Policing.* Washington, DC: Police Foundation, 1998.

———. "Evidence–Based Policing: Social Organization of Information for Social Control." In *Crime and Social Organization*, ed. Elin Waring and David Weisburd. New Brunswick, NJ: Transaction Publishers, 2002.

Sherman, Lawrence W., Denise Gottfredson, Doris MacKenzie, John Eck, Peter Reuter, and Shawn Bushway. *Preventing Crime: What Works, What Doesn't, What's Promising: A Report to the United States Congress.* Washington, DC: U.S. Department of Justice, Office of Justice Programs, 1997.

Sherman, Michael, and Gordon Hawkins. *Imprisonment in America: Choosing the Future.* Chicago: University of Chicago Press, 1981.

Simon, Jonathan. "The Ideological Effects of Actuarial Practices." *Law & Society Review* 22 (1988): 771–800.

———. *Governing Through Crime: How the War on Crime Transformed American Democracy and Created a Culture of Fear.* New York: Oxford University Press, 2007.

Smith, Philip. *Punishment and Culture.* Chicago: University of Chicago Press, 2008.

Sontag, Susan. *Regarding the Pain of Others.* New York: Farrar, Straus and Giroux, 2003.

———. "What Have We Done?" *The Guardian*, May 24, 2004. http://www.commondreams.org/views04/0524–09.htm (accessed July 15, 2008).

Sparks, Richard. *Television and the Drama of Crime: Moral Tales and the Place of Crime in Public Life.* Philadelphia: Open University Press, 1992.

Strange, Carolyn, and Michael Kempa. "Shades of Dark Tourism: Alcatraz and Robben Island." *Annals of Tourism Research* 30 (2003): 386–405.

Sullivan, Dennis, and Larry L. Tifft, eds. *Handbook of Restorative Justice: A Global Perspective.* New York: Routledge, 2006.

Surette, Ray. *Media, Crime, and Criminal Justice: Images and Realities.* Pacific Grove, CA: Brooks/Cole, 1992.

Sykes, Gresham M. *The Society of Captives: A Study of a Maximum Security Prison.* Princeton, NJ: Princeton University Press, 1958.

Taguba, M. G. Antonio M. Article 15-6 Investigation of the 800th Military Police Brigade. February 26, 2004. http://www.npr.org/iraq/2004/prison_abuse_report.pdf (accessed January 7, 2009).

Tiso, Giovanni. "The Spectacle of Surveillance: Images of the Panopticon in Science-Fiction Cinema." Unpublished manuscript, 2000. http://homepages.paradise.net.nz/gtiso/filmessay (accessed November 13, 2006).

Trachtenberg, Alan. *Reading American Photographs: Images as History, Mathew Brady to Walker Evans.* New York: Hill & Wang, 1989.

Urry, John. *The Tourist Gaze: Leisure and Travel in Contemporary Societies.* London: Sage Publications, 1990.

Valier, Claire. *Crime and Punishment in Contemporary Culture.* New York: Routledge, 2004.

van den Haag, Ernest. *Punishing Criminals: Concerning a Very Old and Painful Question.* New York: Basic Books, 1975.

Visher, Christy A. "Incapacitation and Crime Control: Does a 'Lock 'em Up' Strategy Reduce Crime?" *Justice Quarterly* 4 (1987): 513–543.

von Hirsch, Andrew. *Doing Justice: The Choice of Punishments—Report of the Committee for the Study of Incarceration.* New York: Hill & Wang, 1976.

Wacquant, Loïc. "Deadly Symbiosis: When Ghetto and Prison Meet and Mesh." *Punishment & Society* 3 (2001): 95–134.

———. "The Militarization of Urban Marginality: Lessons from the Brazilian Metropolis." *International Political Sociology* 2 (2008): 56–74.

———. *Deadly Symbiosis: Race and the Rise of Neoliberal Penality.* Cambridge: Polity Press, 2008.

———. *Urban Outcasts: A Comparative Sociology of Advanced Marginality.* Cambridge: Polity Press, 2008.

———. *Punishing the Poor: The Neoliberal Government of Social Insecurity.* Durham, NC: Duke University Press, 2009.

Whitman, James Q. *Harsh Justice: Criminal Punishment and the Widening Divide between America and Europe.* New York: Oxford University Press, 2003.

Wilks, Judith, and Robert Martinson. "Is the Treatment of Criminal Offenders Really Necessary?" *Federal Probation* 40 (1976): 3–9.

Williams, Patricia J. *The Alchemy of Race and Rights*. Cambridge, MA: Harvard University Press, 1991.

Wilson, David, and Sean O'Sullivan. "Re-theorizing the Penal Reform Functions of the Prison Film: Revelation, Humanization, Empathy, and Benchmarking." *Theoretical Criminology* 9 (2005): 471–491.

Wilson, James Q. *Thinking about Crime*. New York: Basic Books, 1975.

———. "'What Works' Revisited: New Findings on Criminal Rehabilitation." *The Public Interest* 61 (Fall 1980): 3–17.

Wolfson, Adam. "About the Public Interest." *The Public Interest* 159 (Spring 2005): 18–21.

Wootton, Barbara. *Social Science and Social Pathology*. London: Allen & Unwin, 1959.

Young, Alison. *Imagining Crime: Textual Outlaws and Criminal Conversations*. Thousand Oaks, CA: Sage, 1996.

Young, Jock. *The Vertigo of Late Modernity*. Los Angeles: Sage, 2007.

Zedner, Lucia. "Dangers of Dystopias in Penal Theory." *Oxford Journal of Legal Studies* 22 (2002): 341–366.

Zehr, Howard. *Changing Lenses: A New Focus for Crime and Justice*. Scottdale, PA: Herald Press, 1990.

Zimbardo, Philip. *The Lucifer Effect: Understanding How Good People Turn Evil*. New York: Random House, 2007.

Index

About the Author

MICHELLE BROWN is Associate Professor in the Department of Sociology and Anthropology at Ohio University.